Early Buddhist Discourses

Edited, with Translations, by
John J. Holder

Hackett Publishing Company, Inc.
Indianapolis/Cambridge

Printed in the United States of America

18 17 16 15 14 3 4 5 6 7 8

For further information, please address:

Hackett Publishing Company, Inc.
P.O. Box 44937
Indianapolis, IN 46244-0937

www.hackettpublishing.com

Cover design by Abigail Coyle
Text design by Meera Dash
Composition by Agnew's, Inc.

Library of Congress Cataloging-in-Publication Data

Tipitaka. Suttapitaka. Selections. English. 2006.
Early Buddhist discourses / edited, with translations, by John J. Holder.
p. cm.
Includes bibliographical references and index.
ISBN 0-87220-793-5 (cloth) — ISBN 0-87220-792-7 (pbk.)
I. Holder, John J. (John Joseph), 1960– II. Title.

BQ 1192.E53H65 2006
294.3'823—dc22

2005052842

ISBN-13: 978-0-87220-793-6 (cloth)
ISBN-13: 978-0-87220-792-9 (pbk.)

Contents

Acknowledgments

The manuscript for this book was written while I held a visiting research appointment at the Oriental Institute of Oxford University. The research appointment was made possible by a sabbatical leave from St. Norbert College. I am grateful for the support I received from both institutions for this endeavor.

While at Oxford, I was fortunate to have access to other Pāli scholars—no doubt, some of the best Pāli philologists in the world—who reviewed my translations and made suggestions for revisions. Thus, I would like to acknowledge the very generous help of Richard Gombrich, Alex Wynne, and Justin Meiland (now at Mahidol University in Thailand) in the preparation of the manuscript for this book. I am also indebted to Professor Karen Lang (University of Virginia) who, as the publisher's outside reader of the manuscript, offered many excellent suggestions that have been incorporated into the book.

Finally, two of my teachers deserve recognition for the influence they have had on me and thus on this book. The late Venerable K. Ariyasena taught me the Pāli language through a most intensive approach. Whatever skill I have in Pāli is due largely to the hours and hours of patient tutorship he provided to me at his monastery in Sri Lanka. Professor Harry Krebs (Dickinson College) introduced me to Buddhism both as a teacher and as a person whose character epitomizes the principles of Buddhism. This book is a product of the academic and spiritual journey into Buddhism that he instigated in me so many years ago.

General Introduction

The Pāli Canon and Its Significance within Buddhism

This book contains new English translations of twenty philosophically important discourses from the Discourse Basket (*Sutta Piṭaka*) of the Pāli Canon. The Pāli Canon not only contains a substantial amount of textual material that is arguably the most reliable account of the Buddha's teachings but also offers some of the most profound philosophical and religious ideas ever expressed in any tradition at any time.

The Pāli Canon is recognized as a scriptural source for all Buddhist traditions, although it is more closely associated with the Buddhist tradition called "Theravāda"[1] that is prevalent today in the South Asian countries of Sri Lanka, Burma, and Thailand. The Pāli Canon is so-called because it has been preserved in the middle-Indian language called Pāli. Pāli is a close relative to Sanskrit, the language in which some of India's most famous religious texts were written, such as the *Vedas, Upaniṣads,* and the *Bhagavad Gītā.* The use of Pāli, however, is confined to Buddhist texts.

The Pāli Canon is a sizable body of material. The original Pāli version of the canon, as published in romanized script by the Pali Text Society, fills more than fifty volumes. Buddhists and scholars of Buddhism often refer to the canon as the "*Tipiṭaka*" (which literally means "Three Baskets"), because the material is grouped into three very large sections. The Discipline Basket (*Vinaya Piṭaka*) covers the rules and historical events related to the Buddhist monastic community, the "*Saṅgha.*" The Discourse Basket (*Sutta Piṭaka*) contains by far the largest amount of material. It preserves the sermons and teachings of the Buddha and his earliest disciples. The "Higher Teachings" Basket (*Abhidhamma Piṭaka*) offers a systematic and detailed analysis of the Buddha's doctrines. This group of texts contains long lists of Buddhist concepts and philosophically sophisticated explanations that attempt to catalog comprehensively the Buddha's philosophy.

The texts of the Pāli Canon, as they exist today, show clear evidence of having developed over time. Often within a single discourse there are passages that almost certainly were constructed at different times; and some passages were very obviously assembled by interpolating material borrowed from

1 "Theravāda" means "doctrine of the elders." In the past, scholars have called this tradition "Hinayāna" (literally, "lesser vehicle"). But this term is no longer used because it derives from a biased comparison with the other major Buddhist tradition called "Mahāyāna" (literally, "greater vehicle"). Mahāyāna Buddhism developed in India sometime around the first century B.C.E. and forms the basis for contemporary Buddhist schools in east Asia (China, Japan, Korea, and Tibet).

other sources.[2] The canon was preserved only in oral form until the first century B.C.E., when it was first committed to writing in Sri Lanka. According to the Theravāda tradition, the Pāli Canon was settled at the First Council held by the Buddha's monastic disciples in Rājagaha, immediately after the Buddha's passing. And although it is unlikely that this account is true, there is strong evidence that the texts preserve some material that goes back at least as far as the early third or fourth century B.C.E.—about a century after the Buddha's decease. So although almost no one in the scholarly community believes that the Pāli Canon is the verbatim teachings of the historical Buddha, many scholars do think that it provides to a substantial degree the spirit of the teaching of the historical Buddha and may well contain certain passages that recount the Buddha's own words.

Finally, it must be stressed that, whatever the historical facts about the material contained in the Pāli Canon, these texts are essential to any serious study of Buddhism. More than that, they contain ideas that inform and challenge contemporary students of philosophy and religion on a wide variety of issues.

A Survey of Early Buddhism

The aim of a book of primary sources is to bring the reader into contact with the original material in as direct a way as possible so that the reader can make up his or her own mind about the meaning and cogency of the texts. Yet, to understand the ideas of the original texts requires seeing those ideas in relation to other ideas and relating specific doctrines to the larger context of the Buddha's teaching. For this reason, the following survey of the major points of early Buddhism should provide a helpful background to understanding the primary sources.

The Historical Context of the Buddha's Teaching

Buddhism did not arise in a vacuum. The Buddha's teachings were formulated in response to the social and intellectual conditions of ancient India.[3] The fifth and fourth centuries B.C.E.—when the Buddha lived and the canonical

[2] Despite the fact that the canonical texts show evidence of corruptions, interpolations, and reconciliations with other texts, no effort has been made to stratify the texts along these lines in the translations presented here. Even though stratification of the texts may prove very important in answering certain scholarly questions about early Buddhism, it does not suit the purposes of this book.

[3] It must be remembered that the very idea of "India" as a single political or cultural unit is a very recent development that emerged from colonization by Western powers. Ancient India at

literature began to emerge—were times of great philosophical and religious ferment in ancient India. The Pāli Canon shows that the early Buddhists were aware of the literature of the Vedic tradition, its sacrificial cults, and even certain early Upaniṣads. Aside from the strands of Vedic religion and its Brahmanist (Hindu)[4] philosophy, there were materialists, determinists, Jains, and ascetics of various sorts at the time of the Buddha. In short, ancient India at this time was a veritable marketplace of different spiritual and philosophical systems.

The relationships between the ideas of the historical Buddha and those of his contemporaries have been very difficult to sort out, but a much clearer picture seems to be emerging. There is no question that the Buddha borrowed (and reconstructed) some philosophical concepts from other traditions, such as Brahmanism and Jainism. And yet the Buddha charted a very different course in his teaching from those of his contemporaries. Even where the Buddha borrowed a concept from another tradition, he often used the concept to prove a point very much at odds with the tradition from which it was borrowed. Perhaps of most importance, the early Buddhist texts depict the Buddha as engaged in critical dialogue with the other religious teachers and traditions of his day. From these dialogues, the modern reader can readily discern that, despite certain commonalities, the Buddha's *dhamma* contrasts sharply with the general approach of ancient Indian religion as exemplified by Brahmanist doctrines and practices.

The system of social class in ancient India figures prominently in the early Buddhist discourses. The social system of class and caste as we think of it today was not fully developed in the Buddha's time, but Indian society was already divided into four classes (*vaṇṇā*): Brahmins, warriors and leaders (*khattiyas*), merchants and farmers (*vessas*), and laborers (*suddas*). The Brahmin class (priestly guardians of the Vedic religious cults) stands out in the Pāli Canon, because the Buddha singled out for criticism many of the Brahmins' religious doctrines and their claims to spiritual superiority.

In contrast to the Brahmins, the Buddha is identified with a very diverse group of religious seekers and teachers known collectively as "*samaṇas*" (Skt: *śramaṇas*). The *samaṇas* abandoned the domestic or household life and so lived detached from family life. Some *samaṇas* were recluses living deep in the woods or in the mountains, permanently apart from society; yet many

---

the time of the Buddha was divided up into a number of small states, each of which had its own distinctive political system.

[4] Hinduism as we know it today did not exist in the Buddha's day, although many of the key ideas and texts that form the core of Hindu tradition were already evident. The term "Hindu" is of fairly recent, colonial, vintage. For historical reasons, therefore, "Brahmanism" more accurately references the set of traditions that formed the roots of today's Hindu tradition.

of them wandered about amid society. In regard to doctrines and practices, the *samaṇas* were extremely diverse. Aside from the fact that most of them were celibate, begged for their food, and practiced various forms of self-restraint, there is little more that can be said about them as a group.

Life of the Buddha

"Siddhattha Gotama" (Skt: Siddhārtha Gautama) is the name of the person who became the Buddha. The term "Buddha" is an honorific title that simply means "one who is enlightened" or "one who has woken up" to the truth. What makes a person a Buddha, as distinct from other enlightened persons (called *arahants*), is that a Buddha *discovers* and *teaches* the path to enlightenment. According to Buddhist tradition, there have been and will be Buddhas other than Siddhattha Gotama.

What is crucially important about all the Buddhas, however, is that they are human beings. Unlike so many other religious traditions, Buddhism is founded on the teaching of a human being and not of a god or even a prophet of a god. A Buddha is a person who lives life as a perfected human being. His discovery of the *dhamma* and achievement of enlightenment is entirely his own accomplishment as a human being. Thus, Buddhism claims that the highest religious goals are achievable by a human being through one's own effort.

Attaching firm historical dates to the life of the Buddha is a very difficult task. The dates for the life of the Buddha most widely used by scholars up until recently were 566–486 B.C.E., but the latest scholarship suggests a somewhat later period, 484–404 B.C.E. (or thereabouts).[5] Unfortunately, there is virtually no material evidence relating directly to the life or person of the Buddha, and so the dating process depends on using archaeological evidence in conjunction with accounts drawn from certain ancient texts. In the main, scholars attempt to arrive at the dates for the Buddha by working backward from much firmer dates associated with the Mauryan emperor Aśoka, who reigned in the third century B.C.E.[6]

A great number of legends and myths have grown up around the historical Buddha. And although the traditional stories are highly embellished, they probably do contain the basic outlines of the Buddha's life. With these

[5] Gombrich, Richard. "Dating the Buddha: A Red Herring Revealed," in *The Dating of the Historical Buddha Part 2,* Heinz Bechert, ed. (Gottingen, 1992), pp. 237–259.

[6] The coronation of Aśoka appears to have occurred in or near 268 B.C.E.. According to Buddhist tradition, Aśoka converted to Buddhism and contributed greatly to the spread of Buddhism by sending out a series of missions to distant places. Most notably, his son Mahinda, an ordained Buddhist monk, and daughter Sanghamitta, an ordained Buddhist nun, were instrumental in establishing Buddhism in Sri Lanka in approximately 240 B.C.E..

cautionary notes, the following account reviews what seems most likely to be true about the life of the historical Buddha.

Traditional stories of the Buddha's life record that he was born in the town of Kapilavatthu (near the present-day town of Lumbini, just on the Nepalese side of the border between Nepal and India). He was born into a noble (*khattiya*) family. Most sources say that he was a prince and that his father, Suddhodana, was a king among the Sakyan people, although recent scholarship suggests that his father was more likely an elected chief, rather than a king. Siddhattha's mother, Māyā, died soon after his birth, and his aunt, Pajāpatī, became his stepmother and raised him. As tradition has it, he lived a luxurious and sheltered life well into his adulthood. Siddhattha learned the Brahmanical (Vedic) teachings and rituals as would befit a person of his noble class and status. Yet, despite having all the advantages of wealth and power, Siddhattha was profoundly troubled by the great existential problems facing any human life: sickness, old age, and death. Sometime in his early adulthood, he realized that his opulent lifestyle provided no protection from these serious problems. So at the age of twenty-nine, having already married and had a son, Siddhattha gave up everything he knew and became a homeless religious seeker.

For several years, Siddhattha studied meditational techniques and religious philosophy with two of the most accomplished teachers of his time, first with Aḷāra Kālāma and then with Uddaka Rāmaputta.[7] In each case, he soon equaled the meditational states and levels of insight achieved by his teachers, but he found that such techniques, although valuable, did not bring the final enlightenment he sought. So, having left his teachers, he joined a small group of ascetics who practiced extreme forms of self-denial and self-mortification. After several years of this practice, he came to realize that extreme self-denial did not bring enlightenment, either, so he abandoned this path. Emaciated and weak from prolonged austerities, Siddhattha took some food to regain his strength and sat under a ficus tree near the town of Gayā. Here, after great striving, he achieved his Enlightenment by removing the defilements and other corruptions of the mind that lead to suffering and by developing a penetrative understanding of the changing nature of reality (i.e., the doctrine of dependent arising).

Despite some initial reluctance, the Buddha (as he could now be properly called) taught the path he had discovered to many others, some of whom also became enlightened.[8] His first five disciples—his former ascetic colleagues—were converted by the first sermon in the Deer Park at Isipatana,

[7] Although some scholars have raised questions about the religious traditions of these two teachers, it seems most likely that they both belonged to the Brahmanical (Hindu) tradition.

[8] These enlightened persons are called *arahants* ("worthy ones").

near Benares. In that first sermon, the Buddha taught the Four Noble Truths and so set in motion the "wheel of the *dhamma.*" For the next forty-five years, he wandered around the Ganges Valley teaching, establishing the monastic order of monks and nuns (the "*Saṅgha*"), debating philosophy and religion with members of other religious traditions, as well as serving the needs of the people with acts of kindness and compassion. During his long life, the Buddha apparently had contact with a wide array of people, including kings, prostitutes, fellow *samaṇas,* Brahmins, and businesspersons. He died of dysentery at Kusinārā at the age of eighty. An account of the Buddha's last days is preserved in a wonderful discourse called the *Mahāparinibbāna Sutta* in the *Dīgha Nikāya.*

Philosophical and Religious Doctrines

The Buddha's one and only reason for teaching was to show the way to religious liberation, that is, to help others free themselves, as he had freed himself, from the profound suffering that permeates human existence. The Buddha's *dhamma* must always be understood in the context of this religious purpose. But what distinguishes early Buddhism from all other religious traditions is the fact that the Buddha's *dhamma* does not focus on Ultimate Realities or theologies, because, from the perspective of early Buddhism, these pursuits are useless as a means for achieving the ultimate goal of religious liberation. Early Buddhism declares a way to liberation and happiness despite the precarious and changing nature of the world, and does so without falling back on a transcendental realm of security or a saving God. Instead of metaphysics or theology, early Buddhism focuses on the training of human character in terms of moral conduct, mental culture, and wisdom.

The Buddha's Empiricism

Philosophically, the Buddha was an empiricist in the sense that his religious philosophy centered on experience. Experience figures prominently in the Buddha's teaching in at least three ways: first, the experience of suffering is the motivation for seeking a religious path in life (see the First Noble Truth discussed later); second, he taught that experience is the proper way to justify claims to knowledge; and, third, he provided a highly sophisticated psychological account of experience as a way of explaining how suffering arises and how one might gain control over the causes of suffering so as to bring about the cessation of suffering.

Whereas most religious traditions are based on metaphysically speculative doctrines—doctrines for which there is little empirical evidence (e.g., the reality of an afterlife)—the Buddha told his followers that one should believe only those doctrines that can be personally verified in experience. The Buddha reasoned that what cannot be verified in experience has little to contribute to the resolution of the religious issues that confront a person. The urge to speculate beyond what can be empirically verified usually derives from the ego's demands for security and self-aggrandizement. Furthermore, reliance on traditions or the mere authority of a teacher is not an appropriate way to develop or justify a belief, suggested the Buddha, not even in spiritual matters in which other religious traditions call upon "faith."

Experience is central to early Buddhist philosophy in another way. The Pāli Canon contains a remarkably rich and detailed psychological theory of experience—much richer, in fact, than the sensation-oriented empiricism of seventeenth- and eighteenth-century European philosophers, such as John Locke and David Hume. In the early Buddhist view of experience, experience is more than just knowledge, more than cognition. Noncognitive or affective dimensions of experience, such as feelings, dispositions, and habits, play an essential role in understanding the processes of experience, according to the theories set out in the Pāli discourses. No doubt, any philosophy that is serious about tracing the wellsprings of human action must give serious consideration to the fact that choice and perception are rooted in affective dimensions of experience.

The Essence of the Buddha's Teaching: The Four Noble Truths

The Four Noble Truths are the most succinct expression of the Buddha's teaching, or *dhamma.* They are (1) suffering (*dukkha*); (2) the origin of suffering; (3) the cessation of suffering; and (4) the way leading to the cessation of suffering, namely, the Noble Eightfold Path. The Four Noble Truths contain both a diagnosis and a therapy for the spiritual shortcomings of the human condition.

The starting point for Buddhism, its First Noble Truth, is that suffering is inherent in normal human experience. Suffering is the religious problematic, the reason why a person should attempt to live the religious life. This is not a theoretical or abstract matter. The early Buddhist tradition depicts Siddhattha as a flesh-and-blood person who sought the holy life as a means to solve the suffering that arises because of certain unavoidable facts of life, namely, sickness, old age, and death.

The Pāli word for suffering is "*dukkha.*" *Dukkha* is much more than physical pain. It refers to the suffering that occurs on a number of levels: physical pain; psychological distress (e.g., not getting the things one wants); and spiritual/existential anxieties (e.g., the struggle with personal mortality). Because of these complexities, the word *dukkha* is perhaps more accurately translated by terms like "unsatisfactoriness" or "dissatisfaction."[9] The First Noble Truth summarizes the fact of suffering by identifying birth, aging, sorrow, lamentation, pain, despair, and distress as modes of suffering. Suffering is so pervasive, because unenlightened experience is undermined by the transience of all worldly phenomena—whatever a person depends on, or grasps after, turns out to be unsatisfying in the end.

Although suffering is ever-present in an unenlightened person's life, this is not to say that the Buddha failed to recognize that happiness and pleasure exist in the lives of people. He denied only that such happiness is secure and long lasting. So long as a person has not resolved the problems of sickness, old age, and death, suffering will continue to tinge even one's happiest moments.

The fact that suffering is at the center of Buddhism has led some to think of Buddhism as pessimism. It is true that Buddhism does not paint a rosy, untroubled picture of human existence. But Buddhism claims to be realistic—neither unwarrantedly optimistic nor pessimistic. If the Buddhist tradition offered only an analysis of suffering or held that no solution to suffering is possible, then perhaps the pessimism label would be justified. But this is far from the case. The Buddha's teachings suggest that the proper response to the suffering inherent in human existence is not nihilism and despair, but rather the hard work of the holy life that has tangible benefits at each stage of attainment.

From the early Buddhist point of view, human beings are caught up in suffering on a cosmic scale, namely, the cycle of birth-death-rebirth called "*saṃsāra.*" Escaping this cycle is tantamount to religious liberation. A person's actions, mediated by selfishness or attachment to the world, keep one tethered to this cycle. This bondage to *saṃsāra* is governed by the law of karma (Pāli: *kamma*). Karma is not fate or destiny, as the word has come to be used in Western parlance. "Karma" literally means "action," but it refers more specifically to actions that have an impact on a person's moral or spiritual condition—a kind of "moral causation." The idea that the moral quality of an action has a close connection to the moral quality of the results of that action is the essence of karma. According to the law of karma, morally good actions have a strong tendency to produce good or wholesome (*kusala*) results, and morally bad actions have a strong tendency to produce bad or unwholesome (*akusala*) results. On the larger scale, karma plays a central role in Buddhism because a person is spiritually liberated by eliminating the negative accumulations of karma that perpetuate *saṃsāric* existence (i.e., continual rebirth).

[9] Although "unsatisfactoriness" better captures the flavor or nuance of *dukkha,* it is an unwieldy term. For this reason, "suffering" is used to translate *dukkha* in this book.

The Second and Third Noble Truths describe in detail the origin and elimination of suffering. The Second Noble Truth relates that suffering is caused by craving (*taṇhā*). The Third Noble Truth is just the statement that suffering is curable by removing its cause, namely, craving. It sounds so utterly simple, but it is a very complex matter.

The great genius of the early Buddhist analysis of suffering lies in seeing suffering as the result of a *causal pattern* of factors in human experience. The Buddha identified the factors in the causal pattern that lead to suffering so that the process could be controlled and redirected away from suffering and toward wholesome and beneficial outcomes. This doctrine is referred to as "dependent arising" (*paṭiccasamuppāda*), and it is the central philosophical insight of early Buddhism.

The doctrine of dependent arising directly challenges the metaphysical worldview of the Brahmanical tradition. Whereas the sages in the Brahmanical tradition agreed with the Buddha that the world of normal human experience is changing and ephemeral, they posited a transcendent, changeless, monistic, Ultimate Reality (*Brahman*) that stands behind the changing world. The highest spiritual truth in Brahmanism—what the sage strives to realize—is that all existence ultimately has its source in the changeless One, and that the essence of the person (*ātman*) is identical with this One.

The Buddha explicitly rejected the Brahmanist transcendental metaphysics. According to the Buddha, all phenomena are dependently arisen. Everything that exists is a nexus of causal factors. Thus, all phenomena are impermanent; they arise at some point in time and cease to be at another point in time. In light of this, the Buddha did not resort to a transcendental or unchanging realm beyond this world of change. The changing, natural world is the scene of human affairs—it is the "all" and there is no other, as the Buddha put it in the *Sabba Sutta.*[10] And so whatever way human striving might create religious meaning, it must do so *in this changing world,* and not by escaping from this world to abide in a changeless, transcendent Brahman. This position represents a radical break with Brahmanical religion.

The application of the doctrine of dependent arising to the problem of suffering is most powerfully described in the twelvefold formula.[11] The

[10] See Chapter 7 for the complete discourse.

[11] The twelve causal links in the formula are ignorance, dispositions to action, consciousness, mentality-materiality, the six bases of sense, contact, feeling, craving, attachment, becoming, birth, and the mass of suffering (including aging, death, sorrow, lamentation, pain, despair, and distress). See The Greater Discourse on Cause (Chapter 3) and the Discourse to Kaccāyana (in Chapter 7). The Greater Discourse on Cause is considered by many scholars to be the locus classicus of the doctrine of dependent arising, and yet it offers a formulation of dependent arising having only ten causal links. The full twelvefold formula can be found in the Discourse to Kaccāyana and in several other discourses in this volume.

twelvefold formula is given both in forward (arising) and in reverse (ceasing) orders to show how suffering arises and ceases according to a definite pattern of causal links. The importance of the doctrine of dependent arising cannot be exaggerated. By explaining suffering as a product of a causal process, this doctrine provides the all-important means of manipulating the causal process from one that typically produces suffering to one that can be redirected to happiness and religious liberation.

The Buddha succinctly drew the implications of the doctrine of dependent arising in what he referred to as the "three marks of existence." Everything that exists is impermanent (*anicca*), suffering (*dukkha*), and without a permanent Self (*anattā*).

Buddhism's most famous philosophical teaching is probably the "no-Self" doctrine. This doctrine is unique to Buddhism among the world's religions. Most major religions teach that there is an immortal essence at the core of human existence and that, because of this essence, humans can expect some form of continued existence after death. The Buddha rejected such views as philosophically untenable. Although the Buddha would not speculate whether there is or is not a continued existence beyond death for those who achieve enlightenment (unenlightened beings, of course, can expect to be reborn), the speculative and dogmatic belief in an immortal human essence has no empirical warrant and mainly derives from a pernicious form of egoism. Seeking security against death, both for oneself and for loved ones, a person latches onto the belief in immortality. For such reasons, the Buddha asserted that the motivating factors for the belief in a permanent Self are deeply corrupt and must be abandoned in order to achieve religious liberation.

It is important to put the Buddha's theory of human nature into the proper historical and religious context. The Buddha's "no-Self" doctrine was aimed specifically at the Brahmanical concept of permanent Self (Skt: *ātman*), although the main thrust of his arguments might be applied to the idea of a "soul" in the Christian sense as well. The Brahmanical teaching, as recorded in the Upaniṣads, is that the true reality, or "essence," of each person is this permanent Self that has three fundamental properties: permanence, blissfulness, and pure agency.[12] Religious liberation in the Brahmanical tradition is the realization that this permanent Self is one's true identity and that this identity is none other than Brahman (the One, the Absolute, the mysterious source of all Reality).

[12] Agency as a criterion for the permanent Self does not appear in the earliest Upaniṣads. It appears most notably in the *Kaṭha Upaniṣad,* which most scholars believe developed in a period of time somewhat after the life of the Buddha. But since the Buddhist texts attribute this property to the permanent Self, the ideas expressed in this later Upaniṣad may well have been in a nascent stage in the Buddha's time.

The Buddha challenged this view of a permanent Self by using his empirical method and by applying the doctrine of dependent arising. The Buddha considered all of the various components that make up a person (body, feeling, perception, dispositions to action, and consciousness—what are referred to below as the "five aggregates") and found that none of these meet the criteria of a permanent Self in the Brahmanical sense. None of them are permanent. None are perfectly blissful. None completely control themselves, so none demonstrate pure agency. And since these factors are an exhaustive account of what makes up a human being, the permanent Self is nowhere to be found.

Because of the negative emphasis of this no-Self doctrine, some interpreters of early Buddhism have proposed that the Buddha held that there is no self at all. This interpretation is clearly wrong. In fact, such a view is identified as "annihilationism" (a view attributed to Materialism)[13] in the canon and is specifically listed in the *Brahmajāla Sutta*[14] as a wrong view. The no-Self doctrine denies the existence of a self that is a permanent, blissful, pure agent, and yet there is a *positive* teaching about human persons. The Buddha taught that there is a self, but it is a dependently arisen self, composed of the "five aggregates" (*khandhas*)—body, feeling, perception, dispositions to action, and consciousness—rather than a permanent essence. Here, again, the Buddha espoused a "middle way." Between the extremes of a permanent Self and no self at all, the Buddha taught that the self arises as a nexus of causal factors or processes.

The Buddha's Fourth Noble Truth, the Noble Eightfold Path, is referred to as a "middle way" between the extremes of self-indulgent opulence and self-mortifying asceticism. The Buddha had personally experimented with both of these extremes and realized that neither offered a life that solves the problem of suffering. The Noble Eightfold Path is the Buddha's *practical therapy* for living a life by the "middle way"; it comprises the following factors:

1. Right View—understanding the Four Noble Truths and the doctrine of dependent arising

[13] Materialists, known variously as *Cārvākas* and *Lokāyatikas,* were an early reaction to the Brahmanist tradition. Materialist ideas were probably in existence in ancient India for several centuries before the rise of Buddhism. These thinkers held that matter is the ultimate constituent of reality. All phenomena, including consciousness, are reducible to the four basic material elements: earth, water, fire, and air. Although there seems to be some diversity among the Materialists regarding the reality of composite things, they all denied the continuity of the person beyond death, hence they explicitly rejected the Upaniṣadic conception of *ātman* and were referred to in Buddhist literature as "annihilationists." Most Materialists also held that moral judgment is meaningless—a position that the Buddha was at great pains to avoid in *his* rejection of a permanent Self.

[14] See *Dīgha Nikāya* 1.34–35.

2. Right Intention—abandoning intentions based on attachments to sensual pleasures and selfishness; developing intentions based on benevolence and compassion
3. Right Speech—avoiding speech that is false, quarrelsome, hurtful, idle chatter; engaging in speech that is supportive and beneficial to all
4. Right Action—refraining from killing living beings, stealing, and sexual misconduct; performing acts of kindness and compassion
5. Right Livelihood—refraining from livelihoods that involve wrongful speech and action; engaging in livelihoods that develop right speech and action
6. Right Effort—putting forth effort to prevent and undermine unwholesome mental states; instigating and developing wholesome mental states (e.g., loving-kindness)
7. Right Mindfulness—developing constant mindfulness, intense awareness, in reference to the changing and impermanent nature of the body, feelings, mind, and mental objects
8. Right Concentration—developing one-pointedness of mind and the four advanced meditative states (*jhānas*)

In the texts, the Noble Eightfold Path is explicated in terms of three phases of religious training that aim to transform experience through the gradual cultivation of the human personality. The threefold training is the development of moral conduct (*sīla*), mental culture (*samādhi*), and wisdom or insight (*paññā*). The threefold training is progressive and cumulative training. The training is progressive, because the texts relate that the "fruit" or "benefit" of moral conduct is mental culture, and that the "fruit" of mental culture is wisdom (or insight). The training is cumulative, because each step in the training is taken up and transformed in subsequent training, not abandoned or replaced.

Moral conduct includes right speech, right action, and right livelihood. Early Buddhism teaches the gradual development of moral habits through the practice of virtuous living. Virtuous actions are both the product and the cause of a morally virtuous character. For Buddhist laypersons, the Buddha laid out a code of substantive ethics in the form of five precepts. Lay Buddhists should refrain from killing living beings, stealing, sexual misconduct, lying, and taking intoxicants that lead to indolence.

Mental culture includes right effort, right mindfulness, and right concentration. From a Buddhist point of view, the mind is the key factor in the arising and ceasing of suffering. Suffering arises because the unenlightened person allows corrupt mental factors to distort perceptions and volitions. Through proper mental training, especially mindfulness, a person can control one's reactions to the world at the very point where such reactions arise and thus avoid unwholesome tendencies that distort one's perceptions and volitions. With the elimination of unwholesome or defiling tendencies, suffering ceases. The details of the development of mental culture require a very complex psychological account of human experience and action—much more detailed than can be covered here—but it should be apparent from this summary that control of the mind is absolutely central to Buddhist training.

Broadly speaking, meditative practice involves two different types of meditation: *samatha* (calming or serenity) meditation and *vipassanā* (insight) meditation. *Samatha* meditation disciplines emotions and aims at concentration. *Vipassanā* meditation sharpens the understanding to realize dependent arising and its corollaries, and so aims at insight into how things really are. The Buddhist texts refer to a number of highly advanced forms of meditation known as the four *jhānas.* The first *jhana* involves removing all sensual desires and immoral impulses, calming the body, concentrating the mind (but discursive thought remains), and experiencing in all this a sublime joy. The second *jhāna* eliminates discursive thought and, through concentration, produces profound joy and happiness. Mindfulness emerges in the third *jhāna,* and here the meditator experiences happiness and equanimity. In the fourth *jhāna,* there is neither suffering nor happiness, but there are equanimity, mindfulness, and moral purity taken to their highest levels.

Mental culture coupled with moral conduct has the ultimate aim of developing Buddhism's highest virtues (called the *brahmavihāras*): compassion (*karuṇā*), loving-kindness (*mettā*), sympathetic joy (*muditā*), and equanimity (*upekhā*).

Wisdom (or insight) includes right view and right intention. To become an enlightened person, one must fully comprehend the doctrine of dependent arising and its three corollaries, impermanence, suffering, and the doctrine of no (permanent) Self. More specifically, wisdom means understanding precisely how suffering arises and ceases. The realization of the doctrine of dependent arising was the catalyst for the Buddha's enlightenment. The knowledge that leads to the destruction of the defilements (*āsava*s) is the pinnacle of this understanding and is tantamount to achieving religious liberation (*nibbāna*).

The various stages of training together shape the enlightened person. This is what the Buddha meant when he said the following: "Wisdom is purified by morality, and morality is purified by wisdom: where one is, the other is; the moral person has wisdom and the wise person has morality, and the combination of morality and wisdom is called the highest thing in the world."[15]

[15] *Dīgha Nikāya* 1.124.

Finally, it must be stressed that the Buddha's religious therapy falls entirely within the natural, causal framework of dependent arising—this, in fact, was his greatest insight and revolutionary idea. Not only does dependent arising describe the arising of factors within the personality that lead to suffering, but it is also the prescription for achieving religious liberation through taking control over those same causal factors. The religious life in simplest terms is a matter of taking hold of those factors that produce suffering and, by training one's mind, redirecting those factors towards freedom and happiness. Thus, the essence of the Buddhist path is psychological and ethical, rather than metaphysical or theological.

The Enlightened Person and *Nibbāna*

According to the early Buddhist texts, the enlightened person is one who has completely eradicated the fetters that keep a person bound to *saṃsāric* existence (i.e., the cycle of rebirth). An enlightened person is fully liberated by the destruction of the defilements (*āsavas*) and insight into the dependently arisen nature of things. In short, such a person lives having achieved *nibbāna* (Skt: *nirvāṇa*).

The word "*nibbāna*" has a Sanskrit etymology that means to "blow out," as in the blowing out of a fire or flame. Here, "flame" seems to be used as a metaphor for selfish craving. Despite *nibbāna*'s central place within the Buddhist tradition, secondary sources offer widely divergent interpretations of *nibbāna*. What is clear from the Pāli texts is that *nibbāna* is neither a place nor a metaphysical state of being. *Nibbāna* is not the extinguishing of the *person* (as some Western scholars have thought), but only the extinguishing of the flames of craving that assail a person's character. The flames referred to here are the three flames of greed, hatred, and delusion that keep a person bound to a suffering existence. As rebirth is the effect of the defilements of a corrupt mind, *nibbāna* means the end of rebirth and thus an escape from the *saṃsāric* cycle. In the comparatively few canonical passages where *nibbāna* receives a positive description, *nibbāna* is described as sublime and stable happiness, joy, calm, and tranquillity. In simplest terms, *nibbāna* is the solution to the human existential problem, namely, the suffering that permeates life on the physical, psychological, and religious levels. Thus, *nibbāna* is best conceived as a mode of perfected living in this changing world.

Buddhist Social Thought: *Saṅgha* and Society

The *Saṅgha* is the Buddhist monastic community that is responsible for preserving and preaching the *dhamma*. The *Saṅgha* is composed of *bhikkhus* (monks) and *bhikkhunīs* (nuns) for whom ordination is a matter of "going forth" from domestic life to a "homeless" life of balanced simplicity.

The *Saṅgha* was instituted by the Buddha to provide a day-to-day social context for living the religious life. The Buddha laid down very specific rules for the *bhikkhus* and *bhikkhunīs* to follow. These are recorded in the first basket of the Pāli Canon called the *Vinaya Piṭaka.* The heart of the *Vinaya* is the more than two hundred monastic rules (called the *pātimokkha*) that the *bhikkhus* and *bhikkhunīs* chant every two weeks.

Buddhism developed at a time of significant social change in ancient India. However, the Pāli Canon depicts the Buddha as more of a social reformer than a social revolutionary—and even this role was somewhat incidental to the Buddha's focus on religious matters. The Buddha accepted the fourfold system of social class that was evident in his day, but he put all four classes on equal terms. Thus, he rejected class hierarchy and specifically objected to the Brahmin claims to be the highest class.

Although the *Saṅgha* may be held up as an ideal social context for religious striving, the Buddha had no intention of founding a religious community that ignored the spiritual needs of people in society at large. Buddhism includes male and female laity who not only provide material support to the *Saṅgha* but also are enjoined to make spiritual progress by keeping the five precepts referred to above. A Buddhist layperson can even achieve enlightenment (at least in theory), although domestic life is usually considered such a formidable obstacle to religious progress that, in practice, enlightenment would seem very nearly impossible for a person living a domestic life. Since Buddhism is not a "church" having "members," what it means to be a "Buddhist layperson" is somewhat ambiguous. In simplest terms, a "Buddhist layperson" is someone who relies on the "Three Refuges." A person invokes the "Three Refuges" by saying: "I take the Buddha as a refuge. I take the *dhamma* as a refuge. I take the *Saṅgha* as a refuge."

Reading the Early Buddhist Discourses

The aim of this book is to offer the reader a broad understanding of all of the basic doctrines of early Buddhism through reading the canonical sources in translation. Out of the vast amount of material in the Pāli Canon, twenty discourses have been selected that cover all of the major subfields of philosophy addressed within the canon. The discourses are arranged in a sequence, according to the main philosophical issues addressed. The sequence of topics is roughly as follows: biographical and methodological material, metaphysics, meditative practices, epistemology, and ethics and social philosophy. Also, there is at least one reading from each of the four major collections in the Discourse Basket.

The book includes complete discourses (*suttas*), rather than short excerpts, because of the inherent power of the narrative setting in the discourses to convey the Buddha's ideas. Buddhism is fundamentally about human issues that arise in genuine lived experience. The fascinating stories that frame the discourses significantly enliven the study of the doctrines and show them to be relevant to the human condition.

Readers should note that although the Pāli Canon is treated with great reverence by all Buddhists, especially those who practice Theravāda Buddhism, it is not considered the "word of God" or as infallible Truth. The texts record the Buddha himself saying that the teachings should be regarded with an open and a critical mind by his disciples. Likewise, the philosophically minded reader should critically reflect on the ideas presented in these texts. Far from being disrespectful of Buddhism, such critical investigation is encouraged and welcomed in the Buddhist tradition.[16]

A general glossary is provided at the end of the book because early Buddhist texts have many technical and specialized terms with which the reader who is new to the study of Buddhism is likely to be unfamiliar. Many glossary entries are given both in English and in Pāli to facilitate study by the advanced reader. Where variant interpretations or translations of a term are possible, the glossary often mentions the more important variant interpretations or translations.

A selected bibliography of useful secondary resources is provided at the end of the book to supplement the study of the primary texts.

Further Resources for Students and Instructors

A Web site has been developed that offers further support for the study of the early Buddhist texts in this book. The Web site contains the following instructional aids: study and discussion questions keyed to each chapter; maps; and photographs that illustrate the cultural traditions and history of Buddhism. The Web site can be found at www.hackettpublishing.com.

[16] See the Discourse to the Kālāmas (Chapter 2) for the Buddha's views on how to assess religious teachings.

List of Primary Texts

Primary Texts from the Discourse Basket (*Sutta Piṭaka*) of the Pāli Canon

Aṅguttara Nikāya, 5 vols., R. Morris and E. Hardy, eds. (London: Pali Text Society, 1885–1900). Translated as *The Book of Gradual Sayings,* F. L. Woodward and E. M. Hare (London: Pali Text Society, 1932–1936).

Dīgha Nikāya, 3 vols., T. W. Rhys Davids and J. E. Carpenter, eds. (London: Pali Text Society, 1890–1911). Translated as *Dialogues of the Buddha,* T. W. Rhys Davids and C.A.F. Rhys Davids (London: Pali Text Society, 1899–1921).

Majjhima Nikāya, 3 vols., V. Trenckner and R. Chalmers, eds. (London: Pali Text Society, 1887–1901). Translated as *Middle Length Sayings,* I. B. Horner (London: Pali Text Society, 1954–1959).

Saṃyutta Nikāya, 6 vols., L. Feer, ed. (London: Pali Text Society, 1884–1904). Translated as *The Book of the Kindred Sayings,* C.A.F. Rhys Davids and F. L. Woodward (London: Pali Text Society, 1917–1930).

Abbreviations and Notations

PED T. W. Rhys Davids and W. Stede, eds., *Pali-English Dictionary* (London: Pali Text Society, reprinted 1986).

Page numbers for the original Pāli texts are incorporated in the translations and appear in the outside margin next to the text to which they refer. These are keyed to the Pali Text Society editions listed above. Where paragraph numbers are given in the Pali Text Society editions, the paragraph numbers in the translations accord with those given in these editions. In editions where no paragraph numbers are given, paragraph numbers are improvised for ease of reference.

1

Discourse on the Noble Quest

(*Ariyapariyesana Sutta*)[1]

Who was the Buddha? Why did he choose to live a religious life? What are the distinctive factors in the Buddha's path to religious liberation (*nibbāna*)? The Discourse on the Noble Quest provides some of the answers to these questions as it purports to contain the Buddha's own account of significant events in his quest for religious meaning.

This discourse focuses on the Buddha's "going forth" from his opulent domestic life to a life of homelessness in search of release from suffering, the supreme goal of the religious life. The Buddha's enlightenment and his decision to teach the *dhamma* are recounted here. The Buddha's initial reluctance to teach the *dhamma* (until prevailed upon by Brahmā Sahampati) raises some very intriguing questions about the Buddha's self-understanding in regard to his role as a religious teacher. But perhaps more than anything else, these autobiographical passages remind the reader that, although the Buddha was extraordinary in terms of his virtues, mental powers, and religious achievements, he was a human being. According to the early Buddhist tradition, the path blazed by the Buddha is a path available to all human beings who strive assiduously to attain the moral conduct (*sīla*), mental culture (*samādhi*), and wisdom (*paññā*) taught by the Buddha.

As the title of the discourse suggests, the Buddha explains his search for religious fulfillment as the "noble quest." The discourse presents the "noble quest" in contrast to the "ignoble quest." According to the Buddha, the ordinary, unenlightened person is troubled by the vicissitudes of life—the profound existential problems of sickness, old age, and death—for reasons that run much deeper than most people realize. But the unenlightened person seeks happiness in the things "liable to birth," "liable to sickness," and so on, and therefore develops an infatuation with these things. Such behavior is bound to lead to suffering rather than genuine happiness, according to the Buddha. At the core of the ignoble quest is a corrupt mind, a morass of psychological factors, such as egoful attachments and self-indulgent sensualism, that spoils a person's existence and makes it nearly impossible for such a person to overcome the suffering that derives from sickness, old age, and death. Because sickness, old age, and death are unavoidable facts of any

[1] *Majjhima Nikāya* 1.160–175.

human life, these problems prevent the unenlightened person from achieving anything except the most superficial kinds of happiness in life.

The "noble quest," on the other hand, is a way to a sublime happiness, in spite of sickness, old age, and death. The noble quest focuses on the abandonment of selfish attachments and self-indulgent sensualism. In early Buddhism, addiction to sensual pleasure is considered to be among the most insidious causes of selfishness and other moral impurities. For this reason, the development of a mind free from the unwholesome effects of unrestrained sensualism is one of the central aims of the training taught by the Buddha. The destruction of selfish and hedonistic attitudes requires the development of *restraint,* especially the control of sensory experiences that involve sensual pleasure.

This central teaching of early Buddhism is here put into a powerful narrative context. The Buddha recounts why he went forth from domestic life into the religious life and what his experience was as a student under two prominent teachers of his day. According to the Buddha's own account, he mastered the spiritual knowledge and meditative powers of his teachers, Āḷāra Kālāma and Uddaka Rāmaputta. But having equaled or bettered his teachers in terms of knowledge and meditative powers, the Buddha did not achieve the breakthrough to religious liberation that he sought.

Having attained the four *jhānas* and such advanced meditative states as the "plane of no-thing" and the "plane of neither-perception-nor-non-perception," the Buddha finds out that these meditative powers alone are not sufficient by themselves for achieving enlightenment. Only the complete and utter destruction of the defilements of the mind (*āsavas*) leads to the ultimate religious liberation (*nibbāna*). Thus, the Buddha's noble quest is a revolutionary religious path. In contrast to the *metaphysical* path that culminates in knowledge of a transcendent reality or the *theistic* path that emphasizes developing a special relationship with God(s), the Buddha has laid out a spiritual quest for *ethical* transformation that focuses on the training of the mind.

Discourse

160

1. Thus have I heard. At one time, the Exalted One[2] was living in Sāvatthi, in the Jeta forest at Anāthapiṇḍika's park. Then the Exalted One, having dressed early in the morning, took his bowl and robe, and entered Sāvatthi for alms. Then a number of *bhikkhus* approached the venerable Ānanda.

[2] *Bhagavā.* This word is by far the most common term used to refer to the Buddha in the Pāli Canon. In other translations, *bhagavā* is often translated as "Blessed One" or "Lord."

When they had approached the venerable Ānanda, they said this: "It has been a long time, brother Ānanda, since the Exalted One gave a talk on the *dhamma* face-to-face. It would be good, brother Ānanda, if it were possible for us to hear the Exalted One give a talk on the *dhamma* face-to-face."

"In that case, you venerable ones should go to the hermitage of the Brahmin Rammaka. Perhaps there you may get to hear the Exalted One give a talk on the *dhamma* face-to-face."

"Yes, brother," those *bhikkhus* replied to the venerable Ānanda.

Then the Exalted One, having walked about in Sāvatthi for alms, returned from his almsround after his meal, and addressed the venerable Ānanda: "Venerable Ānanda, we will go to the Eastern Park, the palace of Migāra's mother, for the midday's rest."

"Yes, sir," replied the venerable Ānanda to the Exalted One. 161

Then the Exalted One went with the venerable Ānanda to the Eastern Park, to the palace of Migāra's mother, for the midday's rest. Then the Exalted One, having come out of seclusion in the evening, addressed the venerable Ānanda: "Venerable Ānanda, we will go to the Eastern Porch to bathe our limbs."

"Yes, sir," replied the venerable Ānanda to the Exalted One.

Then the Exalted One went with the venerable Ānanda to the Eastern Porch to bathe their limbs. Having bathed his limbs at the Eastern Porch and having emerged from the water, he stood in a single robe drying his limbs.

Then the venerable Ānanda said this to the Exalted One: "Sir, the hermitage of the Brahmin Rammaka is not far. The hermitage of the Brahmin Rammaka is lovely. Beautiful is the hermitage of the Brahmin Rammaka. It would be good, sir, if the Exalted One, out of compassion, were to approach the Brahmin Rammaka."

The Exalted One assented by remaining silent.[3] Then the Exalted One approached the hermitage of the Brahmin Rammaka. At that time a number of *bhikkhus* were sitting down in the Brahmin Rammaka's hermitage talking about *dhamma*. The Exalted One stood outside the door waiting for the discussion to stop. Then, when he saw that they had stopped talking, the Exalted One coughed and knocked on the door. The *bhikkhus* opened the door for the Exalted One. Then the Exalted One entered the Brahmin Rammaka's hermitage and sat down in the appointed seat.

When he was seated, the Exalted One addressed the *bhikkhus:* "When you were sitting down having a discussion just now, *bhikkhus*, what was the discussion among you that was interrupted?"

[3] Remaining silent, that is, stating no objection to a proposed course of action, is a common way of indicating agreement in the early Buddhist texts.

"Sir, our *dhamma* talk that was interrupted earlier was about the Exalted One himself. Then the Exalted One arrived."

"Good, *bhikkhus!* It is fitting, *bhikkhus,* that you—who are young men from good families who have gone forth from home to homelessness out of faith—are seated together talking about the *dhamma.* When you are gathered together, *bhikkhus,* there are two things to be done: discuss *dhamma* or maintain the noble silence.

2. "*Bhikkhus,* there are these two quests: the noble quest and the ignoble quest. What is the ignoble quest? In this regard, someone who is himself liable to birth seeks after what is also liable to birth; being himself liable
162 to old age, seeks after what is also liable to old age; being himself liable to sickness, seeks after what is also liable to sickness; being himself liable to death, seeks after what is also liable to death; being himself liable to sorrow, seeks after what is also liable to sorrow; being himself liable to impurity, seeks after what is also liable to impurity.

"What would you say is liable to birth? Sons and wife are liable to birth; male and female servants are liable to birth; goats and sheep are liable to birth; cocks and pigs are liable to birth; elephants, cows, horses, and mares are liable to birth; gold and silver are liable to birth. These things one attaches to are liable to birth, and this person who is enslaved, infatuated, and addicted to them, being himself liable to birth, seeks after what is also liable to birth.

"What would you say is liable to old age? Sons and wife are liable to old age . . . seeks after what is also liable to old age.

"What would you say is liable to sickness? Sons and wife are liable to sickness . . . seeks after what is also liable to sickness.

"What would you say is liable to death? Sons and wife are liable to death . . . seeks after what is also liable to death.

"What would you say is liable to sorrow? Sons and wife are liable to sorrow . . . seeks after what is also liable to sorrow.

"What would you say is liable to impurity? Sons and wife are liable to impurity; male and female servants are liable to impurity; goats and sheep are liable to impurity; cocks and pigs are liable to impurity; elephants, cows, horses, and mares are liable to impurity, gold and silver are liable to impurity. These things one attaches to are liable to impurity, and this person who is enslaved, infatuated, and addicted to them, being himself liable to impurity, seeks after what is also liable to impurity. This is the ignoble quest.

3. "And what is the noble quest? In that case, someone who is himself
163 liable to birth, having seen the danger in what is liable to birth, seeks the unborn, the unsurpassed escape from bondage that is *nibbāna.* Being himself liable to old age, having seen the danger in what is liable to old age, he

seeks the unaging, the unsurpassed escape from bondage that is *nibbāna.* Being himself liable to sickness, having seen the danger in what is liable to sickness, he seeks the unailing, the unsurpassed escape from bondage that is *nibbāna.* Being himself liable to death, having seen the danger in what is liable to death, he seeks the deathless, the unsurpassed escape from bondage that is *nibbāna.* Being himself liable to sorrow, having seen the danger in what is liable to sorrow, he seeks the sorrowless, the unsurpassed escape from bondage that is *nibbāna.* Being himself liable to impurity, having seen the danger in what is liable to impurity, he seeks the morally pure, the unsurpassed escape from bondage that is *nibbāna.* This is the noble quest.

4. "And I, too, before awakening, when I was not fully awakened and still a *bodhisatta,*[4] being myself liable to birth, sought after what was likewise liable to birth. Being myself liable to old age, I sought after what was likewise liable to old age. Being myself liable to sickness, I sought after what was likewise liable to sickness. Being myself liable to death, I sought after what was likewise liable to death. Being myself liable to sorrow, I sought after what was likewise liable to sorrow. Being myself liable to impurity, I sought after what was likewise liable to impurity.

"Then I had this thought: 'Why do I, being myself liable to birth, seek after what is likewise liable to birth? Why do I, being myself liable to old age, seek after what is likewise liable to old age? Why do I, being myself liable to sickness, seek after what is likewise liable to sickness? Why do I, being myself liable to death, seek after what is likewise liable to death? Why do I, being myself liable to sorrow, seek after what is likewise liable to sorrow? Why do I, being myself liable to impurity, seek after what is likewise liable to impurity? Suppose that, being myself liable to birth, having understood the danger in what is subject to birth, I seek *nibbāna,* the unborn, highest security from bondage. Suppose that being myself liable to old age, having understood the danger in what is subject to old age, I seek *nibbāna,* the unaging, highest security from bondage. Suppose that being myself liable to sickness, having understood the danger in what is subject to sickness, I seek *nibbāna,* the unailing, highest security from bondage. Suppose that being myself liable to death, having understood the danger in what is subject to death, I seek *nibbāna,* the deathless, highest security from bondage. Suppose that being myself liable to sorrow, having understood the danger in what is subject to sorrow, I seek *nibbāna,* the sorrowless, highest security from bondage. Suppose that being myself liable to impurity, having understood the danger in what is subject to impurity, I seek *nibbāna,* the morally pure, highest security from bondage.'

[4] *Bodhisatta* is the term the Buddha used to refer to himself before his enlightenment. It denotes a person who is destined for awakening.

"Then, after a time, when I was a young man, my hair shiny black, endowed with radiant youth, in the prime of life—my unwilling parents wailing tearfully—I shaved off my hair and donned yellow robes, I went forth from home to homelessness.[5] Having gone forth in this way, on a quest for what is good, searching for the unsurpassed, highest, path to peace, I approached Āḷāra Kālāma. When I had approached Āḷāra Kālāma, I said this: 'Good Kālāma, I wish to take up the holy life in this *dhamma* and discipline.'

"Having said this, Āḷāra Kālāma said this to me: 'Let the venerable one live [here]. This *dhamma* is such that, a wise person would soon master it
164 and dwell in it, having understood and realized for himself his teacher's doctrine.' So I very soon and quickly mastered this *dhamma.* I spoke the doctrine of knowledge and the doctrine of the elders, as far as mere lip service and repetition were concerned. I acknowledged—I as well as others—that 'I know and I see.' Then I had this thought: 'Āḷāra Kālāma does not merely proclaim this *dhamma* by means of faith. He proclaims: "Having understood and realized this for myself, I entered into it and dwell in it." Certainly, Āḷāra Kālāma dwells knowing and seeing this *dhamma.*'

"Then I approached Āḷāra Kālāma. Having approached him, I said this to Āḷāra Kālāma: 'To what extent do you, good Kālāma, proclaim this *dhamma,* having understood and realized it for yourself and entered into it?' This having been said, Āḷāra Kālāma proclaimed the plane of no-thing. Then I had this thought: 'It is not only Āḷāra Kālāma who has faith, but I, too, have faith. It is not only Āḷāra Kālāma who has energy, but I, too, have energy. It is not only Āḷāra Kālāma who has mindfulness, but I, too, have mindfulness. It is not only Āḷāra Kālāma who has concentration, but I, too, have concentration. It is not only Āḷāra Kālāma who has wisdom, but I, too, have wisdom. Suppose that I were to strive to achieve this *dhamma* which Āḷāra Kālāma proclaims: 'Having understood and realized this for myself, I entered into and dwell in it.' So very soon and very quickly, I entered into it and dwelled in it, having understood and realized this *dhamma* for myself.

"Then I approached Āḷāra Kālāma. Having approached him, I said this to Āḷāra Kālāma: 'Is it to this extent that you, reverend Kālāma, proclaim this *dhamma* which, having understood and realized it for yourself, you entered it?'

[Āḷāra Kālāma:] "'Friend, it is to that extent that I proclaim this *dhamma* which, having understood and realized it for myself, I entered into it.'

"'Friend, it is to that extent that I, too, entered into and dwell in this *dhamma,* having understood and realized it for myself.'

[5] "Going forth from home to homelessness" means leaving the domestic life for an ascetic or reclusive life devoted to religious goals. Such a practice is part of a number of Indian religious traditions (including Hinduism) and is not a peculiarly Buddhist practice.

[Āḷāra Kalāma:] "'It is profitable for us, friend, it is a gain for us, friend, that we see such a venerable one as this, such a fellow seeker of a holy life. I proclaim this *dhamma* that I have entered, having understood and realized it for myself, is the *dhamma* that you entered and dwell in, having understood and realized it for yourself. That *dhamma* which you entered and dwell 165
in, having understood and realized it for yourself, is the *dhamma* that I proclaim that I have entered, having understood and realized it for myself. This *dhamma* that I know is the *dhamma* that you know. This *dhamma* that you know is the *dhamma* that I know. Whatever I am, that you are. Whatever you are, that I am. Come now, friend, there being both of us, let us look after this group of followers.'

"In this way, Āḷāra Kālāma, my teacher, set me, the student, on the same level as himself. And he honored me with great honors. Then I had this thought: 'This *dhamma* does not lead to aversion, nor to dispassion, nor to cessation, nor to calmness, nor to higher knowledge, nor to awakening, nor to *nibbāna*—only just as far as the achievement of the plane of no-thing.' Not being satisfied with this *dhamma,* I abandoned it and went away.

5. "So, on a quest for what is good, searching for the unsurpassed, highest, path to peace, I approached Uddaka Rāmaputta. Having approached Uddaka Rāmaputta, I said this to him: 'Friend, I wish to take up the holy life in this *dhamma* and discipline.'

"Having said this, Uddaka Rāmaputta said this to me: 'Let the venerable one live [here]. This *dhamma* is such that, a wise person would soon master it and dwell in it, having understood and realized for himself his teacher's doctrine.' So I very soon and quickly mastered this *dhamma.* I spoke the doctrine of knowledge and the doctrine of the elders, as far as mere lip service and repetition were concerned. I acknowledged—I as well as others—that 'I know and I see.' Then I had this thought: 'Rāma[6] did not merely proclaim this *dhamma* by means of faith. He proclaimed: "Having understood and realized this for myself, I entered into it and dwell in it." Certainly, Rāma dwelt knowing and seeing this *dhamma.*'

"Then I approached Uddaka Rāmaputta. Having approached him, I said this to Uddaka Rāmaputta: 'To what extent did Rāma proclaim this *dhamma,* having understood and realized it for himself and entered into it?' This having been said, Uddaka Rāmaputta proclaimed the plane of neither-perception-nor-nonperception. Then I had this thought: 'It is not only
Rāma who had faith, but I, too, have faith. It is not only Rāma who had 166

[6] Apparently, Uddaka's father, Rāma, had been the one who had achieved the high spiritual knowledge that Siddhattha studied under Uddaka. Uddaka himself had not fully achieved this spiritual knowledge. This matter explains why the Buddha compares himself to Rāma and not Uddaka.

energy, but I, too, have energy. It is not only Rāma who had mindfulness, but I, too, have mindfulness. It is not only Rāma who had concentration, but I, too, have concentration. It is not only Rāma who had wisdom, but I, too, have wisdom. Suppose that I were to strive to achieve this *dhamma* which Rāma proclaimed: 'Having understood and realized this for myself, I entered into and dwell in it.' So very soon and very quickly, I entered into it and dwelled in it, having understood and realized this *dhamma* for myself.

"Then I approached Uddaka Rāmaputta. Having approached him, I said this to Uddaka Rāmaputta: 'Friend, is it to this extent that Rāma proclaimed this *dhamma* which, having understood and realized it for himself, he entered it?'

[Uddaka Rāmaputta:] "'Friend, it is to that extent that Rāma proclaimed this *dhamma* which, having understood and realized it for himself, he entered into it.'

"'Friend, it is to that extent that I, too, entered into and dwell in this *dhamma,* having understood and realized it for myself.'

[Uddaka Rāmaputta:] "'It is profitable for us, friend, it is a gain for us, friend, that we see such a venerable one as this, such a fellow seeker of a holy life. The *dhamma* that Rāma proclaimed, which he entered and dwelled in, having understood and realized it for himself, is the *dhamma* that you proclaim, which you have entered and dwelled in, having understood and realized it for yourself. That *dhamma* that you proclaim, which you have entered and dwelled in, having understood and realized it for yourself, is the *dhamma* that Rāma proclaimed, which he entered and dwelled in, having understood and realized it for himself. This *dhamma* that Rāma knew is the *dhamma* that you know. This *dhamma* that you know is the *dhamma* that Rāma knew. Whatever Rāma was, that you are. Whatever you are, that Rāma was. Come now, friend, you look after this group of followers.'

"In this way, Uddaka Rāmaputta, a fellow seeker of the holy life and my teacher, set me, the student, on the same level as himself. And he honored me with great honors. Then I had this thought: 'This *dhamma* does not lead to aversion, nor to dispassion, nor to cessation, nor to calmness, nor to higher knowledge, nor to awakening, nor to *nibbāna*—only just as far as the achievement of the plane of neither-perception-nor-non-perception.' So I turned away from and abandoned this *dhamma,* having not attained enough by this *dhamma.*

6. "So, on a quest for what is good, searching for the unsurpassed, highest, path to peace, I walked in stages through Magadha and arrived at the
167 camp-township of Uruvelā. There I saw a beautiful piece of land, a lovely
wooded grove, a delightful, clear flowing river with beautiful banks and a nearby village that could offer almsfood. Then I had this thought: 'Indeed,

sir, this is a beautiful piece of land, a lovely wooded grove, a delightful, clear flowing river with beautiful banks and a nearby village that could offer alms-food. Indeed, this is enough for the striving of a young man of a good family who is focused on the goal of striving.' So, I sat down there thinking: 'This is enough for striving.'

7. "So—being myself liable to birth, having seen the danger in what is liable to birth, on a quest for *nibbāna,* the unborn, unsurpassed security from bondage—I attained *nibbāna,* the unborn, unsurpassed security from bondage. Being myself liable to old age, having seen the danger in what is liable to old age, on a quest for *nibbāna,* the unaging, unsurpassed security from bondage—I attained *nibbāna,* the unaging, unsurpassed security from bondage. Being myself liable to sickness, having seen the danger in what is liable to sickness, on a quest for *nibbāna,* the unailing, unsurpassed security from bondage—I attained *nibbāna,* the unailing, unsurpassed security from bondage. Being myself liable to death, having seen the danger in what is liable to death, on a quest for *nibbāna,* the deathless, unsurpassed security from bondage—I attained *nibbāna,* the deathless, unsurpassed security from bondage. Being myself liable to sorrow, having seen the danger in what is liable to sorrow, on a quest for *nibbāna,* the sorrowless, unsurpassed security from bondage—I attained *nibbāna,* the sorrowless, unsurpassed security from bondage. Being myself liable to impurity, having seen the danger in what is liable to impurity, on a quest for *nibbāna,* the morally pure, unsurpassed security from bondage—I attained *nibbāna,* the morally pure, unsurpassed security from bondage. The knowledge and vision arose in me: 'My liberation is unshakable. This is the last birth. There is now no rebirth.'[7]

8. "Then I had this thought: 'This *dhamma* that I have attained is deep, difficult to see, difficult to understand, peaceful, excellent, beyond reasoning, subtle, and to be experienced by the wise. But this generation delights in worldly attachment, revels in worldly attachment, and rejoices in worldly attachment. For a generation delighting in worldly attachment, that takes delight in worldly attachment, and rejoices in worldly attachment, this doctrine is hard to see, namely, dependent arising which involves specific conditionality.[8] Also, this doctrine is hard to see, namely, the tranquillizing of all dispositions to action, the renunciation of all attachments, the destruction of craving, dispassion, cessation, and *nibbāna.* So were I to teach this 168
dhamma and others were not to understand me, that would be wearisome

[7] Religious freedom or liberation in both Hindu and Buddhist traditions is conceived as escape from the *saṃsāric* cycle, that is, the round of birth-death-rebirth.

[8] *Idapaccayatā*—literally, "this-conditionality."

and vexing for me.' Moreover, these verses that have never been heard before occurred to me spontaneously:

'I have attained it with difficulty
Enough now of preaching!
By those consumed with lust and hate
This *dhamma* is not easily understood
It goes against the stream, it is subtle, deep, hard to see, and delicate
Those who are slaves to passion will not see it
As they are covered in a mass of darkness.'

9. "Thinking it over in these ways, my mind was inclined toward indifference and not toward teaching the *dhamma.* Then Brahmā Sahampati read my mind with his mind, and he had this thought: 'Sir, the world is lost. Sir, the world is destroyed, inasmuch as the *Tathāgata,* an *arahant,* a fully awakened one, is inclined toward indifference and not toward teaching the *dhamma.*' Then, just as a strong man might stretch out a bent arm or bend back a stretched arm, in the same way Brahmā Sahampati disappeared from the Brahmā-world and appeared in front of me. Then Brahmā Sahampati, having arranged his upper robe over one shoulder, and having saluted me with his hands raised and joined in reverence, said this: 'Sir, let the Exalted One teach the *dhamma!* Let the Well-Farer teach the *dhamma!* There are beings that have a nature with little passion who are wasting away from not hearing the *dhamma.* They will become knowers of the *dhamma.*' This was what Brahmā Sahampati said. Having said this, he said another thing:

'What has appeared in Magadha before
Is an impure *dhamma,* as it was thought up by people with defilements;
Open this door to the deathless.
Let them hear the *dhamma*
To which the stainless one has awoken.
Just as a person standing on a rock at the crest of a mountain
Might watch people all around
Likewise, O wise, all-seeing one, ascend the terraced heights built of *dhamma.*
Released from grief, look down at the people
169 Afflicted with sorrow, oppressed with birth and old age.

Arise hero, conqueror in battle, leader of the caravan who is without debt,
Wander in the world.

O Exalted One, teach the *dhamma*
They will become knowers (of the *dhamma*).'

10. "Then, having heard Brahmā's request, out of compassion for beings, I surveyed the world with the eye of a Buddha.[9] As I surveyed the world with the eye of a Buddha, I saw beings that had a nature with little passion and others that had a nature with much passion, some with acute faculties and others with dull faculties, some with good qualities and others with bad qualities, some easy to teach, and others difficult to teach, and some who lived seeing fear and blame in another world. Just as in a pond of blue, red, or white lotuses,[10] some of the blue, red, or white lotuses that are born in and grow in the water thrive immersed in the water without rising out of it, and some other lotuses that are born in and grow in the water rest on the surface of the water, and some other lotuses that are born in and grow in the water rise out of the water and stand untainted by the water. In the same way, I surveyed the world with the eye of a Buddha, and I saw beings having a nature with little passion and others having a nature with much passion, some with acute faculties and others with dull faculties, some with good qualities and others with bad qualities, some easy to teach and others difficult to teach, and some who live seeing fear and blame in another world. Then I replied to Brahmā Sahampati with the following verse:

'The doors to deathlessness are opened for them, Brahmā,
Let those with ears show their faith.
Thinking it would be an annoyance, Brahmā,
I have not spoken
This *dhamma* that is profound and excellent for humankind.'

11. "Then Brahmā Sahampati thought: 'I have created the opportunity for the Exalted One to teach the *dhamma*.' Then having saluted me and having kept me on his right side,[11] he disappeared right then and there.

12. "I had this thought: 'To whom should I first teach the *dhamma*? Who will quickly understand this *dhamma*?' Then I had this further thought:

[9] According to Buddhist tradition, Buddhas have special sensory and mental powers.

[10] The lotus is an important image in Buddhist literature, especially in the texts of the Mahāyāna tradition. The lotus rises out of the mud and muck of a pond only to thrust forth a flower of unsullied and pristine beauty. But the lotus is still rooted in the pond. Likewise, the *arahant* emerges from the mire of the normal world as a morally purified being. But such a person is still rooted in the world—the Buddhist adept is *in* the world, but not *of* it.

[11] Respect and reverence is shown by keeping the respected person or object always to one's right side.

'This Āḷāra Kālāma is wise, learned, and intelligent and for a long time has
170 had a nature with little passion. Suppose, then, I were to teach Āḷāra Kālāma
the *dhamma* first; he would understand this *dhamma* quickly.' Then a *deva* approached me and said this: 'Āḷāra Kālāma died seven days ago, sir.' Then the knowledge and vision arose in me that 'Āḷāra Kālāma died seven days ago.' Then I had this thought: 'Āḷāra Kālāma was a great man. If he had heard this *dhamma,* he would have understood it quickly.'

"I had this thought: 'To whom should I first teach the *dhamma?* Who will quickly understand this *dhamma?*' Then I had this further thought: 'This Uddaka Rāmaputta is wise, learned, and intelligent and for a long time has had a nature with little passion. Suppose, then, I were to teach Uddaka Rāmaputta the *dhamma* first; he would understand this *dhamma* quickly.' Then a *deva* approached me and said this: 'Uddaka Rāmaputta died last night, sir.' Then the knowledge and vision arose in me that Uddaka Rāmaputta died last night. Then I had this thought: 'Uddaka Rāmaputta was a great man. If he had heard this *dhamma,* he would have understood it quickly.'

"I had this thought: 'To whom should I first teach the *dhamma?* Who will quickly understand this *dhamma?*' Then I had this further thought: 'The group of five monks who looked after me when I was striving were of great service to me. Suppose, then, I were to teach the *dhamma* to that group of five monks first.' Then I had this thought: 'Where is that group of five monks living now?' Then I saw with my *deva*-eye, purified and surpassing that of [normal] humans, that the group of five monks was living in Vārāṇasi (Benares) at the Deer Park in Isipatana. Then having stayed at Uruvelā for as long as was proper, I set out walking by stages to Vārāṇasi.

13. "Then Upaka, an Ājīvika,[12] saw me as I was walking along the main road between Gayā and the place of enlightenment. Having seen me, he said this to me: 'Friend, your faculties are very pure and your skin complexion
very clear and radiant. Under whom, friend, have you gone forth? Who
171 is your teacher? Whose doctrine do you profess?' This having been said, I
replied to Upaka with these verses:

'Conquering all, knowing all, am I.
Undefiled among all things
Renouncing all, I am freed by the destruction of craving.
Having understood all this for myself, whom should I declare as
my teacher?

I have no teacher
There is no equal to me

[12] Ājīvikas were naked wandering ascetics.

In the world, with its *devas,*
There is no person equal to me.

I am an *arahant* in the world
I am the unsurpassed teacher
I alone am the fully enlightened one
I have become cooled and blissful.

I go to the city of Kāsi
To turn the wheel of *dhamma*
In a world that has become blind
I will beat the drum of deathlessness.'

[Upaka said:] 'In which case, friend, you claim that you are an *arahant,* an infinite victor.'

'Victors are those like me
Who have attained the destruction of defilements
Evil things have been conquered by me
Therefore, Upaka, I am a victor.'

"This having been said, Upaka said: 'May it be so, friend.' Having said that, he shook his head and went away taking a different road.

14. "Then I set out walking by stages to the Deer Park at Isipatana in Vārāṇasi. And there I approached the group of five monks.[13] The group of five monks saw me approaching at a distance. Having seen me, they came to an agreement among themselves: 'Friend, this religious wanderer Gotama is coming. He lives in luxury and has wavered in his striving. He has gone back to a life of luxury, so he should not be greeted nor should we stand up out of respect for him, nor should we receive his bowl or robe. Yet perhaps a seat should be put out so he can sit down, if he wants.' But as I approached, the group of five monks was not able to keep the agreement. Some of them came out to meet me and received my bowl and robe. Some of them prepared a seat. Some of them brought water for washing feet. And they addressed me by name and with the word 'friend.' When they had spoken thus, I said this to the group of five monks: 'Monks, do not address the *Tathāgata* by name or with the word "friend." Monks, the *Tathāgata* is an *arahant,* a fully enlightened one. Listen, monks, the deathless has been 172

[13] The text reads "*bhikkhū,*" but here the term is translated as "monks," rather than left untranslated, as when it refers specifically to Buddhist monks. The reason for this treatment is that at this point in the discourse, no Buddhist ordination has occurred.

attained. I will instruct you. I will teach you the *dhamma.* If you practice in the way in which I advise you, you will soon attain the goal for which young men of good families rightly go forth from home to homelessness—that unsurpassed goal of the holy life[14] here in this very world—and you will dwell in it, having entered it by understanding and realizing it for yourselves.'

"When this had been said, the group of five monks said this to me: 'But, friend Gotama, by this conduct, practice, and performance of austerities you did not attain any superior human states, any knowledge and vision befitting a noble one. So how is it now, having reverted to living in luxury and wavering in striving, that you will have attained any superior human states, any knowledge and vision befitting a noble one?'

"When this had been said, I said this to the group of five monks: 'Monks, the *Tathāgata* is not one who lives in luxury. He has not wavered in his striving or reverted to luxury. The *Tathāgata* is an *arahant,* a fully enlightened one. Listen, monks, the deathless has been attained. I will instruct you. I will teach you the *dhamma.* If you practice in the way in which I advise you, you will soon attain the goal for which young men of good families rightly go forth from home to homelessness—that unsurpassed goal of the holy life here in this very world—and you will dwell in it, having entered it by understanding and realizing it for yourselves.' And a second time, the group of five monks said this to me: 'But, friend Gotama, by this conduct, practice, and performance of austerities you did not attain any superior human states, any knowledge and vision befitting a noble one. So how is it now, having reverted to living in luxury and wavering in striving, that you will have attained any superior human states, any knowledge and vision befitting a noble one?' And a second time, *bhikkhus,* I said to the group of five monks: 'Monks, the *Tathāgata* is not one who lives in luxury. He has not wavered in his striving or reverted to luxury. The *Tathāgata* is an *arahant,* a fully enlightened one. Listen, monks, the deathless has been attained. I will instruct you. I will teach you the *dhamma.* If you practice in the way in which I advise you, you will soon attain the goal for which young men of good families rightly go forth from home to homelessness—that unsurpassed goal of the holy life here in this very world—and you will dwell in it, having entered it by understanding and realizing it for yourselves.

"So a third time the group of five monks said this to me: 'But, friend Gotama, by this conduct, practice, and performance of austerities you did not attain any superior human states, any knowledge and vision befitting a noble one. So how is it now, having reverted to living in luxury and wavering

[14] *Brahmacariya.*

in striving, that you will have attained any superior human states, any knowledge and vision befitting a noble one?'

"When this had been said, I said this to the group of five monks: 'You know me by personal acquaintance, monks, have I ever spoken like this before?'

"'No, sir.'

"'Monks, the *Tathāgata* is an *arahant,* a fully enlightened one. Listen, monks, the deathless has been attained. I will instruct you. I will teach you the *dhamma.* If you practice in the way in which I advise you, you will soon attain the goal for which young men of good families rightly go forth from home to homelessness—that unsurpassed goal of the holy life here in this very world—and you will dwell in it, having entered it by understanding 173
and realizing it for yourselves.'

"And I was able to convince the group of five monks. Then I would teach two monks, while three monks went for alms. And the six of us lived on the alms the three had brought back. Sometimes I would teach three monks, while two monks went for alms. And the six of us lived on the alms the two brought back.

"Then the group of five monks, having been taught in this way and instructed in this way: being themselves liable to birth, having known the danger in what is liable to birth, seeking *nibbāna,* the unborn, unsurpassed security from bondage—they attained *nibbāna,* the unborn, unsurpassed security from bondage. Being themselves liable to old age . . . they attained *nibbāna,* the unaging, unsurpassed security from bondage. Being themselves liable to sickness . . . they attained *nibbāna,* the unailing, unsurpassed security from bondage. Being themselves liable to death . . . they attained *nibbāna,* the deathless, unsurpassed security from bondage. Being themselves liable to sorrow . . . they attained *nibbāna,* the sorrowless, unsurpassed security from bondage. Being themselves liable to impurity, having known the danger in what is liable to impurity, seeking *nibbāna,* the morally pure, unsurpassed security from bondage—they attained *nibbāna,* the morally pure, unsurpassed security from bondage. Knowledge and vision arose in us: 'Our liberation is unshakable. This is the last birth. There is now no rebirth.'

15. "*Bhikkhus,*[15] there are these five types of sensual pleasure. What are the five? Visible objects cognizable by the eye, alluring, desirable, pleasing, likable, connected with sense desire, and enticing; sounds cognizable by the ear . . . smells cognizable by the nose . . . tastes cognizable by the tongue . . . tangibles cognizable by the body, alluring, desirable, pleasing, likable,

[15] At this point, the group of five can be referred to as "*bhikkhus*" because they have been converted to the Buddhist path. Compare this passage with the account in the "Mahāvagga" of the Discipline Basket. See *Vinaya* 1.8–14.

connected with sense desire, and enticing. These are the five types of sensual pleasure.

"Regarding those religious wanderers and Brahmins who experience these five types of sensual pleasure, who are tied to them, infatuated by them, addicted to them, who do not see the danger in them, and who do not know an escape from them, it should be understood that: 'They have come to calamity, come to misfortune. The Evil One (Māra) does with them as he pleases.' Just as in the forest a deer might be lying down bound up in a heap of snares. In such a case, it should be understood about the deer that: 'It has come to calamity, come to misfortune. The hunter does with it as he pleases.' For when the hunter comes, it will not go away as it wishes. So, too, regarding those religious wanderers and Brahmins who experience these five types of sensual pleasure, who are tied to them, infatuated by them, addicted to them, who do not see the danger in them, and who do not know an escape from them, it should be understood that: 'They have come to calamity, come to misfortune. The Evil One does with them as he pleases.'

"Regarding those religious wanderers and Brahmins who experience these five types of sensual pleasure, but who are not tied to them, not infatuated by them, not addicted to them, who see the danger in them, and who know
174 an escape from them, it should be understood that: 'They have not come to calamity, not come to misfortune. The Evil One cannot do with them as he pleases.' Just as in the forest a deer might not be lying down bound up in a heap of snares. In such a case, it should be understood about the deer that: 'It has not come to calamity, come to misfortune. The hunter cannot do with it as he pleases.' For when the hunter comes, it will go away as it wishes. So, too, regarding those religious wanderers and Brahmins who experience these five types of sensual pleasure, who are not tied to them, not infatuated by them, not addicted to them, who see the danger in them, and who know an escape from them, it should be understood that: 'They have not come to calamity, not come to misfortune. The Evil One cannot do with them as he pleases.'

16. "Just as a deer in a forest roams the slopes of the forest confidently, stands confidently, sits down confidently, and sleeps confidently. What is the reason for this? It is beyond the hunter's grasp. In the same way, having become detached from sensual pleasures, detached from unwholesome mental states, a *bhikkhu* lives, having entered the first *jhāna,* which is accompanied by reasoning and cogitation, wherein there is joy and happiness born of detachment. This *bhikkhu* is called one who has made Māra blind and, having deprived Māra's eyesight of its range, he lives unseen by the Evil One.

"Again, in a further case, by the calming of reasoning and cogitation, internally purified, a *bhikkhu* lives, having entered the second *jhāna,* which has a one-pointed mind that is devoid of reasoning and cogitation and wherein there is joy and happiness born of concentration.[16] This *bhikkhu* is called one who has made Māra blind and, having deprived Māra's eyesight of its range, he lives unseen by the Evil One.

"Again, in a further case, dwelling in equanimity, and with the cessation of joy, mindful and fully aware, a *bhikkhu* lives, having entered the third *jhāna,* wherein he experiences happiness with the body and that which the noble ones describe as: 'He who has equanimity and mindfulness lives happily.' This *bhikkhu* is called one who has made Māra blind and, having deprived Māra's eyesight of its range, he lives unseen by the Evil One.

"Again, in a further case, abandoning both happiness and suffering, from the extinction of the elation and despair he felt formerly, a *bhikkhu* lives, having entered the fourth *jhāna,* wherein there is neither suffering nor happiness, but the purity of mindfulness and equanimity. This *bhikkhu* is called one who has made Māra blind and, having deprived Māra's eyesight of its range, he lives unseen by the Evil One.

"Again, in a further case, by completely passing beyond the perception of physicality, by the extinguishing of repugnant perceptions, by giving no attention to perceptions of diversity,[17] thinking 'space is infinite,' a *bhikkhu* lives having entered into the plane of infinite space. This *bhikkhu* is called one who has made Māra blind and, having deprived Māra's eyesight of its range, he lives unseen by the Evil One.

"Again, in a further case, by passing completely beyond the plane of infinite space, thinking 'consciousness is infinite,' a *bhikkhu* lives having entered into the plane of infinite consciousness. This *bhikkhu* is called one who has made Māra blind and, having deprived Māra's eyesight of its range, he lives unseen by the Evil One.

"Again, in a further case, by completely passing beyond the plane of infinite consciousness, thinking 'there is not anything,' a *bhikkhu* lives having entered into the plane of no-thing. This *bhikkhu* is called one who has made Māra blind and, having deprived Māra's eyesight of its range, he lives unseen by the Evil One.

"Again, in a further case, by completely passing beyond the plane of nothing, a *bhikkhu* lives having entered into the plane of neither-perception-nor- 175
nonperception. This *bhikkhu* is called one who has made Māra blind and, having deprived Māra's eyesight of its range, he lives unseen by the Evil One.

[16] *Samādhi.*

[17] Apparently, this means ignoring the normal kind of differentiating experience in which one experiences a plurality of beings in the world. Instead, one experiences everything as a unified plenum.

"Again, in a further case, by completely passing beyond the plane of neither-perception-nor-non-perception, a *bhikkhu* lives having entered into the cessation of perception and feeling. Having seen this by his wisdom, the defilements[18] are completely destroyed. This *bhikkhu* is called one who has made Māra blind and, having deprived Māra's eyesight of its range, he lives unseen by the Evil One. He has crossed beyond his attachment to the world. He walks confidently, stands confidently, sits down confidently, and sleeps confidently. What is the reason for this? He is beyond the grasp of the Evil One."

17. This was said by the Exalted One. Delighted, those *bhikkhus* rejoiced in what the Exalted One had said.

[18] *Āsavas.* These are the mental factors that distort perceptions and corrupt the mind. There are three basic defilements: greed, hatred, and delusion.

2

Discourse to the Kālāmas

(*Kālāma Sutta*[1])

This discourse begins with a common problem: different religious teachers make vastly different claims about religious truth and the practices necessary to achieve religious goals, so how does one know which one is right? What criteria can one use to determine who is telling the truth? This is the problem posed by the Kālāmas to the Buddha, and, no doubt, it remains a problem for many religious inquirers today. Compounding the problem is the tendency of most religious traditions to claim to have exclusive ownership of the highest religious truth.

In responding to the Kālāmas, the Buddha demonstrates his empiricism and balanced teaching methods. Moreover, the Buddha stands out (perhaps, even alone) among religious teachers for his antidogmatic treatment of religious doctrines. Most religions, of course, hold that their scriptures or the pronouncements of their spiritual leaders are ultimate truths and should be accepted unquestioningly by the faithful. But in this discourse, the Buddha makes it clear that he disagrees with traditions that require unquestioning faith in scriptures or spiritual leaders. Instead, he proposes that there should be proper *reasons* for accepting a doctrine, even a religious doctrine. According to the Buddha, an objective assessment of a doctrine should look carefully at what sort of results are likely, if one were to act in accordance with the doctrine. A doctrine should be accepted only to the extent that the doctrine can be verified in the person's own experience as one that leads to wholesome and happy consequences. Even the authority of the Buddha and the Buddhist texts, therefore, should not be a matter of blind faith. The canonical Buddhist texts are certainly revered by Buddhists, but if one takes the Buddha at his word, the texts are to be read critically and the teachings contained in the texts subjected to reflection and empirical assessment. Today, this position would be called "religious empiricism."

This discourse also gives a detailed description of the noble disciple—a person freed from the defilements of greed, hatred, and delusion. Such a person develops the cardinal virtues of Buddhism: loving-kindness, compassion, sympathetic joy, and equanimity. Significantly, the noble disciple has access to the four "comforts" that offer spiritual solace to a person. Among

[1] *Aṅguttara Nikāya* 1.188–193

the profound, existential problems that cause many people anxiety are such matters as whether or not there is an afterlife or whether actions are rewarded or punished according to the merits of the action. But these problems do not trouble the trained noble disciple. Such a person has achieved "comfort" because the noble disciple thinks that whether or not there is an "afterworld," and whether or not there are rewards and punishments for actions (i.e., karmic results), one should purify oneself from moral stains and do good. In other words, the rationale for morally good actions is intrinsic and can be found in this very world. The noble disciple is neither plied with promises of an afterlife nor guaranteed great rewards for moral actions, as in many other religious traditions.

Discourse

188

1. Thus have I heard. At one time, the Exalted One was walking on tour in Kosala with a large contingent of *bhikkhus* and arrived at a town named Kesaputta. The Kālāmas of Kesaputta heard that the recluse Gotama, son of the Sakyans, the one who went forth from the Sakyan clan, had arrived. And this good report was spread about concerning the venerable Gotama; the Exalted One is described as: "an *arahant,* a fully awakened one, endowed with knowledge and virtue, a Well-Farer, a knower of the world, an unsurpassed charioteer of human beings who are like horses to be tamed, a teacher of *devas* and human beings, a Buddha, an Exalted One. He makes known this world—with its *devas,* Māras, Brahmās, religious wanderers, and Brahmins—to the present generation of *devas* and humans beings, having understood and realized this for himself. He teaches the *dhamma* which is beautiful in the beginning, beautiful in the middle, and beautiful in the end, in spirit as well as in letter. He makes known the pure religious life that is complete in its entirety. It would be a good thing to see such an *arahant* as that."

2. Then the Kālāmas of Kesaputta approached the Exalted One. Having approached him, some of them saluted him and sat down to one side. Some of them exchanged greetings with the Exalted One, conversed courteously with him, and when finished, sat down to one side. Some others stretched out their clasped hands in a gesture of reverence and then sat down to one side. Still others announced their names and clans, and then sat down to one side. Some others remained silent and then sat down to one side. When he was seated to one side, one of the Kālāmas of Kesaputta said this to the Exalted One:

"There are, sir, certain recluses and Brahmins who come to Kesaputta. They explain and proclaim only their own doctrines, while the doctrines of others they abuse, despise, treat with contempt, and condemn. Also, sir,
189 there are other recluses and Brahmins who come to Kesaputta. These also

explain and proclaim their own doctrines, while the doctrines of others they abuse, despise, treat with contempt, and condemn. Sir, we are in doubt and perplexity about this. Who among these honorable recluses speaks the truth, and who speaks what is false?"

3. "Indeed, it is proper to be in doubt, Kālāmas, and to be perplexed. When there is a doubtful situation, perplexity arises.

"In such cases, do not accept a thing by recollection, by tradition, by mere report, because it is based on the authority of scriptures, by mere logic or inference, by reflection on conditions, because of reflection on or fondness for a certain theory, because it merely seems suitable, nor thinking: 'The religious wanderer is respected by us.' But when you know for yourselves: 'These things are unwholesome, blameworthy, reproached by the wise, when undertaken and performed lead to harm and suffering'—these you should reject.

4. "What do you think, Kālāmas? When greed arises within a person, is it to one's benefit or to one's detriment?"

"To one's detriment, sir."

"So, Kālāmas, does this greedy person, being overpowered by greed and having lost control over his mind, kill living beings, take what is not given, go with another's wife, tell lies, and encourage others to do the same, which things are to his detriment and suffering for a long time?"

"Yes, sir."

5. "What do you think, Kālāmas? When hatred arises within a person, is it to one's benefit or to one's detriment?"

"To one's detriment, sir."

"So, Kālāmas, does this hateful person, being overpowered by hate and having lost control over his mind, kill living beings, take what is not given, go with another's wife, tell lies, and encourage others to do the same, which things are to his detriment and suffering for a long time?"

"Yes, sir."

6. "What do you think, Kālāmas? When delusion arises within a person, is it to one's benefit or to one's detriment?"

"To one's detriment, sir."

"So, Kālāmas, does this deluded person, being overpowered by delusion 190
and having lost control over his mind, kill living beings, take what is not given, go with another's wife, tell lies, and encourage others to do the same, which things are to his detriment and suffering for a long time?"

"Yes, sir."

7. "What do you think, Kālāmas? Are these things wholesome or unwholesome?"

"Unwholesome, sir."

"Are they blameworthy or not blameworthy?"

"Blameworthy, sir."

"Are they reproached by the wise or commended by the wise?"

"Reproached by the wise, sir."

"If these things are undertaken and performed, do they lead to one's detriment and suffering or not, or how is it in this matter?"

"Sir, if these things are undertaken and performed, they lead to harm and suffering. That is the way it is in this matter, in our opinion."

8. "So then, Kālāmas, regarding what I said just now: 'Do not accept a thing by recollection, by tradition, by mere report, because it is based on the authority of scriptures, by mere logic or inference, by reflection on conditions, because of reflection on or fondness for a certain theory, because it merely seems suitable, nor thinking: "The religious wanderer is respected by us." But, Kālāmas, when you know for yourselves: "These things are unwholesome, blameworthy, reproached by the wise, when undertaken and performed lead to one's detriment and suffering"—these you should reject.' Having said this, this is the reason for what I said.

9. "Here, Kālāmas, do not accept a thing by recollection, by tradition, by mere report, because it is based on the authority of scriptures, by mere logic or inference, by reflection on conditions, because of reflection on or fondness for a certain theory, because it merely seems suitable, nor thinking: 'The religious wanderer is respected by us.' But, Kālāmas, when you know for yourselves: 'These things are wholesome, not blameworthy, commended by the wise, when undertaken and performed lead to one's benefit and happiness'—you should live undertaking these things.

10. "What do you think, Kālāmas? When non-greed arises within a person, is it to one's benefit or to one's detriment?"

"To one's benefit, sir."

"So, Kālāmas, does this non-greedy person, not being overpowered by greed and having control over one's mind, not kill living beings, not take what is not given, not go with another's wife, not tell lies, and encourage
191 others to do the same, which things are to one's benefit and happiness for a long time?"

"Yes, sir."

11. "What do you think, Kālāmas? When non-hatred arises within a person, is it to one's benefit or to one's detriment?"

"To one's benefit, sir."

"So, Kālāmas, does this non-hateful person, not being overpowered by hate and having control over one's mind, not kill living beings, not take what is not given, not go with another's wife, not tell lies, and encourage others to do the same, which things are to one's benefit and happiness for a long time?"

"Yes, sir."

12. "What do you think, Kālāmas? When non-delusion arises within a person, is it to one's benefit or to one's detriment?"

"To one's benefit, sir."

"So, Kālāmas, does this non-deluded person, not being overpowered by delusion and having control over his mind, not kill living beings, not take what is not given, not go with another's wife, not tell lies, and encourage others to do the same, which things are to one's benefit and happiness for a long time?"

"Yes, sir."

13. "What do you think, Kālāmas? Are these things wholesome or unwholesome?"

"Wholesome, sir."

"Are they blameworthy or not blameworthy?"

"Not blameworthy, sir."

"Are they reproached by the wise or commended by the wise?"

"Commended by the wise, sir."

"If these things are undertaken and performed, do they lead to one's benefit and happiness or not, or how is it in this matter?"

"Sir, if these things are undertaken and performed, they lead to one's benefit and happiness. That is the way it is in this matter, in our opinion."

14. "So then, Kālāmas, regarding what I just now said: 'In such cases, do not accept a thing by recollection, by tradition, by mere report, because it is based on the authority of scriptures, by mere logic or inference, by reflection on conditions, because of reflection on or fondness for a certain theory, because it merely seems suitable, nor thinking: "The religious wanderer is respected by us." But, Kālāmas, when you know for yourselves: "These things are wholesome, not blameworthy, commended by the wise, when undertaken and performed lead to one's benefit and happiness"—you should live undertaking these.' Having said this, this is the reason for what I said." 192

15. "Now, Kālāmas, as a noble disciple is one who is freed from covetousness and malevolence, not confused in mind, attentive and mindful, with a heart filled with loving-kindness, he lives, having pervaded one direction with such a heart, and likewise a second direction, a third direction, and a fourth direction. Upward, downward, across, everywhere, and in every way, throughout the whole world, he lives endowed with a loving-kindness that is widespread, great, boundless, free from hatred, and untroubled. With a heart filled with compassion, he lives, having pervaded one direction with such intentions, and likewise a second direction, a third direction, and a

fourth direction. Upward, downward, across, everywhere, and in every way, throughout the whole world, he lives endowed with a compassion that is widespread, great, boundless, free from hatred, and untroubled. With a heart filled with sympathetic joy, he lives, having pervaded one direction with such a heart, and likewise a second direction, a third direction, and a fourth direction. Upward, downward, across, everywhere, and in every way, throughout the whole world, he lives endowed with a sympathetic joy that is widespread, great, boundless, free from hatred, and untroubled. With a heart filled with equanimity, he lives, having pervaded one direction with such a heart, and likewise a second direction, a third direction, and a fourth direction. Upward, downward, across, everywhere, and in every way, throughout the whole world, he lives endowed with an equanimity that is widespread, great, boundless, free from hatred, and untroubled.

"Indeed, Kālamas, a noble disciple is thus freed in mind from hatred, untroubled in mind, unstained in mind, pure in mind, and in this world has attained the following four comforts.

16. "[The noble disciple thinks:] 'If there is an after-world, if there is the fruit and result of actions that are good or evil, then I will be reborn at the breaking up of the body, after death, in a place that is happy, a heavenly world.' This is the first comfort he attains. He thinks: 'If there is no after-world, no fruit and result of actions that are good or evil, then here in the visible world I will keep myself free from hatred, untroubled, free from vexation, and happy.' This is the second comfort he attains. He thinks: 'If I were to do an action that results in something bad, but I did not intend to do something bad to anyone, then how will suffering touch me who does nothing bad?' This is the third comfort he attains. He thinks: 'If I were to do an action that involves nothing bad, then I would see myself as pure in both ways.'[2] This is the fourth comfort he attains.

"Indeed, Kālamas, a noble disciple is thus freed in mind from hatred, untroubled in mind, unstained in mind, pure in mind, and in this visible world has attained those four comforts."

17. "So it is, Exalted One. So it is, Well-Farer. Indeed, sir, a noble disciple is thus freed in mind from hatred, untroubled in mind, unstained in
193 mind, pure in mind, and in this visible world has attained these four comforts.[3] Indeed, sir, a noble disciple is thus freed in mind from hatred, untroubled in mind, unstained in mind, pure in mind, and in this visible world has attained those four comforts.

2 "Both ways" means pure in terms of both intentional and nonintentional results of actions.

3 The four comforts are repeated verbatim.

"Wonderful, sir! Wonderful, sir! It is just as if someone were to make upright what was turned upside down, or were to uncover what was covered over, or were to explain the way to those who are lost, or were to hold up an oil lamp in the darkness saying 'those endowed with eyes will see the visible objects.' Just so, the Exalted One makes known the *dhamma* by diverse methods. We here go to the Exalted One for refuge, and also to the *dhamma* and to the *Saṅgha.* Let the Exalted One accept as lay followers those of us who have gone for refuge, from this day forth as long as we live."

3

The Greater Discourse on Cause

(*Mahānidāna Sutta*)[1]

This discourse provides what many scholars deem the most comprehensive analysis of the central doctrine of Buddhism, namely, dependent arising (*paṭiccasamuppāda*). The importance of the doctrine of dependent arising cannot be overstated. Elsewhere, the Buddha is quoted as saying: "One who perceives dependent arising perceives the *dhamma;* and one who perceives the *dhamma,* perceives dependent arising."[2] In short, all other parts of the Buddha's teaching may be seen as grounded on the Buddha's teaching of dependent arising.

According to the early Buddhist tradition, the catalyst for the Buddha's enlightenment was his penetrative insight into the dependently arisen nature of all that exists. All existing things are conditioned by other things. Everything changes. Nothing is permanent; nothing has a self-subsisting nature like the Hindu conception of *ātman* or Brahman (or the Platonic notion of a "Form"). Neither the self nor anything else in the world exists immutably, independently, or permanently. Instead, all things arise, evolve, and eventually dissipate, because of complex causal conditions.

The doctrine of dependent arising is the "middle way" applied to metaphysics. It stands between the theories of a transcendent Absolute Reality (e.g., the Hindu "Brahman") and metaphysical nihilism, or between eternalism and annihilationism (the Materialist[3] view that the person ceases at death). From the point of view of dependent arising, things *do exist,* but only as complex, interdependent, changing processes.

Insight into dependent arising illuminates specifically the processes whereby suffering arises and ceases in a person. It was the Buddha's application of this insight to his own situation that led to his attainment of enlightenment or *nibbāna.* By realizing that there is nothing anywhere that is permanent enough to grasp onto for security, he understood that one is faced with only one alternative: to avoid suffering, one must stop grasping onto things as if they were permanent and secure (especially the belief in a permanent Self). In brief, one must *let go.*

[1] *Dīgha Nikāya* 2.55–71.

[2] *Majjhima Nikāya* 1.190–191.

[3] See note 13 in the General Introduction.

As it specifically applies to the arising and ceasing of suffering, the doctrine of dependent arising is usually presented in the Pāli Canon in terms of the "twelvefold formula." In this discourse, however, the formula has only ten "causal links" (*nidānas*).[4]

By analyzing the arising and ceasing of suffering in terms of a causal chain, the Buddha intends to provide a means of controlling and eliminating suffering altogether. The arising of craving (*taṇhā*) from feeling (*vedanā*) is perhaps the most crucial link in the causal chain because it is at that point in the chain that the process can be redirected away from suffering to more beneficial results. Because the connection between craving and feeling is so critical to gaining control over the processes of experience, the discourse presents a secondary sequence of dependent arising that is interpolated between these two links.

Special attention should be given to the fact that dependent arising commences where psycho-physicality[5] and consciousness mutually condition one another. In other words, there is no single factor from which the chain of causal links arises, and yet there is no infinite regress of causes either. This fact suggests an approach to causation that is nonlinear, a theory of mutual conditionality, rather than a linear sequence of mechanical causes. The fact that consciousness mutually conditions psycho-physicality not only is a way to avoid an infinite regress in the causal chain but also shows that consciousness and the other mental phenomena are emergent features of natural processes and not imposed from a transcendent, supernatural realm of pure Spirit.

Perhaps most surprising from a religious point of view, the doctrine of dependent arising implies that religious liberation is neither the knowledge of a transcendent reality, nor an identification of one's true Self (*ātman*) with the Absolute (*Brahman*), nor even a beatific relationship with God. Religious liberation in early Buddhism is not a matter of being liberated from a lower metaphysical state by passing to a higher metaphysical state. It is, instead, an ethical and a psychological transformation that takes place in this changing world. By cutting off the psychological roots of suffering, one escapes the bonds of *saṃsāric* existence, namely, the rounds of birth-death-rebirth. This is, from the early Buddhist point of view, nothing other than religious freedom (*nibbāna*).

The discourse also offers one of the more philosophically interesting accounts of the Buddha's arguments against the belief in a permanent Self.

4 The causal links "ignorance" (*avijjā*) and "dispositions to action" (*saṅkhara*) that occur in the twelvefold version of the formula are omitted from the tenfold version in this discourse.

5 "Psycho-physicality" (*nāma-rūpa*) is the Buddha's way of referring to mental and bodily processes. Other translators render this term as "name and form" or "mental-materiality."

The application of dependent arising to considerations about human nature is at the core of the Buddha's teaching, so these sections are no mere afterthought. Those who declare a permanent Self, such as the Brahmanical concept of *ātman,* must hold that such a Self is either material or immaterial and is either limited or unlimited. Taking up all four possible combinations of these characteristics of a permanent Self, the Buddha shows the *bhikkhus* that none of them represents a plausible view of the person.

The last sections of the discourse describe the seven stations of consciousness, the two planes of higher experience, and the eight stages of liberation. These successive stations and stages appear to be accounts of what the trained disciple can expect to experience as one follows the training and becomes more and more adept in wisdom (through the stations of consciousness) and meditational techniques (through the stages of liberation). The end result for those who master these two types of training is liberation in "both ways": liberation both by wisdom (or higher knowledge) and by meditative concentration. As the discourse boldly declares, liberation in both ways is the penultimate achievement of the practice of Buddhism.

Discourse

55

1. Thus have I heard. At one time, the Exalted One was staying among the Kurus in a town called Kammāsadhamma. Then the venerable Ānanda approached the Exalted One. And having approached him, he greeted him respectfully and sat down to one side. When he had sat down to one side, Ānanda said this: "It is wonderful, sir. It is marvelous how profound this dependent arising[6] is, and how profound it appears! And yet it appears to me as clear as clear can be!"

"Do not say that, Ānanda! Do not say that! This dependent arising is profound and appears profound. It is through not understanding and not penetrating this doctrine that this generation has become like a tangled ball of string, covered with blight, tangled like coarse grass, and unable to pass beyond states of woe, ill destiny, ruin, and the round of birth-and-death.

2. "If you are asked: 'Is there something specific on which aging-and-death are dependent?' you should answer: 'There is.' If someone were to ask: 'Dependent on what is there aging-and-death?' you should answer: 'Dependent on birth, there is aging-and-death.'

"If you are asked: 'Is there something specific on which birth is dependent?' you should answer: 'There is.' If someone were to ask: 'Dependent on

[6] *Paṭiccasamuppāda.*

what is there birth?' you should answer: 'Dependent on becoming, there is birth.'

"If you are asked: 'Is there something specific on which becoming is dependent?' you should answer: 'There is.' If someone were to ask: 'Dependent on what is there becoming?' you should answer: 'Dependent on attachment, there is becoming.' 56

"If you are asked: 'Is there something specific on which attachment is dependent?' you should answer: 'There is.' If someone were to ask: 'Dependent on what is there attachment?' you should answer: 'Dependent on craving, there is attachment.'

"If you are asked: 'Is there something specific on which craving is dependent?' you should answer: 'There is.' If someone were to ask: 'Dependent on what is there craving?' you should answer: 'Dependent on feeling, there is craving.'

"If you are asked: 'Is there something specific on which feeling is dependent?' you should answer: 'There is.' If someone were to ask: 'Dependent on what is there feeling?' you should answer: 'Dependent on contact, there is feeling.'

"If you are asked: 'Is there something specific on which contact is dependent?' you should answer: 'There is.' If someone were to ask: 'Dependent on what is there contact?' you should answer: 'Dependent on psycho-physicality, there is contact.'

"If you are asked: 'Is there something specific on which psycho-physicality is dependent?' you should answer: 'There is.' If someone were to ask: 'Dependent on what is there psycho-physicality?' you should answer: 'Dependent on consciousness, there is psycho-physicality.'

"If you are asked: 'Is there something specific on which consciousness is dependent?' you should answer: 'There is.' If someone were to ask: 'Dependent on what is there consciousness?' you should answer: 'Dependent on psycho-physicality, there is consciousness.'

3. "Thus, dependent on psycho-physicality, there is consciousness, and dependent on consciousness, there is psycho-physicality; dependent on psycho-physicality, there is contact; dependent on contact, there is feeling; dependent on feeling, there is craving; dependent on craving, there is attachment; dependent on attachment, there is becoming; dependent on becoming, there is birth; dependent on birth, there is aging-and-death; dependent on aging-and-death, there is sorrow, lamentation, pain, despair, and distress. 57
Thus there is the arising of this whole mass of suffering.

4. "I have said: 'Dependent on birth, there is aging-and-death,' and this is the way that it should be understood that aging-and-death is dependent

on birth. If there were no birth at all, anywhere, of anybody or in any state—namely, of *devas* in the state of *devas,* of *gandhabbas* in the *gandhabba* state, of *yakkhas* in the state of *yakkhas,* of ghosts in the ghostly state, of humans in the human state, of quadrupeds in the state of quadrupeds, of birds in the state of birds, of reptiles in the reptile state—if there were absolutely no birth at all of all these beings in these various states, then, from the cessation of birth, would aging-and-death be evident?"

"No, sir."

"Therefore, Ānanda, this is the cause, the source, the origin, the condition for aging-and-death—namely, birth."

5. "I have said: 'Dependent on becoming, there is birth,' and this is the way that it should be understood that birth is dependent on becoming. If there were no becoming at all, anywhere, of anybody or in any state—namely, the becoming of pleasures, the becoming of the material, or the becoming of the immaterial—if there were absolutely no becoming at all, then, from the cessation of becoming, would birth be evident?"

"No, sir."

"Therefore, Ānanda, just this is the cause, the source, the origin, the condition for birth—namely, becoming."

6. "I have said that 'Dependent on attachment, there is becoming,' and this is the way that it should be understood that becoming is dependent on
58 attachment. If there were no attachment at all, anywhere, by anybody in any state—namely, attachment to sensual pleasure, attachment to speculative views, attachment to rite-and-ritual, attachment to theories of the permanent Self[7]—if there were absolutely no attachment at all, then, from the cessation of attachment, would becoming be evident?"

"No, sir."

"Therefore, Ānanda, just this is the cause, the source, the origin, the condition for becoming—namely, attachment."

7. "I have said that 'Dependent on craving, there is attachment,' and this is the way that it should be understood that attachment is dependent on craving. If there were no craving at all, anywhere, by anybody in any state—namely, craving for sights, craving for sounds, craving for smells, craving for tastes, craving for tangibles, craving for mental objects—if there were absolutely no craving at all, then, from the cessation of craving, would attachment be evident?"

"No, sir."

"Therefore, Ananda, just this is the cause, the source, the origin, the condition for attachment, namely, craving."

[7] *Attā.*

8. "I have said that 'Dependent on feeling, there is craving,' and this is the way that it should be understood that craving is dependent on feeling. If there were no feeling at all, anywhere, by anybody, in any state—namely, feelings born of eye-contact, ear-contact, nose-contact, tongue-contact, body-contact, and mind-contact—if there were absolutely no feeling at all, then, from the cessation of feeling, would craving be evident?"

"No, sir."

"Therefore, Ānanda, just this is the cause, the source, the origin, the condition for craving—namely, feeling.

9. "Thus, craving is dependent upon feeling; pursuit is dependent upon craving;[8] gain is dependent upon pursuit; decision-making is dependent upon gain; desire and passion are dependent on decision-making; indulgence is dependent on desire and passion; possessiveness is dependent on
indulgence; stinginess is dependent on possessiveness; protecting possessions 59
is dependent on stinginess; and many evil and unwholesome activities[9] such as taking up sticks and swords, quarreling, disputes, contention, strife, slander, and lies arise because of protecting possessions.

10. "I have said that 'Many evil and unwholesome activities such as taking up sticks and swords, quarreling, disputes, contention, strife, slander, and lies arise because of protecting possessions.' And this is the way that it should be understood that many evil and unwholesome activities such as taking up sticks and swords, quarreling, disputes, contention, strife, slander, and lies arise because of protecting possessions. If there were no protecting of possessions at all, anywhere, by anybody, in any state, if there were absolutely no protecting of possessions, then, from the cessation of protecting of possessions, would there arise these many evil and unwholesome activities, such as taking up sticks and swords, quarreling, disputes, contention, strife, slander, and lies?"

"No, sir."

"Thus, Ānanda, this is the reason, the cause, the origin, and the condition for these many unwholesome states, such as taking up sticks and swords, quarreling, disputes, contention, strife, slander, and lies—namely, protecting possessions.

11. "I have said that 'protecting of possessions is dependent on stinginess.' And this is the way that it should be understood that protecting of possessions is dependent on stinginess. If there were no stinginess at all,

[8] From this point through the next ten sections, the text gives a secondary or subsidiary sequence of dependent arising that lies between craving and feeling in the primary sequence of dependent arising.

[9] The word *dhammā* usually translates as "mental objects," but the context requires rendering the term as "activities." In the Buddha's view, activities are motivated by mental factors.

anywhere, by anybody, in any state, if there were absolutely no stinginess of any sort at all, then, from the cessation of stinginess, would protecting of possessions be evident?"

"No, sir."

"Thus, Ānanda, this is the reason, the cause, the origin, and the condition for protecting possessions—namely, stinginess.

12. "I have said that 'stinginess is dependent on possessiveness.' And this is the way that it should be understood that stinginess is dependent on pos-
60 sessiveness. If there were no possessiveness at all, anywhere, by anybody, in any state, if there were absolutely no possessiveness of any sort at all, then, from the cessation of all possessiveness, would stinginess be evident?"

"No, sir."

"Thus, Ānanda, this is the reason, the cause, the origin, and the condition for stinginess—namely, possessiveness.

13. "I have said that 'possessiveness is dependent on indulgence.' And this is the way that it should be understood that possessiveness is dependent on indulgence. If there were no indulgence at all, anywhere, by anybody, in any state, if there were absolutely no indulgence of any sort at all, then, from the cessation of all indulgence, would possessiveness be evident?"

"No, sir."

"Thus, Ānanda, this is the reason, the cause, the origin, and the condition for possessiveness—namely, indulgence.

14. "I have said that 'indulgence is dependent on desire and passion.' And this is the way that it should be understood that indulgence is dependent on desire and passion. If there were no desire and passion at all, anywhere, by anybody, in any state, if there were absolutely no desire and passion of any sort at all, then, from the cessation of all desire and passion, would indulgence be evident?"

"No, sir."

"Thus, Ānanda, this is the reason, the cause, the origin, and the condition for indulgence—namely, desire and passion.

15. "I have said that 'desire and passion are dependent on decision-making.' And this is the way that it should be understood that desire and passion are dependent on decision-making. If there were no decision-making at all, anywhere, by anybody, in any state, if there were absolutely no decision-making of any sort at all, then, from the cessation of all decision-mak-
61 ing, would desire and passion be evident?"

"No, sir."

"Thus, Ānanda, this is the reason, the cause, the origin, and the condition for desire and passion—namely, decision-making.

16. "I have said that 'decision-making is dependent upon gain.' And this is the way that it should be understood that decision-making is dependent upon gain. If there were no gain at all, anywhere, by anybody, in any state, if there were absolutely no gain of any sort at all, then, from the cessation of all gain, would decision-making be evident?"

"No, sir."

"Thus, Ānanda, this is the reason, the cause, the origin, and the condition for decision-making—namely, gain.

17. "I have said that 'gain is dependent upon pursuit.' And this is the way that it should be understood that gain is dependent upon pursuit. If there were no pursuit at all, anywhere, by anybody, in any state, if there were absolutely no pursuit of any sort at all, then, from the cessation of all pursuit, would gain be evident?"

"No, sir."

"Thus, Ānanda, this is the reason, the cause, the origin, and the condition for gain—namely, pursuit.

18. "I have said that 'pursuit is dependent upon craving.' And this is the way that it should be understood that pursuit is dependent upon craving. If there were no craving at all, anywhere, by anybody, in any state—such as craving for pleasure, craving for becoming,[10] craving for non-becoming—if there were absolutely no craving of any sort at all, then, from the cessation of all craving, would pursuit be evident?"

"No, sir."

"Thus, Ānanda, this is the reason, the cause, the origin, and the condition for pursuit, namely, craving. Hence, these two things become a pair and
so become united as one by feeling. 62

19. "I have said that 'dependent on contact, there is feeling.' And this is the way that it should be understood that feeling is dependent on contact If there were no contact at all, anywhere, by anybody, in any state—such as eye-contact, ear-contact, nose-contact, tongue-contact, body-contact, mind-contact—if there were absolutely no contact at all, then, from the cessation of contact, would feeling be evident?"

"No, sir."

"Thus, Ānanda, this is the reason, the cause, the origin, and the condition for feeling—namely, contact.

20. "I have said that 'dependent on psycho-physicality, there is contact.' And this is the way that it should be understood that contact is dependent

[10] The word *bhava* might also be translated as "rebirth" in this context. Of course, were *bhava* to be translated as "rebirth," it would imply that there is a future life. Such a translation would give the passage a substantially different meaning.

on psycho-physicality. By whatever properties, characteristics, signs, or indications the mentality-factor is conceived, would there be evident, in the absence of such properties, characteristics, signs, or indications, any conception of the materiality-factor?"

"No, sir."

"By whatever properties, characteristics, signs, or indications the materiality-factor is conceived, would there be evident, in the absence of such properties, characteristics, signs, or indications, any conception of sensory reaction on the part of the mentality-factor?"

"No, sir."

"By whatever properties, characteristics, signs, or indications the mentality-factor and the materiality-factor are conceived, would there be evident, in the absence of such properties, characteristics, signs, or indications, any conception of either of these, or of sensory reaction?"

"No, sir."

"By whatever properties, characteristics, signs, or indications the mentality-factor is conceived, would there be evident, in the absence of these properties, characteristics, signs, or indications, any contact?"

"No, sir."

"Therefore, Ānanda, just this, namely psycho-physicality, is the root, the cause, the origin, the condition for contact.

21. "I have said: 'Dependent on consciousness, there is psycho-physical-
63 ity.' And this is the way that it should be understood that psycho-physicality is dependent on consciousness. If consciousness were not to come into the mother's womb, would psycho-physicality develop there?"

"No, sir."

"Or if consciousness entered the mother's womb, but was deflected, would psycho-physicality come to birth in this life?"

"No, sir."

"And if the consciousness of a tender young being, boy or girl, were cut off, would psycho-physicality grow, develop, and mature?"

"No, sir."

"Therefore, Ānanda, just this is the root, the cause, the origin, the condition of psycho-physicality—namely, consciousness.

22. "I have said: 'Dependent on psycho-physicality, there is consciousness.' And this is the way that it should be understood that consciousness is dependent on psycho-physicality. If consciousness did not find a resting-place in psycho-physicality, would there subsequently be an arising and a coming-to-be of birth, aging, death, and suffering?"

"No, sir."

"Therefore, Ānanda, just this is the root, the cause, the origin, the condition

of consciousness—namely, psycho-physicality. Thus far, then, we can trace birth and decay, death, falling into other states, and being reborn; thus far extends the way of designation, of explanation; thus far is the sphere of understanding; thus far the round goes for our existence here [in this life]— 64
namely, psycho-physicality together with consciousness.

23. "In what ways do those who declare a permanent Self explain it? Some of those who declare a permanent Self explain it as material and limited: 'My Self is material and limited.' Some of those who declare a permanent Self explain it as material and unlimited: 'My Self is material and unlimited.' Some of those who declare a permanent Self explain it as immaterial and limited: 'My Self is immaterial and limited.' Some of those who declare a permanent Self explain it as immaterial and unlimited: 'My Self is immaterial and unlimited.'

24. "Whoever declares a permanent Self and explains it as material and limited, either explains the Self as material and limited now or explains that it is going to be so.[11] Or such a person thinks: 'Though it is not so now, I will construct it so it is like that.' That being the case, that is enough said about those who dwell on the speculation that the Self is material and limited.

"Whoever declares a permanent Self and explains it as material and unlimited, either explains the Self as material and unlimited now or explains that it is going to be so. Or such a person thinks: 'Though it is not so now, I will construct it so it is like that.' That being the case, that is enough said about those who dwell on the speculation that the Self is material and unlimited.

"Whoever declares a permanent Self and explains it as immaterial and limited, either explains the Self as immaterial and limited now or explains that it is going to be so. Or such a person thinks: 'Though it is not so now, I will construct it so it is like that.' That being the case, that is enough said about those who dwell on the speculation that the Self is immaterial and limited.

"Whoever declares a permanent Self and explains it as immaterial and unlimited, either explains the Self as immaterial and unlimited now or explains that it is going to be so. Or such a person thinks: 'Though it is not so now, I will construct it so it is like that.' That being the case, that is enough 65
said about those who dwell on the speculation that the Self is immaterial and unlimited.

"In these ways, those who declare a permanent Self explain it.

25. "In what ways do those who do not declare a permanent Self explain the matter? Some of those who do not declare a permanent Self do not

[11] Using the variant reading *tathā bhāviṃ* for *tattha bhāviṃ* in the Pali Text Society edition.

explain it as material and limited with the words: 'My Self is material and limited.' Some of those who do not declare a permanent Self do not explain it as material and unlimited with the words: 'My Self is material and unlimited.' Some of those who do not declare a permanent Self do not explain it as immaterial and limited with the words: 'My Self is immaterial and limited.' Some of those who do not declare a permanent Self do not explain it as immaterial and unlimited with the words: 'My Self is immaterial and unlimited.'

26. "Whoever does not declare a permanent Self and does not explain it as material and limited, neither explains the Self as material and limited now nor explains that it is going to be so. Or such a person does not think: 'Though it is not so now, I will construct it so it is like that.' That being the case, that is enough said about those who do not dwell on the speculation that the Self is material and limited.

"Whoever does not declare a permanent Self and does not explain it as material and unlimited, neither explains the Self as material and unlimited now nor explains that it is going to be so. Or such a person does not think: 'Though it is not so now, I will construct it so it is like that.' That being the case, that is enough said about those who do not dwell on the speculation that the Self is material and unlimited.

"Whoever does not declare a permanent Self and does not explain it as immaterial and limited, neither explains the Self as immaterial and limited now nor explains that it is going to be so. Or such a person does not think: 'Though it is not so now, I will construct it so it is like that.' That being the case, that is enough said about those who do not dwell on the speculation that the Self is immaterial and limited.

"Whoever does not declare a permanent Self and does not explain it as immaterial and unlimited, neither explains the Self as immaterial and unlimited now nor explains that it is going to be so. Or such a person does not
66 think: 'Though it is not so now, I will construct it so it is like that.' That being the case, that is enough said about those who do not dwell on the speculation that the Self is immaterial and unlimited.

"In these ways, those who do not declare a permanent Self explain the matter.

27. "In what ways does one who considers the permanent Self consider it? One considering the permanent Self as feeling considers it in these words: 'Feeling is my Self.' Or one considering the permanent Self as feeling considers it in these words: 'Feeling is not my Self, my Self insentient.' Or one considering the permanent Self considers it in these words: 'My Self is not feeling, nor is my Self insentient. My Self feels, my Self has a feeling nature.' In such ways, do those who consider the permanent Self explain it.

28. "In this connection, the one who says: 'Feeling is my Self' should be questioned: 'There are these three kinds of feeling, friend: pleasant feeling, painful feeling, and neither-painful-nor pleasant feeling.[12] Of these three kinds of feeling, which do you consider the Self?'

"When one feels a pleasant feeling, at that moment, one neither experiences a painful feeling nor a neither-painful-nor-pleasant feeling—one feels only a pleasant feeling at that time. When one feels a painful feeling, at that moment, one experiences neither a pleasant feeling nor a neither-painful-nor-pleasant feeling—one feels only a painful feeling at that time. When one feels a neither-painful-nor-pleasant feeling, at that moment, one experiences neither a pleasant feeling nor a painful feeling—one feels only a neither-painful-nor-pleasant feeling at that time.

29. "Also, pleasant feeling is impermanent, a composite, dependently arisen, of a nature to be destroyed, of a nature to decay, of a nature to fade,
of a nature to cease. Painful feeling, too, is impermanent, a composite, 67
dependently arisen, of a nature to be destroyed, of a nature to decay, of a nature to fade, of a nature to cease. And yet again, a neither-painful-nor-pleasant feeling is impermanent, a composite, dependently arisen, of a nature to be destroyed, of a nature to decay, of a nature to fade, of a nature to cease.

"If one who experiences a pleasant feeling thinks 'this is my Self,' when that same pleasant feeling ceases, one will think 'my Self has disappeared.' If one who experiences a painful feeling thinks 'this is my Self,' when that same painful feeling ceases, one will think 'my Self has disappeared.' If one who experiences a neither-painful-nor-pleasant feeling thinks 'this is my Self,' when that same neither-painful-nor-pleasant feeling ceases, one will think 'my Self has disappeared.'

"So it is that one considering the permanent Self, considers it in this world as impermanent, full of pleasure and pain, and as having an arising and decaying nature. Therefore, on account of this, it is not acceptable to consider that: 'Feeling is my Self.'

30. "In another case, Ānanda, the one who says: 'Feeling is not my Self, my Self is insentient,' should be questioned: 'Friend, where there is no feeling of any kind, would it be possible there to say that "I am"?' [To which such a person would reply:] 'No, sir, it would not.'

"Therefore, on account of this, it is not acceptable to consider that: 'Feeling is not my Self, my Self is insentient.'

31. "In another case, Ānanda, the one who says: 'My Self is not feeling, nor is my Self insentient. My Self feels, my Self has a feeling nature,' should be asked: 'Friend, were feelings of any kind, of any sort, in any way, to cease

[12] In other words, a *neutral* feeling.

without remainder, if there were no feeling at all and if feeling were to cease, would it be possible there to say "I am this"?' [To which such a person would reply:] 'No, sir, it would not.'

68 "Therefore, on account of this, it is not acceptable to consider that: 'My Self is not feeling, nor is my Self insentient. My Self feels, my Self has a feeling nature.'

32. "When a *bhikkhu* does not consider feeling as the permanent Self, nor considers the Self as without feeling, nor considers 'my Self feels, my Self has a feeling nature'—if he is without such considerations—he does not grasp after anything in this world. Not attached, he does not tremble. Not trembling, he personally achieves *nibbāna.* He knows that 'birth is destroyed, the holy life has been fulfilled, done is what had to be done, there is no further state of existence.'

"If, concerning the *bhikkhu* whose mind is thus freed, someone were to say: 'The *bhikkhu* holds the speculative view that "The *Tathāgata* exists after death"'—that would not be proper. If someone were to say: 'He holds the view that "The *Tathāgata* does not exist after death"'—that would not be proper. If someone were to say: 'He holds the view that "The *Tathāgata* both does and does not exist after death"'—that would not be proper. If someone were to say: 'He holds the view that "The *Tathāgata* neither does nor does not exist after death"'—that would not be proper.

"What is the reason for this? Because whatever verbal expression there is, whatever process of verbal expression there is, whatever language there is, whatever process of language there is, whatever concept there is, whatever process of conception there is, whatever wisdom there is, whatever sphere of wisdom there is, whatever round of rebirth there is, whatever evolving of the round there is—by understanding that, the *bhikkhu* is freed. Being freed by understanding that, it would not be proper to say that he holds the view 'one does not know and one does not see.'

33. "There are these seven stations of consciousness and these two planes. What are the seven?

69 "There are beings who are diverse in body, and diverse in intelligence—such as human beings, some *devas,* and some who live in a state of misery after death. This is the first station of consciousness.

"There are beings who are diverse in body, but the same in intelligence—such as the *devas* of the Brahmā-order who are reborn at the level of the first *jhāna.* This is the second station of consciousness.

"There are beings who are the same in body, but diverse in intelligence—such as the *devas* of streaming radiance.[13] This is the third station of consciousness.

[13] *Ābhassarā.*

"There are beings who are the same in body, and the same in intelligence—such as the *devas* of the luminous realm.[14] This is the fourth station of consciousness.

"There are beings who, from completely passing beyond the perception of visible form, from the passing away of sensory reaction, from non-attention to the diversity of perceptions, think 'space is infinite' and who have reached the plane of infinite space. This is the fifth station of consciousness.

"There are beings who, through completely passing beyond the plane of infinite space, think 'consciousness is infinite' and who have reached the plane of infinite consciousness. This is the sixth station of consciousness.

"There are beings who, through completely passing beyond the plane of infinite consciousness, think 'there does not exist anything' and who have reached the plane of no-thing. This is the seventh station of consciousness.

"The plane of insentient beings is the first plane, the plane of neither-perception-nor-non-perception beings is the second plane.

34. "In a case where there is that first station of consciousness, wherein beings are diverse in body and diverse in intelligence—such as humans, some *devas,* and some who live in a state of misery after death—for those who know that, know its origin, know its passing away, know its satisfaction, know its danger, who know the escape from it, would it be proper for them to delight in it?" 70

"No, sir, it would not."

"Ānanda, in a case where there is that second station of consciousness, wherein beings are diverse in body, but the same in intelligence—such as the *devas* of the Brahmā-order who are reborn at the level of the first *jhāna*—for those who know that, know its origin, know its passing away, know its satisfaction, know its danger, who know the escape from it, would it be proper for them to delight in it?"

"No, sir, it would not."

"Ānanda, in a case where there is that third station of consciousness, wherein beings are the same in body, but diverse in intelligence—such as the *devas* of streaming radiance—for those who know that, know its origin, know its passing away, know its satisfaction, know its danger, who know the escape from it, would it be proper for them to delight in it?"

"No, sir, it would not."

"Ānanda, in a case where there is that fourth station of consciousness, wherein beings are the same in body, and the same in intelligence—such as the *devas* of the luminous realm—for those who know that, know its origin, know its passing away, know its satisfaction, know its danger, who know the escape from it, would it be proper for them to delight in it?"

14 *Subhakiṇṇā.*

"No, sir, it would not."

"Ānanda, in a case where there is that fifth station of consciousness, wherein beings, from completely passing beyond the perception of visible form, from the passing away of sensory reaction, from non-attention to the diversity of perceptions, think 'space is infinite' and who have reached the plane of infinite space—for those who know that, know its origin, know its passing away, know its satisfaction, know its danger, who know the escape from it, would it be proper for them to delight in it?"

"No, sir, it would not."

"Ānanda, in a case where there is that sixth station of consciousness, wherein beings who, through completely passing beyond the plane of infinite space, think 'consciousness is infinite' and who have reached the plane of infinite consciousness—for those who know that, know its origin, know its passing away, know its satisfaction, know its danger, who know the escape from it, would it be proper for them to delight in it?"

"No, sir, it would not."

"Ānanda, in a case where there is that seventh station of consciousness, in which one has completely passed beyond the plane of infinite consciousness, thinking 'there does not exist anything' and having reached the plane of nothing—for those who know that, know its origin, know its passing away, know its satisfaction, know its danger, who know the escape from it, would it be proper for them to delight in it?"

"No, sir, it would not."

"Ānanda, in the case of the plane of insentient beings, for those who know that, know its origin, know its passing away, know its satisfaction, know its danger, who know the escape from it, would it be proper for them to delight in it?"

"No, sir, it would not."

"Ānanda, in the case of the plane of neither-perception-nor-non-perception, for those who know that, know its origin, know its passing away, know its satisfaction, know its danger, who know the escape from it, would it be proper for them to delight in it?"

"No, sir, it would not."

"Ānanda, when a *bhikkhu* has understood things as they really are—in regard to these seven stations of consciousness and two planes, their origin, their passing away, their satisfaction, their danger, and the escape from them—then he becomes free. He is called a *bhikkhu* who has been freed by wisdom.[15]

35. "There are these eight stages of liberation, Ānanda. What are the eight?

[15] *Paññā.* This term can also be translated as "insight."

"One who is material sees material objects. This is the first stage of liberation.

"One who has perception of immaterial objects internally sees material objects externally. This is the second stage of liberation. 71

"One who is intent on the word 'beautiful.' This is the third stage of liberation.

"One who passes completely beyond the perception of visible objects, with the passing away of sensory reaction and with non-attention to the diversity of perceptions, thinks 'space is infinite,' and lives having entered into the plane of infinite space. This is the fourth stage of liberation.

"One who passes completely beyond the plane of infinite space thinks 'consciousness is infinite,' and lives having entered into the plane of infinite consciousness. This is the fifth stage of liberation.

"One who passes completely beyond the plane of infinite consciousness thinks 'there does not exist anything,' and lives having entered into the plane of no-thing. This is the sixth stage of liberation.

"One who passes completely beyond the plane of no-thing lives having entered into the plane of neither-perception-nor-non-perception. This is the seventh stage of liberation.

"One who passes completely beyond the plane of neither-perception-nor-non-perception lives having entered into the cessation of perception and feeling. This is the eighth stage of liberation.

36. "When a *bhikkhu* has entered upon these eight stages of liberation—in forward order, or in reverse order, or in both forward and reverse order, so that he enters into and emerges from them whenever he desires—and when his defilements are destroyed, he enters and dwells in the undefiled liberation of the mind and liberation by wisdom, which he has understood and realized by himself *in this world,* such a one is called a *bhikkhu* who is 'liberated in both ways.'[16] And there is no other 'liberation in both ways' that is higher or more excellent than this 'liberation in both ways.'"

This was said by the Exalted One. Delighted, the venerable Ānanda rejoiced in what the Exalted One had said.

[16] Being liberated in "both ways" means liberation achieved both through wisdom (insight) and through meditative concentration.

4

The Greater Discourse on the Foundations of Mindfulness

(*Mahāsatipaṭṭhāna Sutta*)[1]

This discourse contains the most detailed account of meditation in the Pāli Canon. The "foundations of mindfulness" are critical meditative achievements on the path to religious liberation. As meditative practice, mindfulness fits into the second stage of training, mental culture (*samādhi*). Mindfulness is also the seventh factor of the Noble Eightfold Path. By developing mindfulness, a person first observes the various aspects of one's being, then learns to control the mind and its reactions to external and internal stimuli. From a Buddhist point of view, this control of the mind is critical as a way to channel experiences into wholesome directions and thus avoid suffering. The discussion of mindfulness in this discourse does not focus on the specific practices of moral conduct. This is explained by the fact that, as an advanced meditative technique, mindfulness presumes the development of moral conduct.

The discourse gives specific instructions for the development of mindfulness regarding four major factors in human experience: the body, feeling, the mind, and mental objects. The Buddha instructs the meditator to "live observing body as body (feeling as feeling, mind as mind, etc.), energetically, self-possessed and mindful, having eliminated both the desire for and despair over the world."[2] The discourse proceeds gradually, sequentially, and cumulatively through all four factors—the achievement at each stage constitutes a "foundation of mindfulness."

The forms of meditation suggested by the Buddha include such widely known practices as breathing and focalization techniques that lead to calm and mental clarity. One begins by merely paying attention to phenomena as they arise and cease within one's experience, not yet judging whether they are good or bad. This method means temporarily pulling back from experience and observing it disinterestedly or dispassionately, seeing each experience for exactly what it is and thereby seeing the full value of each of the possible responses to an experiential situation. But mindfulness goes further. The Buddha describes extending such awareness to all bodily actions and

[1] *Dīgha Nikāya* 2.290–315.

[2] *Dīgha Nikāya* 2.290.

mental phenomena. When walking, one should have mindful awareness of walking. When eating, one should have mindful awareness of eating, and so on. One who possesses mindfulness has mastery over the ebbs and flows of the mind as one senses, feels, thinks, and chooses.

This discourse is also an excellent resource for studying the Four Noble Truths, which describe the essence of the early Buddhist doctrine in its most succinct form. In the Four Noble Truths, the Buddha points out that the religious problem is suffering on a variety of levels; that the underlying causes of suffering are selfish craving and ignorance; that the route to the removal of the problem is the elimination of the causes of suffering; and that the practical therapy, the Noble Eightfold Path, eliminates suffering and provides the foundations for the holy life that culminates in *nibbāna.* The Four Noble Truths are structured like a medical diagnosis and therapy. For this reason, the Buddha is sometimes imagined as a medical doctor who understands the existential sickness inherent in the human condition and who provides an effective (religious) cure.

Discourse

290

1. Thus have I heard. At one time the Exalted One was living among the Kurus. Kammāssadhamma was the name of the market town in Kuru. There the Exalted One addressed the *bhikkhus,* saying: "*Bhikkhus.*"

"Sir," those *bhikkhus* said in response to the Exalted One.

The Exalted One said this: "There is this one path, *bhikkhus,* for the purification of beings, for passing beyond grief and lamentation, for the extinction of suffering and despair, for the attainment of knowledge, for the realization of *nibbāna,* namely, these four foundations for mindfulness.

"What are the four? In a certain case, a *bhikkhu* lives observing the body as body, energetically, self-possessed and mindful, having eliminated both the desire for and the despair over the world. He lives observing feeling as feeling, energetically, self-possessed and mindful, having eliminated both the desire for and the despair over the world. He lives observing the mind as mind, energetically, self-possessed and mindful, having eliminated both the desire for and the despair over the world. He lives observing mental phenomena as mental phenomena, energetically, self-possessed and mindful,
having eliminated both the desire for and the despair over the world. 291

2. "And how, regarding the body, does a *bhikkhu* live observing the body?

"In such a case, a *bhikkhu* who has either gone to the forest, to the root of a tree, or to an empty house, sits down cross-legged and folds his legs, makes his body erect, and with resolve he establishes mindfulness all around him. He breathes in mindfully; he exhales mindfully. Taking in a long breath, he knows 'I am taking in a long breath.' Or, exhaling a long breath, he knows 'I am exhaling a long breath.' Or, taking in a short breath, he knows 'I am taking in a short breath.' Or, exhaling a short breath, he knows 'I am exhaling a short breath.' He trains himself thinking: 'I will breathe in experiencing all of my body.' He trains himself thinking: 'I will exhale experiencing all of my body.' He trains himself thinking: 'I will breathe in calming the processes of my body.' He trains himself thinking: 'I will exhale calming the processes of my body.'

"Just as a skillful turner or turner's apprentice, when he turns a long turn knows 'I am turning a long turn.' Or when he turns a short turn knows 'I am turning a short turn.' Just so, a *bhikkhu* breathing in a long breath, knows 'I am taking in a long breath.' Or, exhaling a long breath, he knows 'I am exhaling a long breath.' Or, taking in a short breath, he knows 'I am taking in a short breath.' Or, exhaling a short breath, he knows 'I am exhaling a short breath.' He trains himself thinking: 'I will breathe in experiencing all of my body.' He trains himself thinking: 'I will exhale experiencing all of my body.' He trains himself thinking: 'I will breathe in calming the processes of my body.' He trains himself thinking: 'I will exhale calming the processes of
292 my body.'

"In such ways, he lives observing the body as body internally.[3] Or, he lives observing the body as body externally.[4] Or, he lives observing the body both internally and externally. Or, he lives observing in the body its arising factors. Or, he lives observing in the body its decaying factors. Thinking 'there is body,' his mindfulness becomes established to the extent necessary for knowledge and awareness. He lives unattached and grasps after nothing in the world. Thus, a *bhikkhu* lives observing the body as body.

3. "Again, in another case, a *bhikkhu* that is walking knows 'I am walking.' Or when standing, he knows 'I am standing.' Or when sitting, he knows 'I am sitting.' Or when lying down, he knows 'I am lying down.' So he knows exactly how his body is disposed.

"In such ways, he lives observing the body as body internally . . . unattached and grasps after nothing in the world. Thus, a *bhikkhu* lives observing the body as body.

4. "Again, in another case, a *bhikkhu* when going back and forth is fully aware of his actions. When looking at something or looking away, he is fully aware of his actions. When bending or stretching [his limbs], he is fully aware of his actions. When carrying his inner and outer robes and his bowl,

[3] *Ajjhattaṃ*. This term usually means "internally" or "subjectively," but here it may mean "in oneself."

[4] *Bahiddhā*. This term usually means "externally" or "objectively," but here it may mean "in others."

he is fully aware of his actions. Whether he is drinking, eating, or tasting, he is fully aware of his actions. When he is defecating or urinating, he is fully aware of his actions. When he is walking, standing, sitting, asleep or awake, speaking or remaining silent, he is fully aware of his actions. 293

"In such ways, he lives observing the body as body internally . . . unattached and grasps after nothing in the world. Thus, a *bhikkhu* lives observing the body as body.

5. "Again, in another case, a *bhikkhu* contemplates the same body—from the soles of his feet upward and from the tip of the hair downward, enveloped by skin and full of many kinds of impurities—thinking: 'In this body, there is the hair of the head, hair of the body, nails, teeth, skin, flesh, tendon, bone, bone marrow, a kidney, a heart, a liver, pleura, spleen, lung, bowel, intestinal tract, stomach, excrement, bile, phlegm, pus, blood, sweat, fat, tears, tallow, saliva, snot, synovial fluid, and urine.

"Just as a provision-bag with two openings may be filled with various kinds of grain, such as: hill rice, unhusked rice, beans, gram, sesame seeds, and husked rice, such that a person endowed with good eyesight would say, having poured these out: 'This is hill rice, unhusked rice, beans, gram, sesame seeds, and husked rice.' In the same way, a *bhikkhu* contemplates the body—from the soles of his feet upward and from the tip of the hair downward, enveloped by skin and full of many kinds of impurities—thinking: 'In this body, there is the hair of the head, hair of the body, nails, teeth, skin, flesh, tendon, bone, bone marrow, a kidney, a heart, a liver, pleura, spleen, 294
lung, bowel, intestinal tract, stomach, excrement, bile, phlegm, pus, blood, sweat, fat, tears, tallow, saliva, snot, synovial fluid, and urine.

"In such ways, he lives observing the body as body internally . . . unattached and grasps after nothing in the world. Thus, a *bhikkhu* lives observing the body as body.

6. "Again, in another case, a *bhikkhu* contemplates the body as it is constituted and as it is disposed, with regard to the elements, thinking: 'In this body, there are the earth-element, the water-element, the fire-element, and the air-element.'

"Just as a skilled butcher, or a butcher's apprentice, having killed a cow and divided the carcass into parts, were to sit down at a major crossroads. In the same way, a *bhikkhu* contemplates the body as it is constituted and as it is disposed, with regard to the elements, thinking: 'In this body, there are the earth-element, the water-element, the fire-element, and the air-element.'

"In such ways, he lives observing the body as body internally . . . unat- 295
tached and grasps after nothing in the world. Thus, a *bhikkhu* lives observing the body as body.

7. "Again, in another case, just as a *bhikkhu* might see a body thrown

aside in a cemetery, having been dead for one, two, or three days, bloated, discolored, and festering—he compares this same body to it, thinking: 'This body, too, has the same nature. In this way it will develop; it is not beyond that.'

"In such ways, he lives observing the body as body internally . . . unattached and grasps after nothing in the world. Thus, a *bhikkhu* lives observing the body as body.

8. "Again, in another case, just as a *bhikkhu* might see a body thrown aside in a cemetery, being eaten by crows, hawks, vultures, dogs, or jackals—he compares this same body to it, thinking: 'This body has the same nature.
296 In this way it will develop; it is not beyond that.'

"In such ways, he lives observing the body as body internally . . . unattached and grasps after nothing in the world. Thus, a *bhikkhu* lives observing the body as body.

9. "Again, in another case, just as a *bhikkhu* might see a body thrown aside in a cemetery, a skeleton with flesh and blood held together by sinew, a skeleton without flesh but smeared in blood and held together by sinew, or a skeleton having lost its flesh and blood but held together by sinew, or only bones having lost whatever held them together, scattered about in all directions, a hand-bone here, a foot-bone there, a leg-bone here, a thigh-
297 bone there, a hip-bone here, a backbone there, and a skull here—he compares this same body to it, thinking: 'This body has the same nature. In this way it will develop; it is not beyond that.'

"In such ways, he lives observing the body as body internally . . . unattached and grasps after nothing in the world. Thus, a *bhikkhu* lives observing the body as body.

10. "Again, in another case, just as a *bhikkhu* might see a body thrown aside in a cemetery, the bones looking white like a conch shell, the bones being piled up for a year, the bones having decayed and been reduced to dust—he compares this same body to it, thinking: 'This body has the same nature. In this way it will develop; it is not beyond that.'

298 "In such ways, he lives observing the body as body internally. Or, he lives observing the body as body externally. Or, he lives observing the body both internally and externally. Or, he lives observing in the body its arising factors. Or, he lives observing in the body its decaying factors. Thinking 'there is body,' his mindfulness becomes established to the extent necessary for knowledge and awareness. He lives unattached and grasps after nothing in the world. Thus, a *bhikkhu* lives observing the body as body.

11. "How does a *bhikkhu* live observing feeling as feeling?

"In this case, a *bhikkhu* experiencing a pleasant feeling knows 'I am experiencing a pleasant feeling.' When experiencing a painful feeling, he knows

'I am experiencing a painful feeling.' When experiencing a feeling that is neither pleasant nor painful, he knows 'I am experiencing a feeling that is neither pleasant nor painful.' Or when experiencing a pleasant physical[5] feeling, he knows 'I am experiencing a pleasant physical feeling.' Or when experiencing a pleasant nonphysical feeling, he knows 'I am experiencing a pleasant nonphysical feeling.' Or when experiencing a painful physical feeling, he knows 'I am experiencing a painful physical feeling.' Or when experiencing a painful nonphysical feeling, he knows 'I am experiencing a painful nonphysical feeling.' Or when experiencing a physical feeling that is neither pleasant nor painful, he knows 'I am experiencing a physical feeling that is neither pleasant nor painful.' Or when experiencing a nonphysical feeling that is neither pleasant nor painful, he knows 'I am experiencing a nonphysical feeling that is neither pleasant nor painful.'

"In such ways, he lives observing feeling as feeling internally. Or, he lives observing feeling as feeling externally. Or, he lives observing feeling as feeling both internally and externally. Or, he lives observing in the feeling its arising factors. Or, he lives observing in the feeling its decaying factors. 299
Thinking 'there is feeling,' his mindfulness becomes established to the extent necessary for knowledge and awareness. He lives unattached and grasps after nothing in the world. Thus, a *bhikkhu* lives observing the feeling as feeling.

12. "How does a *bhikkhu* live observing mind as mind?

"In such a case, a *bhikkhu*

knows a lustful mind 'as a lustful mind'
knows a mind that is free from lust 'as a mind that is free from lust'
knows a hateful mind 'as a hateful mind'
knows a mind that is free of hatred 'as a mind free of hatred'
knows a mind that is filled with confusion 'as a mind filled with confusion'
knows a mind that is free from confusion 'as a mind free from confusion'
knows a focused mind 'as a focused mind'
knows an unfocused mind 'as an unfocused mind'
knows an extensive mind 'as an extensive mind'
knows a mind that is not extensive 'as a mind that is not extensive'
knows a mind that is surpassed 'as a mind that is surpassed'
knows a mind that is unsurpassed 'as a mind that is unsurpassed'

[5] *Sāmisaṃ.*

knows a concentrated mind 'as a concentrated mind'

knows a mind that is not concentrated 'as a mind that is not concentrated'

knows a liberated mind 'as a liberated mind'

knows an unliberated mind 'as an unliberated mind'

"In such ways, he lives observing mind as mind internally. Or, he lives observing mind as mind externally. Or, he lives observing mind as mind both internally and externally. Or, he lives observing in the mind its arising factors. Or, he lives observing in the mind its decaying factors. Thinking 'there
300 is mind,' his mindfulness becomes established to the extent necessary for knowledge and awareness. He lives unattached and grasps after nothing in the world. Thus, a *bhikkhu* lives observing the mind as mind.

13. "How does a *bhikkhu* live observing mental phenomena as mental phenomena?

"In this case, a *bhikkhu* lives observing mental phenomena as mental phenomena relating to the five obstacles. And how does a *bhikkhu* live observing mental phenomena as mental phenomena relating to the five obstacles?

"In this case, if there is sensual desire internally, a *bhikkhu* knows 'sensual desire is within me internally.' If there is no sensual desire internally, he knows 'there is no sensual desire within me internally.' He knows when there is an arising of sensual desire that has not arisen before. He knows when there is an abandoning of sensual desire that has arisen before. And he knows of the non-arising in the future of sensual desire that has been given up.

"Or if there is ill will internally, he knows 'ill will is within me internally.' When there is no ill will internally, he knows 'there is no ill will within me internally.' He knows when there is an arising of ill will that has not arisen before. He knows when there is an abandoning of ill will that has arisen before. And he knows of the non-arising in the future of ill will that has been given up.

"Or if there is sloth and laziness internally, he knows 'sloth and laziness are within me internally.' When there is neither sloth nor laziness internally, he knows 'there is neither sloth nor laziness within me internally.' He knows when there is an arising of sloth and laziness that have not arisen before. He knows when there is an abandoning of sloth and laziness that have arisen before. And he knows of the non-arising in the future of sloth and laziness that have been given up.

"Or if there is agitation and worry internally, he knows 'agitation and
301 worry is within me internally.' When there is no agitation and worry inter-

nally, he knows 'there is no agitation and worry within me internally.' He knows when there is an arising of agitation and worry that has not arisen before. He knows when there is an abandoning of agitation and worry that has arisen before. And he knows of the non-arising in the future of agitation and worry that have been given up.

"Or if there is perplexity internally, he knows 'perplexity is within me internally.' When there is no perplexity internally, he knows 'there is no perplexity within me internally.' He knows when there is an arising of perplexity that has arisen before. He knows when there is an abandoning of perplexity that has not arisen before. And he knows of the non-arising in the future of perplexity that has been given up.

"In such ways, he lives observing mental phenomena as mental phenomena internally. Or, he lives observing mental phenomena as mental phenomena externally. Or, he lives observing mental phenomena as mental phenomena both internally and externally. Or, he lives observing in the mental phenomena their arising factors. Or, he lives observing in the mental phenomena their decaying factors. Thinking 'there are mental phenomena,' his mindfulness becomes established to the extent necessary for knowledge and awareness. He lives unattached and grasps after nothing in the world. Thus, a *bhikkhu* lives observing mental phenomena as mental phenomena relating to the five obstacles.

14. "Again, in another case, a *bhikkhu* lives observing mental phenomena as mental phenomena relating to the five aggregates of attachment.

"How does a *bhikkhu* live observing mental phenomena as mental phenomena relating to the five aggregates of attachment?

"In such a case, a *bhikkhu* thinks: 'Such is the body, such is the origin of the body, such is the extinction of the body—such is feeling, such is the origin of feeling, such is the extinction of feeling—such is perception, such is the origin of perception, such is the extinction of perception—
such are the dispositions to action, such is the origin of dispositions to 302
action, such is the extinction of dispositions to action—such is consciousness, such is the origin of consciousness, such is the extinction of consciousness.'

"In such ways, he lives observing mental phenomena as mental phenomena internally. Or, he lives observing mental phenomena as mental phenomena externally. Or, he lives observing mental phenomena as mental phenomena both internally and externally. Or, he lives observing in the mental phenomena their arising factors. Or, he lives observing in the mental phenomena their decaying factors. Thinking 'there are mental phenomena,' his mindfulness becomes established to the extent necessary for knowledge and awareness. He lives unattached and grasps after nothing in the world. Thus, a *bhikkhu* lives observing mental phenomena as mental phenomena relating to the five aggregates of attachment.

15. "In another case, a *bhikkhu* lives observing mental phenomena as mental phenomena relating to the six internal and external bases of sense.

"How does a *bhikkhu* live observing mental phenomena as mental phenomena relating to the six internal and external bases of sense?

"In this case, a *bhikkhu* knows the eye and he knows visual objects. And whatever fetter arises dependent on both of them—he knows that. And when a fetter arises that has not arisen before—he knows that. And when a fetter is abandoned that previously arose—he knows that. And when a fetter will not arise in the future because it has been abandoned—he knows that. . . . He knows the ear and he knows sounds. . . . He knows the nose and he knows smells. . . . He knows the tongue and he knows tastes. . . . He knows the body and he knows tactile sensations. . . . He knows the mind
303 and he knows mental phenomena. And whatever fetter arises dependent on both of them—he knows that. And when a fetter arises that has not arisen before—he knows that. And when a fetter is abandoned that previously arose—he knows that. And when a fetter will not arise in the future because it has been abandoned—he knows that.

"In such ways, he lives observing mental phenomena as mental phenomena internally . . . unattached and grasps after nothing in the world. Thus, a *bhikkhu* lives observing mental phenomena as mental phenomena relating to the internal and external bases of sense.

16. "Again, in another case, a *bhikkhu* lives observing mental phenomena as mental phenomena relating to the seven factors of enlightenment.

"How does a *bhikkhu* live observing mental phenomena as mental phenomena relating to the seven factors of enlightenment?

"In a case where there is the mindfulness factor of enlightenment internally, a *bhikkhu* knows 'There is the mindfulness factor of enlightenment within me internally.' When there is no mindfulness factor of enlightenment internally, he knows 'There is no mindfulness factor of enlightenment within me internally.' And thus he knows how there has arisen the mindfulness factor of enlightenment that has not arisen before. And he knows how the perfection of the development of the mindfulness factor of enlightenment comes about when it has arisen.

"In a case where there is the *dhamma*-discrimination factor of enlightenment internally . . . the energy factor of enlightenment internally . . . the joy
304 factor of enlightenment internally . . . the serenity factor of enlightenment internally . . . the concentration factor of enlightenment internally . . .

"In a case where there is the equanimity factor of enlightenment internally, a *bhikkhu* knows 'There is the equanimity factor of enlightenment within me internally.' When there is no equanimity factor of enlightenment internally, he knows 'There is no the equanimity factor of enlightenment within me internally.' And thus he knows how there has arisen the equanimity factor of enlightenment that has not arisen before. And he knows how the perfection of the development of the equanimity factor of enlightenment comes about when it has arisen.

"In such ways, he lives observing mental phenomena as mental phenomena internally. Or, he lives observing mental phenomena as mental phenomena externally. Or, he lives observing mental phenomena as mental phenomena both internally and externally. Or, he lives observing in the mental phenomena their arising factors. Or, he lives observing in the mental phenomena their decaying factors. Thinking 'there are mental phenomena,' his mindfulness becomes established to the extent necessary for knowledge and awareness. He lives unattached and grasps after nothing in the world. Thus, a *bhikkhu* lives observing mental phenomena as mental phenomena relating to the seven factors of enlightenment.

17. "Again, in another case, a *bhikkhu* lives observing mental phenomena as mental phenomena relating to the Four Noble Truths.

"How does a *bhikkhu* live observing mental phenomena as mental phenomena relating to the Four Noble Truths?

"In this case, a *bhikkhu* knows as it really is 'this is suffering.' He knows as it really is 'this is the origin of suffering.' He knows as it really is 'this is the cessation of suffering.' He knows as it really is 'this is the path going to the cessation of suffering.' 305

18. "What is the noble truth of suffering?

"Birth is suffering, old age is suffering, death is suffering, grief, lamentation, pain, despair, and distress are suffering; not getting what one wants, that is suffering. In brief, the five aggregates of attachment are suffering.

"What is birth? In whatever beings, of whatever classification of beings, there is birth when there is the production, the coming to be, the coming forth, the appearance of, the aggregates and the emergence of the sense bases. This is called birth.

"What is old age? In whatever beings, of whatever classification of beings, there is old age when there is decrepitude, broken teeth, gray hair, wrinkled skin, the dwindling of the life force, and the decaying of the sense faculties. This is called old age.

"What is death? In whatever beings, of whatever classification of beings, [there is death] when there is decease, passing away, breaking up, disappearing, dying, death, completion of one's time, breaking up of the aggregates, and the casting off of the body. This is called death.

"What is grief? On account of being affected by some kind of misfortune

306 or on account of being afflicted by something painful, one grieves, feels sorrow, is in distress, grieves on the inside, or grieves greatly on the inside. This is called grief.

"What is lamentation? On account of being affected by some kind of misfortune or on account of being afflicted by something painful, one deplores it, laments, cries out, cries out loudly, or laments loudly. This is called lamentation.

"What is pain? Whatever is experienced as painful to the body, disagreeable to the body, and pain that arises from bodily contact that is disagreeable. This is called pain.

"What is despair? Whatever is experienced as painful to the mind, disagreeable to the mind, and pain that arises from mental contact that is disagreeable. This is called despair.

"What is distress? On account of being affected by some kind of misery or on account of being afflicted by something painful, one experiences trou-
307 ble, distress, great trouble, and great distress. This is called distress.

"How is not getting what one wants suffering? For beings liable to birth, a wish such as this arises: 'Oh, if only we were not liable to birth, if only we would not be born.' But this will not be attained by merely wishing for it. This is how not getting what one wants is suffering. For beings liable to old age . . . For beings liable to death . . . For beings liable to illness . . . For beings liable to grief, lamentation, pain, despair, and distress, a wish such as this arises: 'Oh, if only we were not liable to grief, lamentation, pain, despair, and distress, if only there were no coming to grief, lamentation, pain, despair, and distress for us.' But this will not be attained by merely wishing for it. This is how not getting what one wants is suffering.

"And what, in brief, are the five aggregates of attachment that are suffering? Namely, they are: the bodily aggregate of attachment, the feeling aggregate of attachment, the perception aggregate of attachment, the dispositions to action aggregate of attachment, and the consciousness aggregate of attachment. These are, in brief, the five aggregates of attachment that are suffering.

308 "This is called the noble truth of suffering.

19. "What is the noble truth of the origin of suffering?

"That craving which leads to rebirth, accompanied by pleasure and lust, finding delight in this or that, namely, craving for sensual pleasure, craving for becoming,[6] and craving for non-becoming.[7]

"Where does such craving arise when it arises? Where is it established when it settles? From whatever things in the world are enticing and

[6] Or, craving for rebirth.

[7] *Vibhava-taṇhā.* Craving for non-becoming is tantamount to craving for annihilation.

agreeable, here such a craving arises when it arises, and here it is established when it settles.

"What is an enticing or agreeable thing in the world? The eye is an enticing and agreeable thing in the world; here such a craving arises when it arises, and here it is established when it settles. The ear is an enticing and agreeable thing in the world; here such a craving arises when it arises, and here it is established when it settles. The nose is an enticing and agreeable thing in the world; here such a craving arises when it arises, and here it is established when it settles. The tongue is an enticing and agreeable thing in the world; here such a craving arises when it arises, and here it is established when it settles. The body is an enticing and agreeable thing in the world; here such a craving arises when it arises, and here it is established when it settles. The mind is an enticing and agreeable thing in the world; here such a craving arises when it arises, and here it is established when it settles.

"Visible objects are enticing and agreeable things in the world; here such a craving arises when it arises, and here it is established when it settles. Sounds are enticing and agreeable things in the world; here such a craving arises when it arises, and here it is established when it settles. Smells are enticing and agreeable things in the world; here such a craving arises when it arises, and here it is established when it settles. Tastes are enticing and agreeable things in the world; here such a craving arises when it arises, and here it is established when it settles. Tangibles are enticing and agreeable things in the world; here such a craving arises when it arises, and here it is established when it settles. Mental phenomena are enticing and agreeable things in the world; here such a craving arises when it arises, and here it is established when it settles.

"Visual consciousness is an enticing and agreeable thing in the world; here such a craving arises when it arises, and here it is established when it settles. Auditory consciousness . . . Olfactory consciousness . . . Gustatory consciousness . . . Bodily consciousness. . . . Mental consciousness is an enticing and agreeable thing in the world; here such a craving arises when it arises, and here it is established when it settles.

"Eye-contact is an enticing and agreeable thing in the world; here such a craving arises when it arises, and here it is established when it settles. Ear-
contact . . . Nose-contact . . . Tongue-contact . . . Body-contact. . . . Mind- 309
contact is an enticing and agreeable thing in the world; here such a craving arises when it arises, and here it is established when it settles.

"Feeling born of eye-contact is an enticing and agreeable thing in the world; here such a craving arises when it arises, and here it is established when it settles. Feeling born of ear-contact . . . Feeling born of nose-contact . . . Feeling born of tongue-contact . . . Feeling born of body-contact. . . . Feeling born of mind-contact is an enticing and agreeable thing in the world;

here such a craving arises when it arises, and here it is established when it settles.

"Perception of visible objects is an enticing and agreeable thing in the world; here such a craving arises when it arises, and here it is established when it settles. Perception of sounds . . . Perception of smells . . . Perception of tastes . . . Perception of tangibles. . . . Perception of mental phenomena is an enticing and agreeable thing in the world; here such a craving arises when it arises, and here it is established when it settles.

"Intentions regarding visible objects are enticing and agreeable things in the world; here such a craving arises when it arises, and here it is established when it settles. Intentions regarding sounds . . . Intentions regarding smells . . . Intentions regarding tastes . . . Intentions regarding tangibles . . . Intentions regarding mental phenomena are enticing and agreeable things in the world; here such a craving arises when it arises, and here it is established when it settles.

"Craving for visible objects is an enticing and agreeable thing in the world; here such a craving arises when it arises, and here it is established when it settles. Craving for sounds . . . Craving for smells . . . Craving for tastes . . . Craving for tangibles. . . . Craving for mental phenomena is an enticing and agreeable thing in the world; here such a craving arises when it arises, and here it is established when it settles.

"Reflection about visible objects is an enticing and agreeable thing in the world; here such a craving arises when it arises, and here it is established when it settles. Reflection about sounds . . . Reflection about smells . . . Reflection about tastes . . . Reflection about tangibles. . . . Reflection about mental phenomena is an enticing and agreeable thing in the world; here such a craving arises when it arises, and here it is established when it settles.

"Deliberation about visible objects is an enticing and agreeable thing in the world; here such a craving arises when it arises, and here it is established when it settles. Deliberation about sounds . . . Deliberation about smells . . . Deliberation about tastes . . . Deliberation about tangibles. . . . Deliberation about mental phenomena is an enticing and agreeable thing in the world;
310 here such a craving arises, and here it is established when it settles.

"This is called the noble truth of the origin suffering.

20. "What is the noble truth of the cessation of suffering?

"It is the utter cessation and extinction of that craving, its renunciation, its forsaking, release from it, and non-attachment to it.

"Where is such craving abandoned when it is abandoned? Where is it destroyed when it is stopped? Whatever in the world is an enticing and agreeable thing, here this craving is abandoned when it is abandoned, and here it is destroyed when it is stopped.

"What is an enticing and agreeable thing in the world? The eye is an enticing and agreeable thing in the world; here this craving is abandoned when it is abandoned, and here it is destroyed when it is stopped. The ear . . . The nose . . . The tongue . . . The body. . . . The mind is an enticing and agreeable thing in the world; here this craving is abandoned when it is abandoned, and here it is destroyed when it is stopped.

"Visible objects are enticing and agreeable things in the world; here this craving is abandoned when it is abandoned, and here it is destroyed when it is stopped. Sounds . . . Smells . . . Tastes . . . Tangibles. . . . Mental phenomena are enticing and agreeable things in the world; here this craving is abandoned when it is abandoned, and here it is destroyed when it is stopped.

"Visual consciousness is an enticing and agreeable thing in the world; here this craving is abandoned when it is abandoned, and here it is destroyed when it is stopped. Auditory consciousness . . . Olfactory consciousness . . . Gustatory consciousness . . . Bodily consciousness. . . . Mental consciousness is an enticing and agreeable thing in the world; here this craving is abandoned when it is abandoned, and here it is destroyed when it is stopped.

"Eye-contact is an enticing and agreeable thing in the world; here this craving is abandoned when it is abandoned, and here it is destroyed when it is stopped. Ear-contact . . . Nose-contact . . . Tongue-contact . . . Body-contact. . . . Mind-contact is an enticing and agreeable thing in the world; here 311
this craving is abandoned when it is abandoned, and here it is destroyed when it is stopped.

"Feeling born of eye-contact is an enticing and agreeable thing in the world; here this craving is abandoned when it is abandoned, and here it is destroyed when it is stopped. Feeling born of ear-contact . . . Feeling born of nose-contact . . . Feeling born of tongue-contact . . . Feeling born of body-contact. . . . Feeling born of mind-contact is an enticing and agreeable thing in the world; here this craving is abandoned when it is abandoned, and here it is destroyed when it is stopped.

"Perception of visible objects is an enticing and agreeable thing in the world; here this craving is abandoned when it is abandoned, and here it is destroyed when it is stopped. Perception of sounds . . . Perception of smells . . . Perception of tastes . . . Perception of tangibles. . . . Perception of mental phenomena is an enticing and agreeable thing in the world; here this craving is abandoned when it is abandoned, and here it is destroyed when it is stopped.

"Intentions regarding visible objects are enticing and agreeable things in the world; here this craving is abandoned when it is abandoned, and here it is destroyed when it is stopped. Intentions regarding sounds . . . Intentions regarding smells . . . Intentions regarding tastes . . . Intentions regarding tangibles. . . . Intentions regarding mental phenomena are enticing and agreeable things in the world; here this craving is abandoned when it is abandoned, and here it is destroyed when it is stopped.

"Reflection about visible objects is an enticing and agreeable thing in the world; here this craving is abandoned when it is abandoned, and here it is destroyed when it is stopped. Reflection about sounds . . . Reflection about smells . . . Reflection about tastes . . . Reflection about tangibles. . . . Reflection about mental phenomena is an enticing and agreeable thing in the world; here this craving is abandoned when it is abandoned, and here it is destroyed when it is stopped.

"Deliberation about visible objects is an enticing and agreeable thing in the world; here this craving is abandoned when it is abandoned, and here it is destroyed when it is stopped. Deliberation about sounds . . . Deliberation about smells . . . Deliberation about tastes . . . Deliberation about tangibles. . . . Deliberation about mental phenomena is an enticing and agreeable thing in the world; here this craving is abandoned when it is abandoned, and here it is destroyed when it is stopped.

"This is called the noble truth of the cessation of suffering.

21. "What is the noble truth of the path going to the cessation of suffering?

"It is this Noble Eightfold Path, namely: right view, right intention, right speech, right action, right livelihood, right effort, right mindfulness, right concentration.

312 "What is right view? It is knowledge regarding suffering, knowledge regarding the origin of suffering, knowledge regarding the cessation of suffering, and knowledge regarding the path leading to the cessation of suffering. This is called right view.

"What is right intention? It is the intention of renunciation, the intention of non-violence, and the intention of non-hurting. This is called right intention.

"What is right speech? It is abstaining from false speech, abstaining from malicious speech, abstaining from harsh speech, and abstaining from frivolous chatter. This is called right speech.

"What is right action? It is abstaining from taking life, abstaining from taking what is not given, and abstaining from acting wrongly in regard to sense pleasures. This is called right action.

"What is right livelihood? In this case, the noble disciple abandons wrong means of livelihood and arranges to live by right means of livelihood. This is called right livelihood.

"What is right effort? In this case, a *bhikkhu* makes an effort and produces a will so that evil and unskilled mental states do not arise that have not arisen before. For that purpose, he stirs his energy, exerts and applies his mind. With regard to evil and unskilled states that have arisen before, he makes an effort and produces a will to abandon them. For that purpose, he stirs his energy, exerts and applies his mind. With regard to good mental states that have not

arisen before, he makes an effort and produces a will so that they arise. For that purpose, he stirs his energy, exerts and applies his mind. With regard to good mental states that have arisen before, he makes an effort and produces a will so that they will persist, not fade away, become more numerous, increase 313
in abundance, develop, and become perfected. For that purpose, he stirs his energy, exerts and applies his mind. This is called right effort.

"What is right mindfulness? In such a case, a *bhikkhu* lives observing the body as body, energetically, self-possessed, and mindful, having eliminated both the desire for and despair over the world. He lives observing feeling as feeling . . . observing the mind as mind . . . a *bhikkhu* lives observing mental phenomena as mental phenomena, energetically, self-possessed, and mindful, having eliminated both the desire for and despair over the world. This is called right mindfulness.

"What is right concentration? In this case, having become detached from sensual pleasures, detached from unwholesome mental states, a *bhikkhu* lives, having entered the first *jhāna,* which is accompanied by reasoning and cogitation, wherein there is joy and happiness born of detachment. By the calming of reasoning and cogitation, internally purified, a *bhikkhu* lives, having entered the second *jhāna,* which has a one-pointed mind that is devoid of reasoning and cogitation and wherein there is joy and happiness born of concentration.[8] Dwelling in equanimity, and with the cessation of joy, mindful and fully aware, a *bhikkhu* lives, having entered the third *jhāna,* wherein he experiences happiness with the body and that which the noble ones describe as: 'He who has equanimity and mindfulness lives happily.' Abandoning both happiness and suffering, from the extinction of the elation and despair he felt formerly, a *bhikkhu* lives, having entered the fourth *jhāna,* wherein there is neither suffering nor happiness, but the purity of mindfulness and equanimity. This is called right concentration.

"This is called the noble truth of the path leading to the cessation of suffering.

"In such ways, he lives observing mental phenomena as mental phenomena internally. Or, he lives observing mental phenomena as mental phe- 314
nomena externally. Or, he lives observing mental phenomena as mental phenomena both internally and externally. Or, he lives observing in the mental phenomena their arising factors. Or, he lives observing in the mental phenomena their decaying factors. Thinking 'there are mental phenomena,' his mindfulness becomes established to the extent necessary for knowledge and awareness. He lives unattached and grasps after nothing in the world. Thus, a *bhikkhu* lives observing mental phenomena as mental phenomena relating to the Four Noble Truths.

[8] *Samādhi.*

22. "*Bhikkhus,* someone who develops in this way these four foundations for mindfulness for seven rainy seasons may expect one or the other of two results: such a person may become a knower in this very world or, if some support for life remains, that person may become a 'non-returner.' Let alone seven rainy seasons, someone who develops in this way these four foundations for mindfulness for six rainy seasons . . . five rainy seasons . . . four rainy seasons . . . three rainy seasons . . . two rainy seasons . . . one rainy season. . . . Let alone one rainy season, someone who develops in this way these four foundations for mindfulness for seven months . . . for six months . . . for five
315 months . . . for four months . . . for three months . . . for two months . . . for
one month . . . for one half of a month. . . . Let alone one half of a month, someone who develops in this way these four foundations for mindfulness for seven days may expect one or the other of two results: such a person may become a knower in this very world or, if some support for life remains, that person may become a 'non-returner.'

"This is the reason why it was said that: 'There is this one path, *bhikkhus,* for the purification of beings, for passing beyond grief and lamentation, for the extinction of suffering and despair, for the attainment of knowledge, for the realization of *nibbāna,* namely, these four foundations for mindfulness.'"

This was said by the Exalted One. Delighted, those *bhikkhus* rejoiced in what the Exalted One had said.

5

The Greater Discourse on the Destruction of Craving

(*Mahātaṇhāsankhaya*)[1]

This discourse is one of the most philosophically important discourses in the whole of the Pāli Canon because it puts together many of the key doctrines and practices of early Buddhism: the doctrine of dependent arising, the analysis of consciousness as dependent on modes of sense experience, the theory of the "nutriments," the Buddha's view of the conception and growth of a human being, monastic training and ethics, the removal of the five obstacles of sense experience, and the higher meditative states called the four *jhānas*. But among these many important doctrines, the destruction of craving (*taṇhā*) is singled out as the key to redirecting human experience away from unwholesome states and toward wholesome states, in effect, eliminating suffering. Thus, the aim of this discourse is to demonstrate that the destruction of craving is nothing less than the most crucial step toward the attainment of religious liberation. Here, again, the early Buddhist texts make ethical and psychological transformation—not metaphysical knowledge—the focus of the religious path.

According to the Buddha's detailed causal analysis of the arising and cessation of suffering, craving arises at the most critical juncture. In the ordinary, corrupted mind, craving arises as a result of feeling (*vedanā*). By themselves, feelings are neither bad nor good—they are merely pleasant, painful, or neutral. But when feelings are filtered through a defiled mind, a person reacts to feelings by developing cravings that invariably lead to suffering. In contrast, a person having a liberated or morally purified mind reacts to feelings by developing wholesome mental states like equanimity and dispassion that lead to tranquillity and happiness.

As the title of the discourse suggests, the practices involved in the destruction of craving are the main focus of the discourse. These practices emphasize the development of a thorough understanding and control of sense experience. Beyond restraint in sense experience, the destruction of craving requires various moral practices: refraining from killing, stealing, lying, and so on, and the commission of acts of love, kindness, and compassion.

[1] *Majjhima Nikāya* 1.256–271.

Typical of early Buddhism, the discourse demonstrates that the practice of virtuous actions goes hand in hand with the psychological training of the mind.

The Buddha's view of consciousness and the human person runs very much against the stream of most other philosophical and religious traditions, especially the Upaniṣadic theory of the *ātman* (a theory that the real Self is a permanent, blissful, pure agent, identical with consciousness). From Plato's conception of the soul as rational intellect to Descartes' view of mind as a thinking substance (*res cogitans*) distinct from the body, philosophers in the West have offered various metaphysical explanations of human consciousness. And yet, in contrast to all these theories, the Buddha saw consciousness as an impermanent, dependently arisen process—not a substance at all. Despite the fact that consciousness is an important and a distinctive factor in the formation of a personal identity, it is not necessary to consider it as a permanent essence. Consciousness, as the Buddha saw it, is not a spiritual interloper in a physical world, but an emergent phenomenon that arises out of the complex interactions of sensory faculties and sensory objects.

The Buddha's position regarding consciousness was probably very difficult for his followers to grasp. After all, the Buddha taught a doctrine of rebirth, and if consciousness is not a permanent personal essence, how can there be rebirth? Since consciousness is closely associated with personal identity, what is it that is reborn and links the new life with past lives, if not a permanent consciousness? Furthermore, how can one talk about religious salvation if there is no permanent identity that experiences it? Without a doctrine that describes a blissful continuity of the person beyond death, can the Buddha offer any solace regarding existential problems like old age and death? It was questions like these that drove the *bhikkhu* Sāti to his misconception of the Buddha's teaching. Given the strong attraction of a theory of a permanent consciousness, and the unrelenting influence of the Upaniṣadic tradition with its doctrine of *ātman,* the Buddha must have been at great pains to reinforce among the *bhikkhus* his teaching that consciousness is a conditioned, impermanent process and is but one among several factors in a dependently arisen personal identity.

Discourse

256

1. Thus have I heard. At one time, the Exalted One was dwelling at Sāvatthi at the Jeta Grove in Anāthapiṇḍika's park. At that time, there was a *bhikkhu* named Sāti, a fisherman's son, in whom had arisen a pernicious view like this: "Thus it is that I understand the *dhamma* taught by the Exalted One: it is this same consciousness, and not another, which transmigrates, which goes through the round of death and rebirth." A number of *bhikkhus*

heard this: "There is a *bhikkhu* named Sāti, a fisherman's son, in whom has arisen a pernicious view like this: 'Thus it is that I understand the *dhamma* taught by the Exalted One: it is this same consciousness, and not another, which transmigrates, which goes through the round of death and rebirth.'"

Then those *bhikkhus* approached Sāti, and having approached him, said this to Sāti: "Is it true that for you, good Sāti, there has arisen a pernicious view like this: 'Thus it is that I understand the *dhamma* taught by the Exalted One: it is this same consciousness, and not another, which transmigrates, which goes through the round of death and rebirth'?"

"It is true, friends, that I understand the *dhamma* of the Exalted One in just that way." Then those *bhikkhus,* wanting to detach him from that pernicious view, cross-examined, pressed for reasons, and questioned Sāti, saying: "Do not speak that way, Sāti! Do not misrepresent the Exalted One! It is not good to misrepresent the Exalted One. The Exalted One would not speak in that manner. In many ways, good Sāti, the Exalted One has said 257
that consciousness is dependently arisen, since, apart from a condition, there is no arising of consciousness."

Nonetheless, although being cross-examined, pressed for reasons, and questioned by these *bhikkhus,* Sāti clung obstinately to that pernicious view and continued to insist on it.

2. When those *bhikkhus* were not able to dissuade Sāti from that pernicious view, they approached the Exalted One. Having approached and greeted the Exalted One, they sat down to one side. When they were seated to one side, those *bhikkhus* said this to the Exalted One: "Sir, there has arisen in Sāti, a pernicious view like this: 'Thus it is that I understand the *dhamma* taught by the Exalted One: it is this same consciousness, and not another, which transmigrates, which goes through the round of death and rebirth.' When, sir, we heard that, we approached Sāti and tried to dissuade him of this pernicious view. But as we were not able to dissuade Sāti from this pernicious view, we now report this matter to the Exalted One."

3. Then the Exalted One addressed a certain *bhikkhu:* "Come, *bhikkhu,* 258
and in my words address the *bhikkhu* Sāti, who is a fisherman's son: 'The teacher calls you, good Sāti.'"

"Yes, sir," that *bhikkhu* assented to the Exalted One. And he approached Sāti. When he had approached him, he said this to Sāti: 'The teacher calls you, good Sāti.'"

"Yes, friend," Sāti, assented to the *bhikkhu.* So he approached the Exalted One. When he had approached and greeted the Exalted One, he sat down to one side. When he was seated to one side, the Exalted One said this to Sāti: "Is it true, Sāti, that there has arisen in you a pernicious view like this: 'Thus it is that I understand the *dhamma* taught by the Exalted One: that which transmigrates, which goes through the round of death and rebirth, is this same consciousness and not another'?"

"Exactly so, sir. This is how I understand the *dhamma* taught by the Exalted One."

"What is that consciousness, Sāti?"

"Sir, it is that which speaks and feels and experiences here and there the result of good and evil actions."

"Do you know anyone, you misguided person, to whom I have taught the *dhamma* in that way? Misguided person, have I not spoken in many ways of consciousness as dependently arisen, since without a condition there would be no arising of consciousness? But you, misguided person, have misrepresented us by your wrong grasp and have injured yourself and have accumulated much demerit. And this, misguided person, will lead to your harm and suffering for a long time."

4. Then the Exalted One addressed the *bhikkhus:* "What do you think, *bhikkhus?* Has this Sāti even a glimmer of this discipline and doctrine?"

"How could he, sir? No, sir."

This having been said, Sāti sat down and became silent, downcast, dejected, with his shoulders drooping, overcome with remorse and bewildered. Then the Exalted One, knowing that Sāti had become downcast and dejected, said this to him: "Misguided person, you will be known by your own pernicious view. In connection with this, I will question the *bhikkhus.*"

Then the Exalted One addressed the *bhikkhus:* "Do you, *bhikkhus,* under-
259 stand the *dhamma* that I teach in the way that this Sāti does who has misrepresented me by his wrong grasp, who has injured himself, and who has accumulated much demerit?"

"No, sir. The Exalted One has explained that consciousness is dependently arisen, since, without a condition, there is no arising of consciousness."

"Good, *bhikkhus.* It is good that you have understood thus the *dhamma* that I teach in this way. For, in many ways, I have said that consciousness is dependently arisen, since, without a condition, there is no arising of consciousness. And this Sāti has misrepresented us by his wrong grasp and injures himself and accumulates much demerit. And this, indeed, will be for the harm and suffering of this misguided man for a long time.

5. "*Bhikkhus,* whatever condition consciousness is dependent on when it arises, by that condition it is reckoned: when consciousness arises dependent on eye and visible objects, it is reckoned as 'visual consciousness'; when consciousness arises dependent on ear and sounds, it is reckoned as 'auditory consciousness'; when consciousness arises dependent on nose and smells, it is reckoned as 'olfactory consciousness'; when consciousness arises dependent on tongue and tastes, it is reckoned as 'gustatory consciousness';

when consciousness arises dependent on body and tangible things, it is reckoned as 'bodily consciousness'; when consciousness arises dependent on mind and mental phenomena, it is reckoned as 'mental consciousness.'

"Just as whatever condition a fire is dependent on when it burns, by that condition it is reckoned: a fire that burns dependent on a log is reckoned as a 'log-fire'; a fire that burns dependent on kindling is reckoned as a 'kindling-fire'; a fire that burns dependent on grass is reckoned as a 'grass-fire'; a fire that burns dependent on dung is reckoned as a 'dung-fire'; a fire that burns dependent on chaff is reckoned as a 'chaff-fire'; a fire that burns dependent on rubbish is reckoned as a 'rubbish-fire.' Just so, whatever condition consciousness is dependent on when it arises, by that condition it is reckoned: when consciousness arises dependent on eye and visible objects, it is reckoned as 'visual consciousness'; when consciousness arises dependent on ear and sounds, it is reckoned as 'auditory consciousness'; when consciousness arises dependent on nose and smells, it is reckoned as 'olfactory 260
consciousness'; when consciousness arises dependent on tongue and tastes, it is reckoned as 'gustatory consciousness'; when consciousness arises dependent on body and tangible things, it is reckoned as 'bodily consciousness'; when consciousness arises dependent on mind and mental phenomena, it is reckoned as 'mental consciousness.'

6. "Do you see, *bhikkhus,* 'this has come to be'?"

"Yes, sir."

"Do you see, *bhikkhus,* 'its origin is that nutriment'?"[2]

"Yes, sir."

"Do you see, *bhikkhus,* 'from the cessation of that nutriment, that which has come to be is subject to cessation'?"

"Yes, sir."

"*Bhikkhus,* does a state of perplexity arise when one doubts 'this has come to be'?"

"Yes, sir."

"*Bhikkhus,* does a state of perplexity arise when one doubts 'its origin is that nutriment'?"

"Yes, sir."

"*Bhikkhus,* does a state of perplexity arise when one doubts 'from the cessation of that nutriment, that which has come to be is subject to cessation'?"

"Yes, sir."

"*Bhikkhus,* by seeing with proper wisdom things as they truly are as regards 'this has come to be,' would perplexity be abandoned?"

"Yes, sir."

[2] *Āhāra.* The nutriments are the supporting requirements that fuel a given phenomenon (e.g., food for the body).

"*Bhikkhus,* by seeing with proper wisdom things as they truly are as regards 'the arising from that as nutriment,' would perplexity be abandoned?"

"Yes, sir."

"*Bhikkhus,* by seeing with proper wisdom things as they truly are as regards 'from the cessation of that nutriment, that which has come to be is subject to cessation,' would perplexity be abandoned?"

"Yes, sir."

"*Bhikkhus,* are you here free from perplexity regarding 'this has come to be'?"

"Yes, sir."

"*Bhikkhus,* are you here free from perplexity regarding 'the arising from that as nutriment'?"

"Yes, sir."

"*Bhikkhus,* are you here free from perplexity regarding 'from the cessation of that nutriment, that which has come to be is subject to cessation'?"

"Yes, sir."

"*Bhikkhus,* do you clearly see, with proper wisdom, as it really is, 'this has come to be'?"

"Yes, sir."

"*Bhikkhus,* do you clearly see, with proper wisdom, as it really is, 'the arising from that as nutriment'?"

"Yes, sir."

"*Bhikkhus,* do you clearly see, with proper wisdom, as it really is, 'from the cessation of that nutriment, that which has come to be is subject to cessation'?"

"Yes, sir."

"*Bhikkhus,* if you cling to, cherish, treasure, or treat passively as mine even this purified and cleansed view, would you understand the *dhamma* as taught in the parable of the raft,[3] which is for the purpose of crossing over and not for the purpose of attachment?"

"No, we would not understand it that way, sir."

261 "But, *bhikkhus,* if you were not to cling to, not to cherish, not to treasure, or not to treat passively as mine this purified and cleansed view, would you understand the *dhamma* as taught in the parable of the raft, which is for the purpose of crossing over and not for the purpose of attachment?"

"Yes, we would understand it that way, sir."

7. "*Bhikkhus,* there are these four nutriments for the maintenance of beings that have come to be or for the support of beings who are seeking birth. What are the four? Physical nutriment (food), either gross or subtle; contact is the second; volition is the third; and consciousness the fourth.

[3] The parable of the raft can be found in section 7 of the Discourse on the Parable of the Water Snake (Chapter 9).

"These four nutriments are from what cause, from what origin, from what are they born, from what are they produced? These four nutriments have craving as their cause, craving as their origin, from craving are born, and from craving they are produced.

"This craving is from what cause, from what origin, from what is it born, from what is it produced? This craving has feeling as its cause, feeling as its origin, from feeling it is born, and from feeling it is produced.

"This feeling is from what cause, from what origin, from what is it born, from what is it produced? This feeling has contact as its cause, contact as its origin, from contact it is born, and from contact it is produced.

"This contact is from what cause, from what origin, from what is it born, from what is it produced? This contact has the six bases of sense[4] as its cause, the six bases of sense as its origin, from the six bases of sense it is born, and from the six bases of sense it is produced.

"These six bases of sense are from what cause, from what origin, from what are they born, from what are they produced? These six bases of sense have psycho-physicality[5] as their cause, psycho-physicality as their origin, from psycho-physicality they are born, and from psycho-physicality they are produced.

"This psycho-physicality is from what cause, from what origin, from what is it born, from what is it produced? This psycho-physicality has consciousness as its cause, consciousness as its origin, from consciousness it is born, and from consciousness it is produced.

"This consciousness is from what cause, from what origin, from what is it born, from what is it produced? This consciousness has dispositions to action as its cause, dispositions to action as its origin, from dispositions to action it is born, and from dispositions to action it is produced.

"These dispositions to action are from what cause, from what origin, from what are they born, from what are they produced? These dispositions to action have ignorance as their cause, ignorance as their origin, from ignorance they are born, and from ignorance they are produced.

"So, *bhikkhus,* dependent on ignorance, there are dispositions to action; dependent on dispositions to action, there is consciousness; dependent on consciousness, there is psycho-physicality; dependent on psycho-physicality, there are the six bases of sense; dependent on the six bases of sense, there is contact; dependent on contact, there is feeling; dependent on feeling, there is craving; dependent on craving, there is attachment; dependent on attachment, there is becoming; dependent on becoming, there is birth; dependent

4 The sense bases are each the combination of a sense faculty and a sense object.

5 *Nāma-rūpa.*

on birth, there is aging-and-death, sorrow, lamentation, pain, despair, and distress. Thus there is the arising of this whole mass of suffering.[6]

8. "This is what I have said. Is this the way you, *bhikkhus,* understand
[*each of these causal linkages?" "That is exactly the way we understand each of*
262 *the causal linkages, sir," those bhikkhus replied.*[7]]

9. "Good, *bhikkhus.* So you speak thus and I also speak thus: when this
263 is, that is; when this arises, that arises—namely, dependent on ignorance,
there are dispositions to action. . . . Thus there is the arising of this whole
mass of suffering.

"But from the complete cessation without remainder of ignorance, there is the cessation of dispositions to action; from the cessation of dispositions to action, there is the cessation of consciousness; from the cessation of consciousness, there is the cessation of the six sense bases; from the cessation of the six sense bases, there is the cessation of contact; from the cessation of contact, there is the cessation of feeling; from the cessation of feeling, there is the cessation of craving; from the cessation of craving, there is the cessation of attachment; from the cessation of attachment, there is the cessation of becoming; from the cessation of becoming, there is the cessation of birth; from the cessation of birth, there is the cessation of old age, death, grief, sorrow, suffering, lamentation, and despair. Thus there is the cessation of this entire mass of suffering.

10. "This is what I have said. Is this the way you, *bhikkhus,* understand
[*the cessation of each of these causal linkages?" "That is exactly the way we under-*
264 *stand the cessation of each of the causal linkages, sir," those bhikkhus replied.*[8]]

11. "Good, *bhikkhus.* So you, *bhikkhus,* speak thus, and I also speak thus: when this is not, that is not; when this ceases, that ceases—namely, from the cessation of ignorance, there is the cessation of dispositions to action. . . . Thus there is the cessation of this entire mass of suffering.

265 12. "Would you, *bhikkhus,* knowing thus and seeing thus look back to
the past in this way: 'Did we exist in the past?' 'Did we not exist in the past?' 'What were we in the past?' 'How were we in the past?' 'Having been what, what were we in the past?'"

"No, not that, sir."

"Would you, *bhikkhus,* knowing thus and seeing thus, look forward to the future in this way: 'Will we exist in the future?' 'Will we not exist in the future?' 'What will we be in the future?' 'How will we be in the future?' 'Having been what, what will we be in the future?'"

[6] This is the full twelvefold formula of dependent arising.

[7] The original text repeats verbatim what the Buddha has just taught them.

[8] The original text again repeats the Buddha's teaching verbatim.

"No, not that, sir."

"Would you, *bhikkhus,* knowing and seeing thus, be inwardly doubtful about the present in this way: 'Do I exist?' 'Do I not exist?' 'Who am I?' 'What am I?' 'This being has come from where?' 'Where will this being go?'"

"No, not that, sir."

"Would you, *bhikkhus,* knowing and seeing thus, speak in this way: 'Our teacher is respected, and out of respect for our teacher, we say this.'"

"No, not that, sir."

"Would you, *bhikkhus,* knowing and seeing thus, speak in this way: 'A religious wanderer speaks in this way, as do other religious wanderers, but we do not say this'?"

"No, not that, sir."

"Would you, *bhikkhus,* knowing and seeing thus, appoint another teacher?"

"No, not that, sir."

"Would you, *bhikkhus,* knowing and seeing thus, return to the religious observances, curious practices, and auspicious ceremonies of ordinary religious wanderers and Brahmins, considering them as the essence [of the holy life]?"

"No, no that, sir."

"Do you, *bhikkhus,* knowing this yourselves, seeing this for yourselves, and finding this out for yourselves, declare that?"

"Yes, sir."

"Good, *bhikkhus.* So you have been guided by me with this *dhamma* that is visible here and now, which is timeless, a come-and-see thing, leading to the goal, to be experienced by the wise for themselves. This is precisely why it has been said that 'This *dhamma* that is visible here and now, which is timeless, a come-and-see thing, leading to the goal, to be experienced by the wise for themselves.'

13. "There are, *bhikkhus,* three things through the union of which conception takes place. In the first case, there is the sexual union of mother and father—but when the mother is not in season and the *gandhabba*[9] is not present, then in that case there is no conception. In a second case, there is 266
the sexual union of the mother and father, and the mother is in season—but the *gandhabba* is not present, then in that case there is no conception in the womb. But in a third case, when there is the sexual union of the mother and father, the mother is in season, and the *gandhabba* is present, through the union of these three things conception takes place in the womb. The mother carries the conceived being in her womb for nine or ten months with great

[9] The word *gandhabba* has no obvious translation. "Embryo" is one possibility. According to some commentators, the *gandhabba* is meant to serve as the factor that provides the continuity of personality in the process of rebirth, linking a new birth with past lives.

anxiety and as a heavy burden. And after the lapse of nine or ten months, the mother gives birth with much anxiety and as a heavy burden. When the child is born, she nourishes it with her own blood. For a mother's milk is called 'blood' in the discipline of a noble one.

"When that child has come of age and his faculties are mature, at that point, he becomes a youngster who plays at games such as toy ploughs, tipcart, turning somersaults, toy windmills, toy measures, toy chariots, and toy bows. And when the child has grown up and his faculties have matured even further, when he is presented with the five sorts of sensual pleasure, the youngster enjoys himself with visible objects cognizable by the eye that are wished for, desirable, pleasing, enticing, connected with pleasure, and exciting; with sounds cognizable by the ear that are wished for, desirable, pleasing, enticing, connected with pleasure, and exciting; with smells cognizable by the nose that are wished for, desirable, pleasing, enticing, connected with pleasure, and exciting; with tastes cognizable by the tongue that are wished for, desirable, pleasing, enticing, connected with pleasure, and exciting; with tangibles cognizable by touch that are wished for, desirable, pleasing, enticing, connected with pleasure, and exciting.

14. "When he sees a visible object with the eye, he becomes attached to the visible object, if it is pleasing, but shuns the visible object, if it is unpleasing. He abides with mindfulness of the body unestablished, with a limited mind, and he does not understand the freedom of mind, the freedom by wisdom, as they really are, wherein those evil and unwholesome states cease without remainder. And so endowed with favoring and opposing, whatever feeling he feels—whether it is pleasant or painful or neither-painful-nor-pleasant—he delights in that feeling, he welcomes it, and remains attached to it. For one who delights in the feeling, who welcomes it and remains attached to it, there arises pleasure. What pleasure there is in the feeling—that is attachment. Dependent on attachment, there is becoming. Dependent on becoming, there is birth. And dependent on birth there are old age, death, grief, sorrow, suffering, lamentation, and despair. Thus there is the arising of this whole mass of suffering.

"When he hears a sound with the ear . . . When he smells a smell with the nose . . . When he tastes a taste with the tongue . . . When he touches a tangible thing with the body . . .

267 "When he knows a mental object with the mind, he becomes attached to the mental object, if it is pleasing, but shuns the mental object, if it is unpleasing. He abides with mindfulness of the body unestablished, with a limited mind, and he does not understand the freedom of mind, the freedom by wisdom, as they really are, wherein those evil and unwholesome states cease without remainder. And so endowed with favoring and opposing, whatever feeling he feels—whether it is pleasant or painful or

neither-painful-nor-pleasant—he delights in that feeling, he welcomes it, and remains attached to it. For one who delights in the feeling, who welcomes it and remains attached to it, there arises pleasure. What pleasure there is in the feeling—that is attachment. Dependent on attachment, there is becoming. Dependent on becoming, there is birth. And dependent on birth there are old age, death, grief, sorrow, suffering, lamentation, and despair. Thus there is the arising of this whole mass of suffering.

15. "Here, a *Tathāgata* arises in this world, an *arahant,* a fully awakened one, endowed with knowledge and virtue, a Well-Farer, a knower of the world, an unsurpassed charioteer of human beings who are like horses to be tamed, a teacher of *devas* and human beings, a Buddha, an Exalted One. He makes known this world—with its *devas,* Māras, Brahmās, including religious wanderers and Brahmins, and generations of *devas* and human beings—having understood and realized this for himself. He teaches the *dhamma* which is beautiful in the beginning, beautiful in the middle, and beautiful in the end, in spirit as well as in letter. He makes known the pure religious life that is completely fulfilled.

"A householder, householder's son, or one who is born to a certain clan, hears that *dhamma* and obtains faith in the *Tathāgata.* Endowed with that faith, he thinks: 'Household life is crowded and dusty; a life gone forth is open air. While living at home, it is not easy to live the higher spiritual life that is completely fulfilled and completely pure like a polished shell. Suppose, having shaved off my hair and beard, and having donned the yellow robe, I were to go forth from home to homelessness.'

"At a later time, abandoning a small fortune or abandoning a large fortune, abandoning a small circle of relatives or abandoning a large circle of relatives, having shaved his hair and beard, and having donned the yellow robes, he goes forth from home to homelessness.

16. "Having thus gone forth, he is endowed with the *bhikkhu*'s training and livelihood. Having given up taking life, he refrains from taking life. Without stick and sword, conscientious and endowed with sympathy, he dwells with compassion toward all living beings. Having given up taking what is not given, he refrains from taking what is not given. Taking only 268
what is given, expecting only what is given, by not stealing, he dwells in purity. Having given up unchastity, he observes a chaste life, living far apart, abstaining from the vulgar practice of sexual intercourse. Having given up false speech, he refrains from false speech. As one who speaks the truth and adheres to the truth, he is reliable, trustworthy, and keeps his word to the world. Having given up malicious speech, he refrains from malicious speech. Having heard something here, he does not repeat it elsewhere to cause dissension. Nor does he, having heard something elsewhere, repeat it here to cause dissension. Thus, he is one who conciliates, promotes friendships,

rejoices in concord, and delights in concord—he speaks words that promote concord. Having given up harsh speech, he refrains from harsh speech. He speaks only such words that are gentle, pleasant to the ear, amiable, charming, polite, agreeable, and pleasing to many people. Having given up talking nonsense, he refrains from talking nonsense. He speaks at the proper time, truthfully, on what is good, on the *dhamma* and the discipline. At the right time, he speaks such words that are worth treasuring, reasonable, moderate, and beneficial.

"He refrains from injuring seeds and plants. He eats once a day. Refraining from eating at night, he refrains from eating at the wrong time. He refrains from dancing, singing, music, and attending shows. He refrains from wearing garlands, perfumes, cosmetics, adornments, or improper decorations. He refrains from using high and large beds. He refrains from accepting gold and silver. He refrains from accepting uncooked grain. He refrains from accepting uncooked meat. He refrains from accepting women and girls. He refrains from accepting male and female slaves. He refrains from accepting goats and sheep. He refrains from accepting chickens and pigs. He refrains from accepting elephants, cattle, horses, and mares. He refrains from accepting fields and land. He refrains from going on errands and sending messages. He refrains from buying and selling. He refrains from false weights, false metals, and false measures. He refrains from bribery, deception, fraud, and crooked ways. He refrains from wounding, executing, binding, highway robbery, plunder, and violence.

"He is content with yellow robes to protect his body and with almsfood to protect his stomach—wherever he goes, he takes only these along. Just as a bird, wherever it flies, flies taking its wings as its sole burden—in just this way a *bhikkhu* is content, with yellow robes to protect his body and with almsfood to protect his stomach—wherever he goes, he takes these along.
269 Endowed by this noble aggregation of virtues, he experiences within himself a faultless happiness.

"When he sees a visible object with the eye, he does not grasp after its sign or its inferior qualities. Were he to dwell with the eye-faculty unrestrained, he would be attacked by evil and unwholesome states of covetousness and grief. For that reason, he enters upon a path of restraint. He guards his eye-faculty and undertakes restraint in regard to his eye-faculty.

"When he hears a sound with the ear . . . When he smells an odor with the nose . . . When he tastes a flavor with the tongue . . . When he touches a tangible with the body . . .

"When he cognizes a mental object with the mind, he does not grasp after its sign or its inferior qualities. Were he to dwell with the mind-faculty unrestrained, he would be attacked by evil and unwholesome states of covetousness and grief. For that reason, he enters upon a path of restraint. He guards his mind-faculty and undertakes restraint in regard to his mind-faculty. Endowed by this noble restraint of the senses, he experiences within himself an unimpaired happiness.

"When going forward and when going back, he acts with full awareness; when looking forward and looking back, he acts with full awareness; when bending and stretching his limbs, he acts with full awareness; when wearing his upper robe, carrying his bowl and outer robe, he acts with full awareness; when eating, drinking, consuming food, and tasting, he acts with full awareness; when defecating and urinating, he acts with full awareness. Whether walking, standing, sitting, sleeping, awake, talking, or remaining quiet, he acts with full awareness.

17. "Endowed by this noble aggregation of virtues, endowed by this noble restraint of the faculties, and possessing this noble mindfulness and full awareness, he resorts to a secluded lodging: a forest, a root of a tree, a mountain, a mountain cave, a ravine, a cemetery, a place deep in the forest, an unsheltered place, or a heap of straw. When he returns from the almsround, after his meal, he sits down crossing his legs. He holds his body erect and establishes mindfulness all around him. Having given up covetousness for the world, he dwells with a mind free from covetousness. He purifies his mind of covetousness. Having given up ill will and anger, he dwells with a mind free from ill will and anger. Compassionate for the welfare of all beings, he purifies his mind of ill will and anger. Having given up sloth and laziness, he dwells with a mind free from sloth and laziness. He purifies his mind of sloth and laziness. Having given up agitation and worry, he dwells undisturbed. With a mind inwardly calmed, he purifies his mind of agitation and worry. Having given up perplexity, he dwells having crossed over from perplexity. As one with no doubts regarding wholesome things, he purifies his mind from perplexity. 270

18. "Having given up these five obstacles, impurities of the mind that weaken wisdom, detached from sensual pleasures, detached from unwholesome states of mind, he lives, having entered into the first *jhāna,* which is accompanied by reasoning and cogitation, wherein there is joy and happiness born of detachment.

"Again, in a further case, by the calming of reasoning and cogitation, internally purified, a *bhikkhu* lives, having entered the second *jhāna,* which has a one-pointed mind that is devoid of reasoning and cogitation and wherein there is joy and happiness born of concentration.

"Again, in a further case, dwelling in equanimity, and with the cessation of joy, mindful and fully aware, a *bhikkhu* lives, having entered the third *jhāna,* wherein he experiences happiness with the body and that which the noble ones describe as: 'He who has equanimity and mindfulness lives happily.'

"Again, in a further case, abandoning both happiness and suffering, from the extinction of the elation and despair he felt formerly, a *bhikkhu* lives, having entered the fourth *jhāna,* wherein there is neither suffering nor happiness, but the purity of mindfulness and equanimity.

19. "When he sees a visible object with the eye, he does not become attached to it, if it is pleasant, and he does not shun the visible object, if it is unpleasant. He abides with mindfulness of the body established, with an unlimited mind, and he understands the freedom of mind, the freedom by wisdom, as they really are, wherein those evil and unwholesome states cease without remainder. And so having abandoned favoring and opposing, whatever feeling he feels—whether it is pleasant or painful or neither-painful-nor-pleasant—he does not delight in that feeling, he does not welcome it, and he does not remain attached to it. As he does not do so, delight in feeling ceases in him. From the cessation of delight in feeling, attachment ceases. From the cessation of attachment, becoming ceases. From the cessation of becoming, birth ceases. From the cessation of birth, old age, death, grief, sorrow, suffering, lamentation, and despair cease. Thus ceases this whole mass of suffering.

"When he hears a sound with the ear . . . When he smells a smell with the nose . . . When he tastes a taste with the tongue . . . When he touches a tangible thing with the body . . .

"When he cognizes a mental object with the mind, he does not become attached to the mental object, if it is pleasing, and he does not shun the mental object, if it is unpleasing. He abides with mindfulness of the body established, with an unlimited mind, and he understands the freedom of mind, the freedom by wisdom, as they really are, wherein those evil and unwholesome states cease without remainder. And so having abandoned favoring and opposing, whatever feeling he feels—whether it is pleasant or painful or neither-painful-nor-pleasant—he does not delight in that feeling, he does not welcome it, and he does not remain attached to it. As he does not do so, delight in feeling ceases in him. From the cessation of delight in feeling, attachment ceases. From the cessation of attachment, becoming ceases. From the cessation of becoming, birth ceases. From the cessation of birth, old age, death, grief, sorrow, suffering, lamentation, and despair cease. Thus ceases this whole mass of suffering.

"This, *bhikkhus,* you should keep in mind as the freedom through the
271 destruction of craving in brief. But the *bhikkhu* Sāti, who is a fisherman's son, is caught in the great net of craving, in the tangle of craving."

20. This was what the Exalted One said. Delighted, those *bhikkhus* rejoiced in the words of the Exalted One.

6

Discourse of the Honeyball

(*Madhupiṇḍika Sutta*)[1]

This short discourse contains some of the most philosophically profound ideas in the Pāli Canon. The discourse relates a highly sophisticated theory of knowledge and experience that is consistent with the Buddha's doctrine of dependent arising. Most theories of experience rely on the separation of consciousness and the experienced world as distinct metaphysical entities. And according to the position known in philosophy as mind-body dualism (a view that is by far the most common position among people generally), consciousness and the external world are composed of distinct substances. From the point of view of early Buddhism, however, experience does not involve metaphysically distinct entities composed of different substances. Instead, in early Buddhism, experience is explained functionally and holistically, that is, as a complex *whole* phenomenon wherein the subject and object are *mutually interdependent* (not separate entities) and all distinctions between subject and object are *functional* (rather than "metaphysical") distinctions.

According to this discourse, experience at the most basic level involves three necessary components: a sense faculty, a sense object, and a particular mode of sensory consciousness (e.g., visual consciousness) that arises dependent on the sense faculty and sense object. Consciousness is thus not a supernatural interloper in a physical world, but a complex, natural factor that arises under certain complex conditions. And yet these three components (sense faculty, object, and mode of consciousness) are not sufficient by themselves to be "experience." There must be the meeting of these three in just the right way; this is called "contact" (*phassa*).

This subtle and philosophically sophisticated theory of experience is put to use in this discourse to explain how obsessions arise in the ordinary, untrained human mind. When the tripartite, functional components of experience are in contact, the result is feeling. And from feeling eventually derive the obsessive propensities that instigate unwholesome actions. Hence, the early Buddhists did not develop a theory of experience for its own sake. Rather, the theory of experience is a response to the demand for an explanation of the religious problematic, namely, suffering. The great

[1] *Majjhima Nikāya* 1.108–114.

achievement, then, in this discourse is the explanation of suffering as the result of identifiable causal processes in experience. Consistent with the theory of dependent arising, experience can account for the arising and ceasing of suffering without reference to metaphysically independent or subsistent entities.

Discourse

108

1. Thus have I heard. At one time the Exalted One was living among the Sakyans in Kapilavatthu at Nigrodha's park. Then the Exalted One, having dressed early in the morning, taking his bowl and robe, entered Kapilavatthu for alms. After he had walked in Kapilavatthu for alms, eaten his meal, and returned from the almsround, he went to the Great Wood for the day's rest. Having entered into the Great Wood, he sat down at the root of a small *marmelos* tree.

Daṇḍapāni,[2] the Sakyan, who was walking about and wandering around, also entered the Great Wood. Having also entered into the Great Wood, he approached the Exalted One at the small *marmelos* tree. When he had approached the Exalted One, he exchanged courtesies, friendly talk, and greetings with him, and then stood to one side leaning on his stick. Standing to one side, Daṇḍapāni said this to the Exalted One: "What is the teaching of the religious wanderer, what does he point out?"

"According to my teaching, sir, there is no disputing with anyone in the world, in a world with its *devas,* Māras and Brahmās, and in this generation of religious wanderers and Brahmins, *devas* and men; such [a teaching] holds that perceptions do not obsess that Brahmin[3] who dwells detached from sensual pleasures, without uncertainty, who has cut off worry and is devoid of craving for becoming or non-becoming.[4] This, friend, is my teaching; this is what I point out."

109 When this had been said, Daṇḍapāni shook his head, wagged his tongue, raised three wrinkles on his forehead, and went away leaning on his stick.

2. Then, when the Exalted One had emerged from seclusion in the evening, he approached Nigrodha's park. Having reached the park, he sat down in the appointed seat. After he sat down, the Exalted One addressed the *bhikkhus* [*recounting verbatim his actions and the encounter with Daṇḍapāni*].

3. When this had been said, a certain *bhikkhu* said this to the Exalted One: "What, sir, is this teaching that 'the Exalted One does not dispute with

[2] This name means "stick-in-hand."

[3] Here the word "Brahmin" refers to a person living the holy life, not the social class.

[4] That is, without craving for rebirth or annihilation.

anyone in the world, in a world with its *devas,* Māras and Brahmās, and in this generation of religious wanderers and Brahmins, *devas* and men?' And, how is it, sir, that 'perceptions do not obsess the Exalted One, that Brahmin who dwells detached from sensual pleasures, without uncertainty, who has cut off worry and is devoid of craving for becoming or non-becoming?'"

"Whatever is the cause, *bhikkhu,* by which mentally proliferated perceptions and (obsessive) notions[5] assail a person, if there is nothing here to rejoice at, to welcome, to hold onto, then this is the end of the propensity to attachment, the end of the propensity to aversion, the end of the propen- 110
sity to speculative views, the end of the propensity to perplexity, the end of the propensity to conceit, the end of the propensity to passion for becoming, the end of the propensity to ignorance, the end of taking up a stick, taking up a weapon, quarreling, disputing, contention, accusation, slander, and false speech. Here these evil unwholesome states cease without remainder."

4. This was said by the Exalted One. Having said this, the Well-Farer stood up from his seat and entered the dwelling. Then, not long after the departure of the Exalted One, these *bhikkhus* had this thought: "Brothers, the Exalted One has recited this recital in brief but has not explained the meaning in detail. He rose from his seat, and entered the dwelling after saying: 'Whatever is the cause, *bhikkhu,* by which mentally proliferated perceptions and (obsessive) notions assail a person. . . . Here these evil unwholesome states cease without remainder.' But who would be able to explain in detail the meaning of this recital which the Exalted One recited in brief, but the meaning of which he did not explain?"

5. Then those *bhikkhus* had this thought: "The venerable Mahākaccāna is praised and honored by the Teacher, and by wise fellow followers of the holy life. The venerable Mahākaccāna would be able to explain in detail the meaning of this recital which the Exalted One recited in brief, but the meaning of which he did not explain. Suppose we were to approach the venerable Mahākaccāna and, having approached the venerable Mahākaccāna, we were to ask him the meaning of this."

Then those *bhikkhus* approached the venerable Mahākaccāna. When they had approached the venerable Mahākaccāna, they exchanged courtesies and friendly greetings with him, and sat down to one side. When they were seated to one side, those *bhikkhus* said this to the venerable Mahākaccāna: "Brother Kaccāna, the Exalted One has recited this recital in brief but did

[5] *Papañcasaññāsaṅkhā.* The word *papañca* is something of an enigma. Until recently, most translators followed the PED and rendered the phrase as "obsessions," but recent scholarship has suggested the translation "mental proliferation." The term *papañca* (Skt: *prapañca*) has a more well-defined meaning as mental proliferation in the Mahāyāna literature that comes several centuries after the Pāli Canon.

not explain the meaning in detail. He rose from his seat and entered the dwelling after saying: 'Whatever is the cause, *bhikkhu,* by which mentally proliferated perceptions and (obsessive) notions assail a person. . . . Here these evil unwholesome states cease without remainder.' Then, brother Kaccāna, not long after the departure of the Exalted One, we had this thought: 'Brothers, the Exalted One has recited this recital in brief but has not explained the meaning in detail. He rose from his seat and entered the dwelling after saying: . . . . But who would be able to explain in detail the meaning of this recital which the Exalted One recited in brief, but the meaning of which he did not explain?' Then, brother Kaccāna, we had this thought: 'The venerable Mahākaccāna is praised and honored by the
111 Teacher, and by wise fellow followers of the holy life. The venerable Mahākaccāna would be able to explain in detail the meaning of this recital which the Exalted One recited in brief, but the meaning of which he did not explain. Suppose we were to approach the venerable Mahākaccāna and, having approached the venerable Mahākaccāna, we were to ask him the meaning of this.' Let the venerable Mahākaccāna explain it."

6. "Brothers, it is just like a person roaming about looking for the pith,[6] seeking the pith, on a quest for the pith, passing by the root of a great standing tree, passing by the trunk, that person might think that the pith is to be sought in the branches and foliage. Just so is this situation of the venerable ones—having had the Teacher face-to-face and having ignored the Exalted One, you think that I should be asked the meaning of this. But, brothers, the Exalted One knowing, he knows; seeing, he sees—he has become sight, he has become knowledge, he has become the *dhamma,* he has become Brahmā—the propounder, the speaker, the leader to the goal, the giver of the deathless, the lord of the *dhamma,* the *Tathāgata.* When you were with the Exalted One, that was the time when you should have asked him the meaning of this. You should have learned it the way the Exalted One would have explained it to you."

"Certainly, brother Kaccāna, the Exalted One knowing, he knows; seeing, he sees—he has become sight, he has become knowledge, he has become the *dhamma,* he has become Brahmā—the propounder, the speaker, the leader to the goal, the giver of the deathless, the lord of the *dhamma,* the *Tathāgata.* When we were with the Exalted One, that was the time when we should have asked him the meaning of this. We should have learned it the way the Exalted One would have explained it to us. But the venerable Mahākaccāna is praised and honored by the Teacher and by the wise who live the holy life. The venerable Mahākaccāna would be able to explain in detail the meaning of this recital which the Exalted One recited in brief, but the meaning of

[6] *Sāra.* In other words, the "essence" or the "core."

which he did not explain. Let the venerable Mahākaccāna explain it, if it is not troublesome."

"Then, brothers, listen, pay careful attention, and I will speak."

"Yes, brother," those *bhikkhus* said to Mahākaccāna in assent.

7. So the venerable Mahākaccāna said this: "Brothers, the Exalted One recited this recital in brief but did not explain the meaning in detail. He rose from his seat and entered the dwelling after saying: 'Whatever is the cause, *bhikkhu,* by which mentally proliferated perceptions and (obsessive) notions assail a person, if there is nothing here to rejoice at, to welcome, to hold onto, then this is the end of the propensity to attachment, the end of the propensity to aversion, the end of the propensity to speculative views, the end of the propensity to perplexity, the end of the propensity to conceit, the end of the propensity to passion for becoming, the end of the propensity to ignorance, the end of taking up a stick, taking up a weapon, quarreling, disputing, contention, accusation, slander, and false speech. Here these evil unwholesome states cease without remainder.'—of that recital which the Exalted One recited in brief, but the meaning of which he did not explain, I understand the meaning in full in this way:

"Visual consciousness arises dependent on the eye and visible objects. The meeting of the three is contact. Dependent on contact, there is feeling. What one feels, that one perceives. What one perceives, that one reasons about. 112
What one reasons about, that one mentally proliferates.[7] What one mentally proliferates, that is the cause by which mentally proliferated perceptions and (obsessive) notions assail a person in regard to visible objects cognizable by the eye, in the past, future, and present.

"Auditory consciousness arises dependent on the ear and sounds; the meeting of the three is contact. . . . Olfactory consciousness arises dependent on the nose and smells; the meeting of the three is contact. . . . Gustatory consciousness arises dependent on tongue and tastes; the meeting of the three is contact. . . . Bodily consciousness arises dependent on body and tangible objects; the meeting of the three is contact. . . .

"Mental consciousness arises dependent on mind and mental objects. The meeting of the three is contact. Dependent on contact, there is feeling. What one feels, that one perceives. What one perceives, that one reasons about. What one reasons about, that one mentally proliferates. What one mentally proliferates, that is the cause by which mentally proliferated perceptions and (obsessive) notions assail a person in regard to mental objects cognizable by the mind, in the past, future, and present.

"When there is an eye, a visible object, and visual consciousness, in that situation one could point out a manifestation of contact. When there is a

[7] *Papañceti.*

manifestation of contact, in that situation one could point out a manifestation of feeling. When there is a manifestation of feeling, in that situation one could point out a manifestation of perception. When there is a manifestation of perception, in that situation one could point out a manifestation of reasoning. When there is a manifestation of reasoning, in that situation one could point out a manifestation of the activities of mentally proliferated perceptions and (obsessive) notions.

"When there is an ear, sound, and auditory consciousness, in that situation one could point out a manifestation of contact. . . . When there is a nose, smell, and olfactory consciousness, in that situation one could point out a manifestation of contact. . . . When there is a tongue, taste, and gustatory consciousness, in that situation one could point out a manifestation of contact. . . . When there is a body, a tangible object, and bodily consciousness, in that situation one could point out a manifestation of contact. . . .

"When there is a mind, mental object, and mental consciousness, in that situation one could point out a manifestation of contact. When there is a manifestation of contact, in that situation one could point out a manifestation of feeling. When there is a manifestation of feeling, in that situation one could point out a manifestation of perception. When there is a manifestation of perception, in that situation one could point out a manifestation of reasoning. When there is a manifestation of reasoning, in that situation one could point out a manifestation of the activities of mentally proliferated perceptions and (obsessive) notions.

"When there is no eye, no visual object, or no visual consciousness, in that situation one could *not* point out a manifestation of contact. When there is no manifestation of contact, in that situation one could *not* point out a manifestation of feeling. When there is no manifestation of feeling, in that situation one could *not* point out a manifestation of perception. When there is no manifestation of perception, in that situation one could *not* point out a manifestation of reasoning. When there is no manifestation of reasoning, in that situation one could *not* point out a manifestation of the activities of mentally proliferated perceptions and (obsessive) notions.

"When there is no ear, no sound or auditory consciousness, in that situation one could *not* point out a manifestation of contact. . . . When there is no nose, no smell, or no olfactory consciousness, in that situation one could *not* point out a manifestation of contact. . . . When there is no tongue, no taste, or no gustatory consciousness, in that situation one could *not* point out a manifestation of contact. . . . When there is no body, no tangible object, or no bodily consciousness, in that situation one could *not* point out a manifestation of contact. . . .

"When there is no mind, no mental object, or no mental consciousness, in that situation one could *not* point out a manifestation of contact. When there is no manifestation of contact, in that situation one could *not* point out a manifestation of feeling. When there is no manifestation of feeling, in that situation one could *not* point out a manifestation of perception. When there is no manifestation of perception, in that situation one could *not* point out a manifestation of reasoning. When there is no manifestation of reasoning, in that situation one could *not* point out a manifestation of the activities of mentally proliferated perceptions and (obsessive) notions.

"Brothers, the Exalted One recited this recital in brief, but has not explained 113
the meaning in detail. He rose from his seat and entered the dwelling after saying: 'Whatever is the cause, *bhikkhu,* by which mentally proliferated perceptions and (obsessive) notions assail a person. . . . Here these evil unwholesome states cease without remainder.' Of that recital which the Exalted One recited in brief, but the meaning of which he did not explain, I understand the meaning in full in this way. But if you venerable ones wish, when you have approached the Exalted One, you can ask him the meaning of this, so you can learn it the way the Exalted One explains it to you."

8. Then those *bhikkhus,* having delighted and rejoiced in what the venerable Mahākaccāna said, arose from their seats and approached the Exalted One. When they had approached the Exalted One, they greeted him and sat down to one side. When they were seated to one side, those *bhikkhus*
[*recounted to him verbatim everything that had transpired up to this point*]. Sir, 114
the venerable Mahākaccāna explained the meaning to us by these methods, by these words, and in these terms."

"*Bhikkhus,* venerable Mahākaccāna is learned and has great wisdom. For, if you were to ask me the meaning of this, I, too, would have explained it exactly as Mahākaccāna explained it. Indeed, this is the meaning of that recital, and thus you should grasp it."

9. When this had been said, the venerable Ānanda said this to the Exalted One: "Sir, just as a person overcome by hunger and tiredness might obtain a honeyball, from each bite of which this person would obtain a sweet and delicious flavor, in the same way, a *bhikkhu* whose mind has an intelligent nature would, by investigating the meaning of this discourse on *dhamma* with his wisdom, be able to obtain delight and mental satisfaction from each bit. By what name, sir, should one call this discourse on the *dhamma?*"

"Regarding that, Ānanda, you may remember this discourse on the *dhamma* as the 'The Honeyball Discourse.'"

10. The Exalted One said this. Delighted, the venerable Ānanda rejoiced in what the Exalted One had said.

7

Short Discourses from the *Saṃyutta Nikāya*

The *Saṃyutta Nikāya* is a multivolume collection of discourses organized roughly by major topic that draws much of its material from other parts of the Discourse Basket (*Sutta Piṭaka*) of the Pāli Canon. This chapter presents five short, but very important, discourses from this large body of material.

The Discourse to Kaccāyana may well be the most important discourse on metaphysics in the Pāli Canon. Ostensibly, the discourse is the Buddha's clarification of "right view," but, in fact, the discourse provides a succinct account of the "middle way" as it applies to metaphysics. The metaphysical position advocated by the Buddha stands between the extremes of absolute existence and absolute non-existence—more specifically, between the "eternalism" of the Upaniṣadic teaching that *ātman*-Brahman is a transcendent ultimate Reality and the "annihilationism" that denies the continuous existence of anything (especially the Materialists' denial of the continuity of the human person). The Buddha asserts that such metaphysical extremes are the result of inclinations or biases brought on by a selfishly corrupt mind. A person who is not biased by a corrupt mind avoids these extremes and understands the "middle way" in metaphysical terms as the twelvefold formula of dependent arising.

Soon after his enlightenment, the Buddha sought out a group of five of his former companions to deliver his first sermons on the *dhamma*. These were the Buddha's ascetic colleagues who considered Siddhattha a "backslider" when he left them and gave up the austere religious life. A Discourse to the First Five Disciples recounts one of these sermons. In this discourse, the Buddha analyzes the metaphysical aspects of human nature. In particular, he criticizes and rejects the Upaniṣadic claim that there is a Self (*attā;* Skt: *ātman*) that is permanent, blissful, and a completely autonomous agent. These three qualities (permanence, blissfulness, and agency) that purportedly make up such a Self are compared with what the Buddha takes to be a comprehensive list of the five constituents of the human person, namely, body, feeling, perception, dispositions to action, and consciousness—collectively called the five aggregates (*khandhas*). But none of these constituents of the person, taken individually or collectively, fulfill any of the three criteria for a permanent Self, hence the concept of a permanent Self is rejected by the Buddha. This cluster of arguments is referred to as the Buddha's "no-Self" (*anattā*) doctrine.

The Verses of Sister Vajirā is among the most famous accounts of the early Buddhist doctrine of "no-Self." This passage is also important because it shows that there were women among the earliest followers of the Buddha who became adept at comprehending and practicing the Buddha's *dhamma.* Here, Māra (the Evil One), tries to disrupt the concentration of the nun Vajirā by trying to trick her into admitting that a permanent Self exists. Māra does this by asking her questions about the "person" that presume the existence of such a Self. Sister Vajirā sees the danger in Māra's questions and responds by asking Māra why he assumes that there is a "person" in the metaphysically substantial or permanent sense. Māra, she says, has adopted a wrong speculative view—the "person" is only an aggregation of processes. Then Sister Vajirā relates the "chariot simile" (a simile that is better known from the Questions of King Milinda[1]) just as the word "chariot" is used to designate an assemblage of parts (it does not refer to a permanent essence), so, too, the term "person" is a convention used to designate the presence of the five aggregates (body, feeling, perception, dispositions to action, and consciousness).

In the Discourse on the All, the Buddha transforms the metaphysical conception of the "All" in the Upaniṣadic tradition ("All" = "Brahman") into an epistemological concept, an empirical limitation on experience and knowledge. The "All" is not Reality, but the comprehensive range of the possibilities of experience, particularly, sense experience. This passage makes a strong case for the view that the Buddha's philosophy is a form of empiricism. Nevertheless, the Buddha does not offer an analysis of experience for its own sake; rather, his epistemology serves his ethical and religious concerns. In a mind defiled by lust, hatred, and delusion, the "All" is burning—a metaphor for the fact that sensory experiences typically instigate a chain of addictive behaviors that inevitably leads to suffering. The alternative, suggested by the Buddha, is to abandon all attachment to sense experiences.

The last passage is entitled "Feelings That Should Be Seen and the Dart." This short discourse provides important insight into the critical role of feeling (*vedanā*) in the evolving process of human experience. The primary aim of early Buddhism is the shaping and transforming of a person's mind from a corrupted state to an enlightened state. This involves more than just knowledge, however. So, contrary to the emphasis on "knowing" (cognition) in most philosophical traditions, early Buddhist philosophy recognizes the importance of noncognitive (or "affective") dimensions of experience in ethical and religious practices. In particular, Buddhist training focuses on the careful cultivation of noncognitive dimensions of the mind, such as "feeling."

[1] The Verses of Sister Vajirā is the basis for (and directly quoted in) a longer discussion of the "chariot simile" in the Questions of King Milinda –a quasi-canonical compendium of early Buddhist philosophy presented as a dialogue between the Bactrian king Milinda (Greek: Menander) and the *bhikkhu* Nagasena. See T. W. Rhys Davids, *The Questions of King Milinda,* Part I (New York: Dover Publications, 1963), pp. 40–45.

This passage also answers one of the more perplexing problems about the lived experience of the trained noble disciple. If a noble disciple experiences an abiding peace and tranquillity, a freedom from the sufferings of the world, does such a person continue to have feelings? If so, how does the noble disciple avoid painful feelings that would destroy one's inner tranquillity? If not, is the noble disciple anything more than an anesthetized zombie? The Buddha attempts to resolve this problem by contrasting the ordinary person with the noble disciple. Whereas the untrained, ordinary person feels two feelings, both a bodily and a mental feeling, the noble disciple feels only the bodily feeling (especially if it is an unpleasant feeling) and not the mental feeling. In other words, the noble disciple still feels but does not allow such feelings to cause a secondary feeling that might disturb the tranquillity of his or her mind.

Discourse to Kaccāyana
(*Kaccāyanagotta Sutta*)[2]

16

17 1. Dwelling at Sāvatthi.

2. At that time, the venerable Kaccāyana approached the Exalted One. When he had approached the Exalted One, he greeted him courteously and sat down to one side.

3. When he was seated to one side, the venerable Kaccāyana said this to the Exalted One: "'Right view, right view,' it is said, sir. To what extent is there right view?"

4. "This world, Kaccāyana, is, for the most part, inclined toward two [views]: existence and non-existence.

5. "For the one who sees with right wisdom the arising of the world as it really is, the idea of non-existence in regard to the world does not occur. For the one who sees with right wisdom the ceasing of the world as it really is, the idea of existence in regard to the world does not occur.

6. "For the most part, the world is bound by approach, attachment, and inclination. But one who does not follow that approach and attachment, that determination of mind, that inclination and disposition, who does not cling to or adhere to the view 'this is my self,' who thinks 'the arising of suffering is what arises, the ceasing of suffering is what ceases'—such a person does not doubt and is not perplexed. Herein, one's knowledge is not dependent on others. To this extent, there is 'right view.'

[2] *Saṃyutta Nikāya* 2.16–17.

7. "'Everything exists'—this is one extreme. 'Everything does not exist'—this is the second extreme.

"Without approaching either of these extremes, the *Tathāgata* teaches the *dhamma* by the middle:

"Dependent on ignorance, there are dispositions to action; dependent on dispositions to action, there is consciousness; dependent on consciousness, there is psycho-physicality; dependent on psycho-physicality, there are the six bases of sense; dependent on the six bases of sense, there is contact; dependent on contact, there is feeling; dependent on feeling, there is craving; dependent on craving, there is attachment; dependent on attachment, there is becoming; dependent on becoming, there is birth; dependent on birth, there is aging-and-death, sorrow, lamentation, pain, despair, and distress. Thus there is the arising of this whole mass of suffering.[3]

"But from the complete cessation without remainder of ignorance, there is the cessation of dispositions to action; from the cessation of dispositions to action, there is the cessation of consciousness; from the cessation of consciousness, there is the cessation of the six sense bases; from the cessation of the six sense bases, there is the cessation of contact; from the cessation of contact, there is the cessation of feeling; from the cessation of feeling, there is the cessation of craving; from the cessation of craving, there is the cessation of attachment; from the cessation of attachment, there is the cessation of becoming; from the cessation of becoming, there is the cessation of birth; from the cessation of birth, there is the cessation of old age, death, sorrow, lamentation, pain, despair, and distress. Thus there is the cessation of this entire aggregation of suffering."

A Discourse to the First Five Disciples[4]

66

1. A certain occasion at the Deer Park in Vārāṇasi (Benares).

2. There the Exalted One addressed the group of five *bhikkhus*. He said this:

3. "The body, *bhikkhus*, is not the permanent Self.[5] Were the body the permanent Self, then this body would not lead to affliction. And it would be possible in regard to the body to say: 'Let my body be thus, let my body not be thus.'

[3] This is the full twelvefold formula of dependent arising.

[4] *Saṃyutta Nikāya* 3.66–68.

[5] *Anattā*. Literally, "not Self."

4. "Inasmuch as the body is not the permanent Self, thus the body leads to affliction. And it is not possible in regard to the body to say: 'Let my body be thus, let my body not be thus.'

5. "Feeling is not the permanent Self. Were feeling the permanent Self,
67 then this feeling would not lead to affliction. And it would be possible in regard to feeling to say: 'Let my feeling be thus, let my feeling not be thus.'

6. "Inasmuch as feeling is not the permanent Self, thus feeling leads to affliction. And it is not possible in regard to feeling to say: 'Let my feeling be thus, let my feeling not be thus.'

7. "Perception is not the permanent Self. Were perception the permanent Self, then this perception would not lead to affliction. And it would be possible in regard to perception to say: 'Let my perception be thus, let my perception not be thus.'

8. "Inasmuch as perception is not the permanent Self, thus perception leads to affliction. And it is not possible in regard to perception to say: 'Let my perception be thus, let my perception not be thus.'

9. "Dispositions to action are not the permanent Self. Were dispositions to action the permanent Self, then these dispositions to action would not lead to affliction. And it would be possible in regard to dispositions to action to say: 'Let my dispositions to action be thus, let my dispositions to action not be thus.'

10. "Inasmuch as dispositions to action are not the permanent Self, thus dispositions to action lead to affliction. And it is not possible in regard to dispositions to action to say: 'Let my dispositions to action be thus, let my dispositions to action not be thus.'

11. "Consciousness is not the permanent Self. Were consciousness the permanent Self, then this consciousness would not lead to affliction. And it would be possible in regard to consciousness to say: 'Let my consciousness be thus, let my consciousness not be thus.'

12. "Inasmuch as consciousness is not the permanent Self, thus consciousness leads to affliction. And it is not possible in regard to consciousness to say: 'Let my consciousness be thus, let my consciousness not be thus.'

13. "What do you think, *bhikkhus?* Is the body permanent or impermanent?"

"Impermanent, sir."

"And that which is impermanent, is it painful or pleasant?"

"Painful, sir."

"And in regard to that which is impermanent, painful, and subject to change, is it proper that it be viewed as 'This is mine. I am this. This is my permanent Self.'?"

"No, indeed, sir."

14. "What do you think, *bhikkhus?* Is feeling permanent or impermanent?"

"Impermanent, sir."

"And that which is impermanent, is it painful or pleasant?"

"Painful, sir."

"And in regard to that which is impermanent, painful, and subject to change, is it proper that it be viewed as 'This is mine. I am this. This is my permanent Self.'?"

"No, indeed, sir."

15. "What do you think, *bhikkhus?* Is perception permanent or impermanent?"

"Impermanent, sir."

"And that which is impermanent, is it painful or pleasant?"

"Painful, sir."

"And in regard to that which is impermanent, painful, and subject to change, is it proper that it be viewed as 'This is mine. I am this. This is my permanent Self.'?"

"No, indeed, sir."

16. "What do you think, *bhikkhus?* Are dispositions to action permanent or impermanent?"

"Impermanent, sir."

"And that which is impermanent, is it painful or pleasant?"

"Painful, sir."

"And in regard to that which is impermanent, painful, and subject to change, is it proper that it be viewed as 'This is mine. I am this. This is my permanent Self.'?"

"No, indeed, sir."

17. "What do you think, *bhikkhus?* Is consciousness permanent or impermanent?"

"Impermanent, sir."

"And that which is impermanent, is it painful or pleasant?" 68

"Painful, sir."

"And in regard to that which is impermanent, painful, and subject to change, is it proper that it be viewed as 'This is mine. I am this. This is my permanent Self.'?"

"No, indeed, sir."

18. "Therefore, *bhikkhus,* whatever body there is—whether in the past, present, or future, internal or external, gross or subtle, inferior or superior, far or near—should be looked on by one who has right wisdom as 'All body is not mine. I am not this. This is not my permanent Self.'

19. "Therefore, whatever feeling there is—whether in the past, present, or future, internal or external, gross or subtle, inferior or superior, far or near—should be looked on by one who has right wisdom as 'All feeling is not mine. I am not this. This is not my permanent Self.'

20. "Therefore, whatever perception there is—whether in the past, present, or future, internal or external, gross or subtle, inferior or superior, far or near—should be looked on by one who has right wisdom as 'All perception is not mine. I am not this. This is not my permanent Self.'

21. "Therefore, whatever dispositions to action there are—whether in the past, present, or future, internal or external, gross or subtle, inferior or superior, far or near—should be looked on by one who has right wisdom as 'All dispositions to action are not mine. I am not these. These are not my permanent Self.'

22. "Therefore, whatever consciousness there is—whether in the past, present, or future, internal or external, gross or subtle, inferior or superior, far or near—should be looked on by one who has right wisdom as 'All consciousness is not mine. I am not this. This is not my permanent Self.'

23. "Seeing things in this way, the learned noble disciple is disillusioned with the body, with feeling, with perception, with dispositions to action, and with consciousness. Being disillusioned [with the five aggregates], one detaches oneself from lust. Being freed [from lust], one is liberated. And in a liberated person, there is knowledge of such liberation, for such a person knows that birth is destroyed, the holy life has been lived, done is what was to be done, and that there is nothing further in this present state of existence."

24. This was said by the Exalted One. Delighted, the group of five *bhikkhus* rejoiced in the words of the Exalted One. And while this teaching was being explained, the minds of the *bhikkhus* in the group of five were liberated from the defilements by non-attachment.

Verses of Sister Vajirā
(*Vajirā Sutta*)[6]

296

1. At one time, the Exalted One was dwelling at Sāvatthi in the Jeta Grove in Anāthapiṇḍika's park. Then the *bhikkhunī* (nun) Vajirā dressed herself early in the morning and, taking her bowl and robe, entered Sāvatthi for alms. She then walked about Sāvatthi for alms. After her midday meal, she

6 *Saṃyutta Nikāya* 1.296–297 (older editions: 134–135).

returned from her almsround and went to the Dark Forest[7] for her afternoon rest. Having entered the Dark Forest, she sat down at the foot of a tree for her afternoon rest.

2. Then Māra, the Evil One, approached the *bhikkhunī* Vajirā, desiring to produce fear, paralyzing terror, and horror in her, and thereby disrupt her concentration. When he had approached her, he addressed her with this verse:

> "By whom was this person[8] created?
> Where is a person's maker?
> From where has a person arisen?
> Where does a person cease?"

3. Then Vajirā had this thought: "Who is it that recites this verse? Is it a human being or a nonhuman being?" Then this thought occurred to her: "Māra, the Evil One, has recited this verse, desiring to produce fear, paralyzing terror, and horror in me, and thereby disrupt my concentration."

4. Then Vajirā, having realized that "This is Māra, the Evil One," replied to him with these verses:

> "Why do you assume 'a person'?
> Māra, you have adopted a wrong speculative view. 297
> This is only a heap of processes
> There is no person to be found here.[9]
>
> "Just as the word 'chariot'
> Refers to an assemblage of parts,
> So, 'person' is a convention
> Used when the aggregates are present.
>
> "Only suffering arises
> And suffering remains and disappears
> Nothing other than suffering arises
> Nothing other than suffering ceases."

[7] *Andhavanaṃ.* As *andha* means "blind" as well as "dark," an alternative translation is "Blind Men's Forest."

[8] *Satto.* This term sometimes has the broader meaning "living being." However, the reference to the five aggregates in Vajirā's reply strongly suggests that the term refers here to a human being.

[9] There is no "person" to be found in the sense of a permanent essence or an underlying substance.

5. At that point, realizing that "the *bhikkhunī* Vajirā knows me," Māra was miserable and unhappy, and so he vanished right there.

Discourse on the All
(*Sabba Sutta*)[10]

15

1. At Sāvatthi. There the Exalted One said:

2. "*Bhikkhus,* I will teach you the all [that exists]. Do listen to this.

3. "And what is the all? It is eye and visible objects, ear and sounds, nose and smells, tongue and tastes, body and tangible objects, mind and mental objects. This is called 'the all.'

4. "Whoever would speak in this way—'Rejecting this all, I will declare another all'—would be engaging in mere talk on his part. One would not be able to reply to a question and, further, would come to vexation. What is the reason for this? Because that which one claims would be beyond the scope of (sense) experience.

5. "*Bhikkhus,* I will teach you the doctrine for abandoning the all. Do listen to this.

6. "And what is the doctrine for abandoning the all? The eye is to be abandoned. Visible objects are to be abandoned. Visual consciousness is to
16 be abandoned. Eye-contact is to be abandoned. And whatever feeling that arises from eye-contact—whether pleasant, painful, or neither-painful-nor-pleasant—that, too, should be abandoned.

7. "The ear is to be abandoned. Sounds are to be abandoned. Auditory consciousness is to be abandoned. Ear-contact is to be abandoned. And whatever feeling that arises from ear-contact—whether pleasant, painful, or neither-painful-nor-pleasant—that, too, should be abandoned.

8. "The nose is to be abandoned. Smells are to be abandoned. Olfactory consciousness is to be abandoned. Nose-contact is to be abandoned. And whatever feeling that arises from nose-contact—whether pleasant, painful, or neither-painful-nor-pleasant—that, too, should be abandoned.

9. "The tongue is to be abandoned. Tastes are to be abandoned. Gustatory consciousness is to be abandoned. Tongue-contact is to be abandoned. And whatever feeling that arises from tongue-contact—whether pleasant, painful, or neither-painful-nor-pleasant—that, too, should be abandoned.

10. "The body is to be abandoned. Tangible objects are to be abandoned. Bodily consciousness is to be abandoned. Body-contact is to be abandoned.

[10] *Saṃyutta Nikāya* 4.15–20.

And whatever feeling that arises from body-contact—whether pleasant, painful, or neither-painful-nor-pleasant—that, too, should be abandoned.

11. "The mind is to be abandoned. Mental objects are to be abandoned. Mental consciousness is to be abandoned. Mind-contact is to be abandoned. And whatever feeling that arises from mind-contact—whether pleasant, painful, or neither-painful-nor-pleasant—that, too, should be abandoned.

12. "This is the doctrine for abandoning the all. . . . 17 18

13. "And what is that all which, by knowing it directly, by fully understanding it, by developing dispassion toward it, and by forsaking it, one will be able to destroy suffering?

14. "The eye is that which, by knowing it directly, by fully understanding it, by developing dispassion toward it, and by forsaking it, one will be able to destroy suffering. Visible objects are those that by knowing them directly, by fully understanding them, by developing dispassion toward them, and by forsaking them, one will be able to destroy suffering. Visual consciousness is that which, by knowing it directly, by fully understanding it, by developing dispassion toward it, and by forsaking it, one will be able to destroy suffering. Eye-contact is that which by knowing it directly, by fully understanding it, by developing dispassion toward it, and by forsaking it, one will be able to destroy suffering. And whatever feeling that arises from eye-contact—whether pleasant, painful, or neither-painful-nor-pleasant—is that which, by knowing it directly, by fully understanding it, by developing dispassion toward it, and by forsaking it, one will be able to destroy suffering.

15. "The ear . . . sounds . . . auditory consciousness . . . ear-contact . . . whatever feeling that arises from ear-contact . . .

16. "The nose . . . smells . . . olfactory consciousness . . . nose-contact . . . whatever feeling that arises from nose-contact . . .

17. "The tongue . . . tastes . . . gustatory consciousness . . . tongue-contact . . . whatever feeling that arises from tongue-contact . . .

18. "The body . . . tangible objects . . . bodily consciousness . . . body-contact . . . whatever feeling that arises from body-contact . . .

19. "The mind is that which, by knowing it directly, by fully understanding it, by developing dispassion toward it, and by forsaking it, one will be able to destroy suffering. Mental objects are those that by knowing them directly, by fully understanding them, by developing dispassion toward them, and by forsaking them, one will be able to destroy suffering. Mental consciousness is that which by knowing it directly, by fully understanding it, by developing dispassion toward it, and by forsaking it, one will be able to destroy suffering. Mind-contact is that which by knowing it directly, by

fully understanding it, by developing dispassion toward it, and by forsakng it, one will be able to destroy suffering. And whatever feeling that arises from mind-contact—whether pleasant, painful, or neither-painful-nor-pleasant—is that which, by knowing it directly, by fully understanding it, by developing dispassion toward it, and by forsaking it, one will be able to destroy suffering.

20. "This is that all which, by knowing it directly, by fully understanding it, by developing dispassion toward it, and by forsaking it, one will be
19 able to destroy suffering. . . .

21. At one time the Exalted One was dwelling at Gayā, at Gayā's head, together with a thousand *bhikkhus.*

22. There, the Exalted One addressed the *bhikkhus:* "*Bhikkhus,* all is burning. And what is that all that is burning?

23. "The eye is burning. Visible objects are burning. Visual consciousness is burning. Eye-contact is burning. And whatever feeling that arises from eye-contact—whether pleasant, painful, or neither-painful-nor-pleasant—that, too, is burning. By what are they burning? They are burning by the fire of lust, by the fire of hatred, and by the fire of delusion. Burning, I say, by birth, old age, death, sorrow, lamentation, pain, despair, and distress.

24–25. "The ear is burning. Sounds are burning. Auditory consciousness is burning. Ear-contact is burning. . . . The nose is burning. Smells are burning. Olfactory consciousness is burning. Nose-contact is burning. . . . The tongue is burning. Tastes are burning. Gustatory consciousness is burning.
20 Tongue-contact is burning. . . . The body is burning. Tangible objects are burning. Bodily consciousness is burning. Body-contact is burning. . . .

26. "The mind is burning. Mental objects are burning. Mental consciousness is burning. Mind-contact is burning. And whatever feeling that arises from mind-contact—whether pleasant, painful, or neither-painful-nor-pleasant—that, too, is burning. By what are they burning? They are burning by the fire of lust, by the fire of hatred, and by the fire of delusion. Burning, I say, by birth, old age, death, sorrow, lamentation, pain, despair, and distress.

27. "Seeing things in this way, the learned noble disciple is disillusioned with the eye, with visible objects, with visual consciousness, with eye-contact, and also with whatever feeling arises from eye-contact—whether pleasant, painful, or neither-painful-nor-pleasant. Seeing things in this way, the learned noble disciple is disillusioned with the ear, with sounds, with auditory consciousness, with ear-contact, and also with whatever feeling arises from ear-contact—whether pleasant, painful, or neither-painful-nor-pleasant. Seeing things in this way, the learned noble disciple is disillusioned with the nose, with smells, with olfactory consciousness, with nose-contact, and

also with whatever feeling arises from nose-contact—whether pleasant, painful, or neither-painful-nor-pleasant. Seeing things in this way, the learned noble disciple is disillusioned with the tongue, with tastes, with gustatory consciousness, with tongue-contact, and also with whatever feeling arises from tongue-contact—whether pleasant, painful, or neither-painful-nor-pleasant. Seeing things in this way, the learned noble disciple is disillusioned with the body, with tangible things, with bodily consciousness, with body-contact, and also with whatever feeling arises from body-contact—whether pleasant, painful, or neither-painful-nor-pleasant. Seeing things in this way, the learned noble disciple is disillusioned with the mind, with mental objects, with mental consciousness, with mind-contact, and also with whatever feeling arises from mind-contact—whether pleasant, painful, or neither-painful-nor-pleasant. Being disillusioned [with the senses], one detaches oneself from lust. Being freed [from lust], one is liberated. And in a liberated person, there is knowledge of such liberation, for such a person knows that birth is destroyed, the holy life has been lived, done is what was to be done, and that there is nothing further in this present state of existence."

28. This was said by the Exalted One. Delighted, those *bhikkhus* rejoiced in the words of the Exalted One.

29. And while this teaching was being explained, the minds of the thousand *bhikkhus* were liberated from the defilements by non-attachment.

Feelings That Should Be Seen and the Dart[11]

1. "*Bhikkhus,* there are these three kinds of feeling. What are the three? 207
Pleasant feeling, painful feeling, and neither-painful-nor-pleasant feeling. Pleasant feeling should be seen as suffering. Painful feeling should be seen as a dart. Neither-painful-nor-pleasant feeling should be seen as impermanent.

2. "When a *bhikkhu* has seen pleasant feeling as suffering, painful feeling as a dart, and neither-painful-nor-pleasant feeling as impermanent, then he is called a *bhikkhu* who sees rightly. Such a person has cut off craving, severed the fetters, completely broken through conceit, and thus has made an end of suffering."

3. One who has seen the pleasant as suffering
Has seen the painful as a dart,
And has seen the impermanent neither-painful-nor-pleasant
feeling as peaceful
That is the *bhikkhu* who sees rightly.

[11] *Saṃyutta Nikāya* 4.207–210.

He fully understands feelings.
He abandons feelings.
He is without defilement in this very life.
Standing in *dhamma* at the breaking up of the body
The master of knowledge cannot be reckoned.

4. "The unlearned ordinary person experiences a pleasant feeling, a painful feeling, or a neither-painful-nor-pleasant feeling.

208 5. "The learned noble disciple also experiences a pleasant feeling, a painful feeling, or a neither-painful-nor-pleasant feeling.

6. "In such a case, *bhikkhus,* what then is the distinction, disparity, or difference between the learned noble disciple and the unlearned ordinary person?"

"Sir, our teachings are rooted in the Exalted One, guided by the Exalted One, and we take refuge in the Exalted One. It would be good if the Exalted One were to explain the meaning of this statement. Having heard it from the Exalted One, we will grasp it."

7. "The unlearned ordinary person, when touched by an unpleasant feeling, grieves, is wearied, laments, weeps beating one's chest, and becomes confused. Such a person feels two feelings, a bodily one and a mental one.

8. "Just as a person might be pierced by a dart and then might be pierced by a second dart. In that case, one would feel two feelings from the darts. Thus, the unlearned ordinary person, when touched by an unpleasant feeling, grieves, is wearied, laments, weeps beating one's chest, and becomes confused. Such a person feels two feelings, a bodily one and a mental one.

"Being touched by that same painful feeling, one develops aversion toward it. And when one develops an aversion toward a painful feeling, the underlying tendency to aversion toward painful feeling lies behind it. Being touched by a painful feeling, one seeks delight in sensual pleasure. What is the reason for this? The unlearned ordinary person does not understand the escape from painful feeling other than sensual pleasure. The underlying tendency of lust is what lies behind this delighting in sensual pleasure. One does not understand as it truly is the origin, the extinction, the satisfaction, the disadvantage, and the escape from these feelings. Not understanding as it truly is the origin, the extinction, the satisfaction, the disadvantage, and the escape from these feelings, the underlying tendency to ignorance is what lies behind neither-painful-nor-pleasant feeling. If one feels a pleasant feeling, one feels it as a person who is attached to it. If one feels a painful feeling,
209 one feels it as a person who is attached to it. If one feels a neither-painful-nor-pleasant feeling, one feels it as a person who is attached to it. This is called an unlearned ordinary person who is attached by birth, death, grief,

sorrow, suffering, lamentation, and despair. I say that this is one who is attached to suffering.

9. "The learned noble disciple, when touched by an unpleasant feeling, does not grieve, is not wearied, does not lament, does not weep beating one's chest, and does not become confused. Such a person feels only one feeling, a bodily one, but not a mental one.

10. "Just as a person might be pierced by a dart, but might not be pierced by a second dart. In that case, one would feel only one feeling from the one dart. Thus, the learned noble disciple, when touched by an unpleasant feeling, does not grieve, is not wearied, does not lament, does not weep beating one's chest, and does not become confused. Such a person feels only one feeling, a bodily one, but not a mental one.

"Being touched by that same painful feeling, one does not develop aversion toward it. And having no aversion toward a painful feeling, the underlying tendency to aversion toward painful feeling does not lie behind it. Being touched by a painful feeling, one does not seek delight in sensual pleasure. What is the reason for this? The noble disciple understands the escape from painful feeling other than sensual pleasure. As one does not delight in sensual pleasure, the underlying tendency of lust does not lie behind this. Such a person understands as it truly is the origin, the extinction, the satisfaction, the disadvantage, and the escape from these feelings. Understanding as it truly is the origin, the extinction, the satisfaction, the disadvantage, and the escape from these feelings, the underlying tendency to ignorance does not lie behind neither-painful-nor-pleasant feeling. If one feels a pleasant feeling, one feels it as a person who is detached from it. If one feels a painful feeling, one feels it as a person who is detached from it. 210
If one feels a neither-painful-nor-pleasant feeling, one feels it as a person who is detached from it. This is called a noble disciple who is detached from birth, death, sorrow, lamentation, pain, despair, and distress. I say that this is one who is detached from suffering.

11. "This is the distinction, disparity, or difference between the learned noble disciple and the unlearned ordinary person.

12. One who is endowed with wisdom,
A person of great learning,
Does not experience (mentally) feelings
That are painful or pleasant.
This is the great distinction in regard to what is wholesome
Between the wise and the ordinary person.

One who has fathomed the *dhamma*,
A person of great learning,

Sees the world with this difference:
Such a person's mind is not disturbed by pleasing things
Nor by undesirable things is that person repulsed.

By one's disinclination, dislike, and opposition
They are scattered, extinguished, and exist no more.
Having understood the reason
One is free from stain and sorrow
One understands rightly and has gone beyond becoming.

8

The Shorter Discourse to Māluṅkyaputta

(*Cūḷa-māluṇkya Sutta*)[1]

Why live the religious life? Is it necessary that a religion have definite theories about such metaphysical issues as the existence of a soul, the afterlife, or the nature of ultimate reality? These questions are the focus of this short discourse.

The discourse opens with Māluṅkyaputta ruminating about leaving the religious training under the Buddha because the Buddha has not declared to him the answers to a series of metaphysically speculative questions. These questions, collectively referred to as the ten "undeclared questions" (*avyākatā*), recur numerous times in the Pāli Canon. Given the typical view that the religious life depends on belief in certain metaphysical truths, Māluṅkyaputta's demand does not seem unreasonable. Should not a religion offer answers to the questions about the creation and end of the world or the nature of the soul? How can there be salvation without knowledge of such things? Surprisingly, early Buddhism gives an unequivocal "no" in answer to these questions. It is not difficult to understand, therefore, why Māluṅkyaputta is upset and confused.

In response to Māluṅkyaputta's challenging words, the Buddha flatly refuses to teach about these metaphysically speculative issues because the answers are probably unfathomable to a human being—especially as the human mind has been conditioned to misconceive the way that things really are. He states that one might well die before one finds any answers to such questions. Of more importance, the Buddha says that these issues are simply irrelevant to living the religious life. For these reasons, the Buddha sidesteps metaphysics and redirects the religious life toward the practice of moral and psychological transformation.

The Buddha explains his reluctance to engage in metaphysical speculation by one of his most famous parables, the "parable of the arrow." In this parable, the Buddha suggests that a person struck with an arrow should seek immediate medical attention rather than delay by vainly seeking useless information about the person who shot the arrow. Similarly, the sufferings of this life pose an urgent need for treatment, and thus these should be the

[1] *Majjhima Nikāya* 1.426–432.

focus of living the religious life, not the vague, unfathomable, and irrelevant issues of speculative metaphysics.

Discourse

426

1. Thus have I heard. At one time, the Exalted One was dwelling at the Jeta Grove in Anāthapiṇḍika's park. Then a certain thought arose in the mind of the venerable Māluṅkyaputta while he was in seclusion in a lonely place: "These are those speculative views that have been left undeclared by the Exalted One, set aside, and rejected: 'the world is eternal'; 'the world is not eternal'; 'the world is finite'; 'the world is infinite'; 'the life principle[2] is the same as the body'; 'the life principle is different from the body'; 'the *Tathāgata* exists after death'; 'the *Tathāgata* does not exist after death'; 'the *Tathāgata* both exists and does not exist after death'; 'the *Tathāgata* neither does nor does not exist after death.' The Exalted One has not declared these to me. I neither approve of nor pardon the Exalted One for not declaring these to me. And so I will approach the Exalted One and ask him the meaning of this. If the Exalted One will declare the meaning of these speculative views[3] to me, then I will live the religious life under the Exalted One. But if the Exalted One will not declare the meaning of these to me, then I will give
427 up the training and return to the lower (domestic) life."

2. Then the venerable Māluṅkyaputta arose from his seclusion and approached the Exalted One late in the afternoon. When he had approached and saluted the Exalted One, he sat down to one side. When he was seated to one side, the venerable Māluṅkyaputta said this to the Exalted One: "Sir, recently, in this connection, a certain thought arose in my mind while I was in seclusion in a lonely place: 'These are those speculative views that have been left undeclared by the Exalted One, set aside, and rejected: "the world is eternal"; "the world is not eternal"; "the world is finite"; "the world is infinite"; "the life principle is the same as the body"; "the life principle is different from the body"; "the *Tathāgata* exists after death"; "the *Tathāgata* does not exist after death"; "the *Tathāgata* both exists and does not exist after death"; "the *Tathāgata* neither does nor does not exist after death." The Exalted One has not declared these to me. I neither approve of nor pardon the Exalted One for not declaring these to me. And so, I will approach the Exalted One and ask him the meaning of this. If the Exalted One will declare the meaning of these speculative views[4] to me, then I will live the religious life

[2] *Jīva.* This word is sometimes translated as "soul."

[3] The original text here repeats all ten speculative views.

[4] The original text again repeats all ten speculative views.

under the Exalted One. But if the Exalted One will not declare the meaning of these to me, then I will give up the training and return to the lower life.'

"If the Exalted One knows that 'the world is eternal' . . . 'the world is not eternal' . . . 'the world is finite' . . . 'the world is infinite' . . . 'the life principle is the same as the body' . . . 'the life principle is different from the body' . . . 'the *Tathāgata* exists after death' . . . 'the *Tathāgata* does not exist after 428
death' . . . 'the *Tathāgata* both exists and does not exist after death' . . . 'the *Tathāgata* neither does nor does not exist after death,' then let the Exalted One declare such views as he knows to me. If the Exalted One does not know these views, then, not knowing and not seeing these, it would be proper for him to say in respect of each view: 'I do not know, I do not see.'"

3. "Māluṅkyaputta, did I speak to you thus: 'Come, Māluṅkyaputta, live the religious life under me, I will declare to you: "the world is eternal"; "the world is not eternal"; "the world is finite"; "the world is infinite"; "the life principle is the same as the body"; "the life principle is different from the body"; "the *Tathāgata* exists after death"; "the *Tathāgata* does not exist after death"; "the *Tathāgata* both exists and does not exist after death"; "the *Tathāgata* neither does nor does not exist after death"'?"

"No, sir."

"Did you ever speak thus to me: 'Sir, I will live the religious life under the Exalted One, and the Exalted One will declare these speculative views[5] to me'?"

"No, sir."

"So it is, Māluṅkyaputta, that I never said: 'Come, Māluṅkyaputta, live the religious life under me, I will declare to you these speculative views.'[6] This being so, misguided person, who are you, and what are you abandoning?

4. "Māluṅkyaputta, should anyone speak thus: 'I will not live the religious life under the Exalted One, unless the Exalted One will declare to me: "the world is eternal"; "the world is not eternal"; "the world is finite"; "the world is infinite"; "the life principle is the same as the body"; "the life principle is different from the body"; "the *Tathāgata* exists after death"; "the *Tathāgata* does not exist after death"; "the *Tathāgata* both exists and does not exist after death"; "the *Tathāgata* neither does nor does not exist after death"'—these would still be undeclared by the *Tathāgata,* and that person 429
would die. Just as a person—having been pierced by an arrow thickly smeared with poison, and his friends and relatives having procured a surgeon—might speak thus: 'I will not have this arrow withdrawn until I know whether the person who wounded me is either a nobleman, a Brahmin, a merchant-farmer, or a worker.'—or might speak thus: 'I will not have this

[5] The original text again repeats all ten speculative views.

[6] The original text again repeats all ten speculative views.

arrow withdrawn until I know whether the person who wounded me has a certain name and a certain clan.'—or might speak thus: 'I will not have this arrow withdrawn until I know whether the person who wounded me is tall or short or medium height.'—or might speak thus: 'I will not have this arrow withdrawn until I know whether the person who wounded me is black-, brown-, or yellow-skinned.'—or might speak thus: 'I will not have this arrow withdrawn until I know whether the person who wounded me lives in a certain village, town, or city.'—or might speak thus: 'I will not have this arrow withdrawn until I know whether the bow that wounded me is a long bow or a crossbow.'—or might speak thus: 'I will not have this arrow withdrawn until I know whether the bowstring that wounded me is fiber, reed, sinew, hemp, or bark.'—or might speak thus: 'I will not have this arrow withdrawn until I know whether the arrow that wounded me was wild or man-made.'—or might speak thus: 'I will not have this arrow withdrawn until I know whether the arrow that wounded me was fitted with feathers from a vulture, a crow, a hawk, a peacock, or a stork.'—or might speak thus: 'I will not have this arrow withdrawn until I know whether the arrow that wounded me was bound by sinew from an ox, a buffalo, a lion, or a monkey.'—or might speak thus: 'I will not have this arrow withdrawn until I know whether the arrow that wounded me is really an arrow, a hoof-tipped arrow, a curved arrow, an
430 iron shaft, a calf-toothed arrow, or made from oleander (tree).'

"Māluṅkyaputta, this person would still be ignorant of those things and then that person would die. So, too, were any person to speak thus: 'I will not live the religious life under the Exalted One, unless the Exalted One will declare these speculative views[7] to me.' And still these would be undeclared by the *Tathāgata,* and then that person would die.

5. "If there is the speculative view[8] 'the world is eternal,' then the religious life does not arise. If there is the speculative view 'the world is not eternal,' then the religious life does not arise. Whether one holds the speculative view that 'the world is eternal' or the speculative view that 'the world is not eternal,' yet there is birth, there is old age, there is death, and there is sorrow, lamentation, pain, despair, and distress—the destruction of which in this life I do declare.

"If there is the speculative view 'the world is finite,' then the religious life does not arise. If there is the speculative view 'the world is infinite,' then the religious life does not arise. Whether one holds the speculative view that 'the world is finite' or the speculative view that 'the world is infinite,' yet there is birth, there is old age, there is death, and there is sorrow, lamentation, pain, despair, and distress—the destruction of which in this life I do declare.

[7] The original text again repeats all ten speculative views.

[8] *Diṭṭhi.*

"If there is the speculative view 'the life principle is the same as the body,' then the religious life does not arise. If there is the speculative view 'the life principle is different from the body,' then the religious life does not arise. Whether one holds the speculative view that 'the life principle is the same as the body' or the speculative view that 'the life principle is different from the body,' yet there is birth, there is old age, there is death, and there is grief, sorrow, suffering, lamentation, and despair—the destruction of which in this life I do declare.

"If there is the speculative view 'the *Tathāgata* exists after death,' then the religious life does not arise. If there is the speculative view 'the *Tathāgata* does not exist after death,' then the religious life does not arise. Whether one holds the speculative view that 'the *Tathāgata* exists after death' or the speculative view that 'the *Tathāgata* does not exist after death,' yet there is birth, there is old age, there is death, and there is sorrow, lamentation, pain, 431
despair, and distress—the destruction of which in this life I do declare.

"If there is the speculative view 'the *Tathāgata* both exists and does not exist after death,' then the religious life does not arise. If there is the speculative view 'the *Tathāgata* neither does nor does not exist after death,' then the religious life does not arise. Whether one holds the speculative view that 'the *Tathāgata* both exists and does not exist after death' or the speculative view that 'the *Tathāgata* neither does nor does not exist after death,' yet there is birth, there is old age, there is death, and there is sorrow, lamentation, pain, despair, and distress—the destruction of which in this life I do declare.

6. "Therefore, Māluṅkyaputta, you should grasp what is undeclared by me as undeclared, and you should also grasp what is declared by me as declared.

"And what is undeclared by me? 'The world is not eternal' is undeclared by me. 'The world is finite ' is undeclared by me. 'The world is infinite' is undeclared by me. 'The life principle is the same as the body' is undeclared by me. 'The life principle is different from the body' is undeclared by me. 'The *Tathāgata* exists after death' is undeclared by me. 'The *Tathāgata* does not exist after death' is undeclared by me. 'The *Tathāgata* both exists and does not exist after death' is undeclared by me. 'The *Tathāgata* neither does nor does not exist after death' is undeclared by me.

"For what reason are these undeclared by me? Because these are not useful in attaining the goal; they are not fundamental to the religious life and do not lead to aversion, dispassion, cessation, peace, higher knowledge, enlightenment, and *nibbāna*—for these reasons, these are not declared by me.

"And what is declared by me? 'This is suffering'[9] is declared by me. 'This is the origin of suffering' is declared by me. 'This is the cessation of suffering'

[9] *Dukkha.*

is declared by me. 'This is the way leading to the cessation of suffering' is declared by me.

"For what reason are these declared by me? Because these are useful in attaining the goal; they are fundamental to the religious life and lead to aversion, dispassion, cessation, peace, higher knowledge, enlightenment, and *nibbāna*—for these reasons, these are declared by me.

432 "Therefore, Māluṅkyaputta, you should grasp what is undeclared by me as undeclared, and you should also grasp what is declared by me as declared."

7. This was said by the Exalted One. Delighted, the venerable Māluṅkyaputta rejoiced in the words of the Exalted One.

9

Discourse on the Parable of the Water Snake

(*Alagaddūpama Sutta*)[1]

Some parts of the Buddha's teaching are very difficult to understand. The Buddha recognized this fact; he very often described the depth and subtlety of his doctrines. It is no wonder, then, that the texts record that some of the *bhikkhus* suffered from grave misunderstandings of the Buddha's doctrines. In this discourse, the *bhikkhu* Ariṭṭha misunderstands the Buddha's teachings on sensual pleasures (particularly, pleasures deriving from sexual activities). Apparently, Ariṭṭha thinks there is a way to indulge in sexual activities without incurring the ill effects that the Buddha ascribed to sensual indulgence. From what the Buddha says in condemning Ariṭṭha's view, it seems that Ariṭṭha believes that one can avoid the defiling mental conditions that normally motivate sexual activities. This belief would explain why Ariṭṭha holds the pernicious view that the obstacles that have been declared by the Buddha are not in fact obstacles to those who practice them. If one could participate in sensual pleasures without being motivated by lust, passion, or greed, then it might be possible to do so without experiencing the suffering that would normally result from sensualist activities. But the Buddha is emphatic that one cannot indulge in sensual pleasures apart from the defiling mental factors that motivate such actions, hence there is no way to avoid the ill effects of indulging in sensual pleasures for one who indulges in them.

Buddhism is certainly not alone among religious and philosophical traditions in warning about the dangers of sensual pleasures. Plato argued that the philosopher should flee from bodily passions because they impede the mind's intellectual functions.[2] Christian asceticism has many forms, of course, but the sinfulness of sensualism is a regular theme in Christian traditions. In Hinduism, sensual pleasure is an appropriate aim of life for those in the domestic phase of life; but in the higher forms of spiritual life, sensual pleasures must be restrained, if not entirely eliminated.

The question that remains for Buddhists is how far to take the Buddha's admonitions against sensual pleasures. The Buddha's "middle way," after all, is a rejection of the two extremes: opulent living on the one hand and self-mortification (extreme austerity) on the other. So, if the Buddha rejected

1 *Majjhima Nikāya* 1.130–142.

2 See Plato's *Phaedo* 65a–b.

self-mortification and extreme forms of asceticism, his position on the proper role of sensual pleasures cannot involve their complete abandonment, as that would be a position identical to the ascetic extreme.

The Buddha uses this opportunity to add another parable to the many parables found in the canonical texts. Here he offers a simile that compares the dangers of grasping the *dhamma* in the wrong way to the dangers of grasping a poisonous water snake. In applying this parable, the Buddha elaborates on the difference between the improper and the proper study of the *dhamma.* Some persons improperly study the *dhamma* by merely reciting it and using it to criticize others, lacking the wisdom and comprehension to put it into practice. Such is but a hollow exercise and becomes itself an obstacle to living the religious life. This is the result of the wrong grasp of the teachings. Proper study of the *dhamma* means going beyond the mere words of the teaching to a profound understanding of the teachings. Such comprehension of the *dhamma* is no mere intellectual exercise, but necessarily includes the practice of the teachings. This right grasp of the teachings redounds to the great benefit of such a person.

This discourse contains another parable, the "parable of the raft," that is much more famous than the one referred to in the title of the discourse. In this parable, the crossing over from the mundane, unenlightened life to a religiously liberated life (*nibbāna*) is compared with crossing over a river. Like *saṃsāric* existence, the near shore is dangerous and frightening, whereas the farther shore promises peace and security. But, as the Buddha explains, there is neither a bridge nor a boat to use for crossing over. In such a case, a person might build a raft and use it to cross over. But once one has crossed over the river, the raft would become an impediment, if it is retained while walking on land. So when the raft is no longer useful, it should be discarded.

The raft is compared with the *dhamma:* the *dhamma* should be seen as instrumental to achieving religious goals; it is not an absolute to be clung to. So the Buddha says "you should abandon the *dhamma,* all the more what is not the *dhamma.*"[3] This statement has led some interpreters to suggest that the enlightened person, having crossed over from *saṃsāra* to *nibbāna,* does not live by the *dhamma,* that the Buddha's teachings are to be abandoned once enlightenment is attained. But such an interpretation of the parable of the raft is unwarranted. The Buddha does not mean that one gives up living by the *dhamma* after achieving enlightenment. Enlightened existence is not a life beyond good and evil with no ethical and religious principles. The early Buddhist texts consistently affirm that the principles of

[3] *Majjhima Nikāya* 1.135. Richard Gombrich gives a valuable analysis of this line with the same interpretation in *How Buddhism Began: The Conditioned Genesis of the Early Teachings* (London: Athlone Press, 1996), pp. 24–25.

dhamma are intrinsic to the enlightened life. What is to be abandoned is not in fact the *dhamma,* but selfish or dogmatic attachment to the *dhamma* (or any other doctrine). Thus, the parable serves as a reminder that religious doctrines grasped dogmatically can fuel unwholesome states, no matter how "right" the doctrines.

The last half of the discourse offers one of the most detailed accounts in the canonical literature regarding the abandonment of the belief in a permanent Self. The Buddha's critical arguments are aimed directly at the ideas put forward in the *Upaniṣads,* even mimicking them by the expression, "This is mine. I am this. This is my permanent Self." The discourse purports to show that the doctrine of a permanent Self is a pernicious lie that arises because of a person's anxieties over death (worries about annihilation at death, for example) and the perpetuation of the illusion of a permanent Self through self-aggrandizement and acquisitiveness.

Discourse

1. Thus have I heard. At one time, the Exalted One was dwelling at 130
Sāvatthi in the Jeta Grove in Anāthapiṇḍika's park. At that time, there was a *bhikkhu* named Ariṭṭha, who was formerly a vulture trainer,[4] in whom a pernicious view such as this had arisen: "As I understand the *dhamma* taught by the Exalted One, those things that are called obstructions[5] by the Exalted One are not capable of obstructing one who pursues them."

Several *bhikkhus* heard that: "There is a *bhikkhu* named Ariṭṭha, who was formerly a vulture trainer, in whom a pernicious view such as this had arisen: 'As I understand the *dhamma* taught by the Exalted One, those things that are called obstructions by the Exalted One are not capable of obstructing one who pursues them.'"

Then those *bhikkhus* approached Ariṭṭha. When they had approached him, they said this: "Is it true, friend Ariṭṭha, that in you a pernicious view such as this has arisen: 'As I understand the *dhamma* taught by the Exalted One, those things that are called obstructions by the Exalted One are not capable of obstructing one who pursues them'?"

"Yes, it is so, friend, I understand the *dhamma* taught by the Exalted One in exactly that way."

[4] *Gaddhabādhipubbassa.* It is not clear what occupation is indicated by this term, but it is likely that involvement with vultures would suggest a "low" social class.

[5] *Antarāyikā.* Literally, "things that come between," thus "obstructions." On the basis of commentaries and the discussion that takes place later in this discourse, the term refers to sensual pleasures, especially sexual activities.

Then those *bhikkhus,* desiring to dissuade Ariṭṭha from this pernicious view, questioned him, cross-examined him, and pressed him for reasons: "Friend Ariṭṭha, do not say that! Do not misrepresent the Exalted One! It is not good to misrepresent the Exalted One. The Exalted One would not say that. In many different ways, friend Ariṭṭha, the Exalted One has explained certain things as obstructions and how these things are capable of obstructing one who pursues them. The Exalted One has described sensual pleasures as affording little gratification, generating much pain and trouble. And here there is even more danger. The Exalted One has described sensual pleasures by the parable of the skeleton, by the parable of the lump of meat, by the parable of the grass torch, by the parable of the pit of coals, by the parable of dreams, by the parable of borrowed things, by the parable of the fruit of a tree, by the parable of the slaughterhouse, by the parable of the impaling stake, by the parable of the snake's head—in each case demonstrating that sensual pleasures generate much pain and trouble; and here there is even more danger."

And yet, even after having been questioned, cross-examined, and pressed for reasons by those *bhikkhus,* Ariṭṭha still vigorously held onto and clung to this pernicious view saying: "Yes, it is so, friend, as I understand the *dhamma* taught by the Exalted One, things that are called obstructions by the Exalted One are not capable of obstructing one who pursues them."

131 2. When those *bhikkhus* were not able to dissuade Ariṭṭha from this pernicious view, they approached the Exalted One. When they approached the Exalted One, they greeted him and sat down to one side. When they were seated to one side, those *bhikkhus* [*recounted verbatim their conversation with Ariṭṭha to the Exalted One*]. "Since we were not able, sir, to dissuade Ariṭṭha from this pernicious view, we are reporting this matter to the Exalted One."

3. Then the Exalted One addressed a certain *bhikkhu:* "Come, *bhikkhu,* and address the *bhikkhu* Ariṭṭha, who was formerly a vulture trainer, with
132 my words: 'Brother Ariṭṭha, the teacher calls you.'"

"Yes, sir," assented that *bhikkhu* to the Exalted One, and he approached Ariṭṭha. When he had approached Ariṭṭha, he said this: "Friend Ariṭṭha, the teacher calls you."

"Yes, sir," assented Ariṭṭha to that *bhikkhu,* and he approached the Exalted One. When he had approached the Exalted One, he greeted him and sat down to one side. When he was seated to one side, the Exalted One said this to Ariṭṭha: "Is it true, friend Ariṭṭha, that the following pernicious view has arisen in you: 'As I understand the *dhamma* taught by the Exalted One, those things that are called obstructions by the Exalted One are not capable of obstructing one who pursues them'?"

"Yes, it is so, friend. I understand the *dhamma* taught by the Exalted One in exactly that way."

"Do you know anyone, you misguided person, to whom I have taught the *dhamma* in that way? Misguided person, have I not explained in many different ways certain things as obstructions, and how these things are capable of obstructing one who pursues them? I have described sensual pleasures as affording little gratification, generating much pain and trouble. And here there is even more danger. I have described sensual pleasures by the parable of the skeleton, by the parable of the lump of meat, by the parable of the grass torch, by the parable of the pit of coals, by the parable of dreams, by the parable of borrowed things, by the parable of the fruit tree, by the parable of the slaughterhouse, by the parable of the impaling stake, and by the parable of the snake's head—in each case demonstrating that sensual pleasures generate much pain and trouble; and here there is even more danger. But you, misguided person, have misrepresented me by your own wrong grasp, have injured yourself, and have accumulated much demerit. That, misguided person, will be to your harm and suffering for a long time."

Then the Exalted One addressed the *bhikkhus:* "What do you think, *bhikkhus?* Does this *bhikkhu* Ariṭṭha have even a glimmer of this *dhamma* and discipline?"

"How could he, sir? No, sir."

This having been said, Ariṭṭha sat down and became silent, downcast, dejected, with his shoulders drooping, overcome with remorse and bewildered. Then the Exalted One, knowing that Ariṭṭha had become downcast and dejected, said this to him: "Misguided person, you will be known by your own pernicious view. In connection with this, I will question the *bhikkhus.*"

4. Then the Exalted One addressed the *bhikkhus:* "Do you, *bhikkhus,* 133
understand the *dhamma* that I teach in the way that this Ariṭṭha does who has misrepresented me by his wrong grasp, who has injured himself, and who has accumulated much demerit?"

"No, sir. The Exalted One has explained certain things as obstructions in many different ways and how those things are capable of obstructing one who pursues them. The Exalted One has described sensual pleasures as affording little gratification, generating much pain and trouble; and here there is even more danger. The Exalted One has described sensual pleasures by the parable of the skeleton, by the parable of the lump of meat, by the parable of the grass torch, by the parable of the pit of coals, by the parable of dreams, by the parable of borrowed things, by the parable of the fruit tree, by the parable of the slaughterhouse, by the parable of the impaling stake, and by the parable of the snake's head—in each case demonstrating that sensual pleasures generate much pain and trouble; and here there is even more danger."

"Good, *bhikkhus.* It is good that you understand the *dhamma* taught by me in this way. For I have described sensual pleasures as affording little gratification, generating much pain and trouble; and here there is even more danger. I have described sensual pleasures by these many parables—in each case demonstrating that sensual pleasures generate much pain and trouble; and here there is even more danger. But Ariṭṭha has misrepresented me by his own wrong grasp, has injured himself, and has accumulated much demerit. This will be to the harm and suffering of this misguided person for a long time. Indeed, that one can indulge in sensual pleasures apart from sensual desires, apart from the perception of sensual desires, and apart from thoughts of sensual desires—that is impossible.[6]

5. "In a certain case, *bhikkhus,* some misguided persons study the *dhamma,* including the discourses, the chants, the explanations, the verses, the sayings, what has been said, the birth stories, the marvelous teachings, and the miscellanies. But having studied the *dhamma,* they do not examine the meaning of these teachings with intelligence. And for them these teachings that have not been examined with intelligence are accepted without comprehension. Instead, they study the *dhamma* for the purpose of criticizing others and for the purpose of merely quoting; so they do not achieve the good result for which purpose the *dhamma* ought to be studied. These teachings that are poorly grasped lead to harm and suffering for a long time. What is the reason for this? It is because of the wrong grasp of the teachings.

"Just as a person walking about seeking a water snake, going after a water snake, searching for a water snake were to see a large water snake and were to take hold of it by its coil or tail. That water snake, having turned back,
134 might bite that person's hand, arm, or another of that person's limbs. As a result, that person might die or experience pain akin to dying. What is the reason for this? It is because of the wrong grasp of the water snake.

"In the same way, some misguided persons study the *dhamma,* including the discourses, the chants, the explanations, the verses, the sayings, what has been said, the birth stories, the marvelous teachings, and the miscellanies. But having studied the *dhamma,* they do not examine the meaning of these teachings with intelligence. And these teachings that have not been examined with intelligence are accepted without comprehension. Instead, they study the *dhamma* for the purpose of criticizing others and for the purpose of merely quoting; so they do not achieve the good result, for which purpose the *dhamma* ought to be studied. These teachings that are poorly grasped lead to harm and suffering for a long time. What is the reason for this? It is because of the wrong grasp of the teachings.

[6] This is the crucial line refuting Ariṭṭha's misguided view. There can be no indulgence in sensualist activities without the defiling motivating factors (e.g., sensual desire) behind them. Hence there is no way to partake in sensualist activities (particularly sexual activities) without incurring the negative effects of the factors that motivate sensualist activities.

6. "In another case, some young men from good families study the *dhamma,* including the discourses, the chants, the explanations, the verses, the sayings, what has been said, the birth stories, the marvelous teachings, and the miscellanies. But having studied the *dhamma,* they do examine the meaning of these teachings with intelligence. And these teachings that have been examined with intelligence are accepted with comprehension. They do not study the *dhamma* for the purpose of criticizing others, nor for the purpose of merely quoting; so they do achieve the good result for which purpose the *dhamma* ought to be studied. These teachings that are rightly grasped lead to their welfare and happiness for a long time. What is the reason for this? It is because of the right grasp of the teachings.

"Just as a person walking about seeking a water snake, going after a water snake, searching for a water snake, were he to see a large water snake, he might restrain it tightly with a forked stick. Having restrained it tightly by the neck with the forked stick, that water snake might wrap itself around the hand, arm, or other limbs of that person, but from this cause, the person would not die nor experience pain akin to dying. What is the reason for this? It is because of the right grasp of the water snake.

"In the same way, some young men from good families study the *dhamma,* including the discourses, the chants, the explanations, the verses, the sayings, what has been said, the birth stories, the marvelous teachings, and the miscellanies. But having studied the *dhamma,* they do examine the meaning of these teachings with intelligence. These teachings that have been examined with intelligence are accepted with comprehension. They do not study the *dhamma* for the purpose of criticizing others, nor for the purpose of merely quoting; so they do achieve the good result for which purpose the *dhamma* ought to be studied. And these teachings that are rightly grasped lead to their welfare and happiness for a long time. What is the reason for this? It is because of the right grasp of the teachings.

"Therefore, *bhikkhus,* you should understand the meaning of what I have said, and you should remember it in this way. Were you not to understand the meaning of what I have said, you should question me about it or one of the learned *bhikkhus* (if there is one present).

7. "*Bhikkhus,* I will teach you that the *dhamma* is like a raft—for crossing over, not for retaining. Listen and pay careful attention, and I will speak."

"Yes, Exalted One," those *bhikkhus* replied to the Exalted One.

The Exalted One said: "Just as a person walking along a highway might see a great body of water, the near shore dangerous and frightening, the further shore secure and not frightening. But if there were neither a boat nor a bridge to use for crossing over from the near shore to the farther shore, that
person might have this thought: 'This is a great body of water, and the near 135
shore is dangerous and frightening. The farther shore is secure and not

frightening. But there is neither a boat nor a bridge to use for crossing over from the near shore to the farther shore. Suppose that, having collected grass, sticks, branches, and leaves, and having bound them together as a raft, riding on that raft, and making an effort with hands and feet, I should cross over safely to the other shore.' Then that person, having collected grass, sticks, branches, and leaves, and having bound them together as a raft, riding on that raft, and making an effort with hands and feet, might cross over safely to the other shore. Having crossed over, having made the further shore, that person might have this thought: 'Now, this raft has been very useful to me. Riding on this raft, and making an effort with my hands and feet, I crossed over safely to the farther shore. Suppose now that, having put this raft on my head, or having raised it onto my shoulder, I should proceed as I desire.' What do you think, *bhikkhus?* If that person were to act in this way, would that person be doing what should be done with the raft?"

"No, Exalted One."

"In what way should that person act, *bhikkhus,* in order to do what should be done with the raft? Here, it might occur to that person who has crossed over, gone to the farther shore: 'Now, this raft has been very useful to me. Riding on this raft, and making an effort with my hands and feet, I crossed over safely to the farther shore. Suppose now that, having hauled this raft onto dry ground or having left it floating on the water, I should proceed as I desire.' In acting this way, that person would be doing what should be done with the raft. Just as, in the parable of the raft, the *dhamma* taught by me is for crossing over, not for retaining. *Bhikkhus,* by understanding the parable of the raft, you should abandon the *dhamma,* all the more what is not the *dhamma.*[7]

8. "*Bhikkhus,* there are these six standpoints for speculative views. What are the six? In this connection, an uninstructed ordinary person, taking no account of the noble ones, unskilled in the *dhamma* of the noble ones, untrained in the *dhamma* of the noble ones, taking no account of the virtuous person, unskilled in the *dhamma* of the virtuous person, untrained in the *dhamma* of the virtuous person, regards the body[8] as: 'This is mine. I am this. This is my permanent Self.'[9] Such a person regards feeling as: 'This is

[7] This is a much quoted, but often misrepresented, statement. The point here is not that after enlightenment one should abandon the Buddha's teachings—nor is an enlightened person "beyond good and evil"—but simply that one should abandon dogmatic or selfish attachment to any teachings, even the Buddha's.

[8] *Rūpa.* This word here refers to the organic/material processes that comprise the body.

[9] Richard Gombrich suggests that this phrase seems to be the Buddha's denial of the famous *Upaniṣadic* phrase *tat tvaṃ asi* ("you are that" or "that art thou") that identifies the true identity of the person (*ātman*) with the world essence (*Brahman*) (see *Chāndogya Upaniṣad* 6.8.7). The

mine. I am this. This is my permanent Self.' Such a person regards perception as: 'This is mine. I am this. This is my permanent Self.' Such a person regards the dispositions to action as: 'These are mine. I am these. These are my permanent Self.' Such a person regards consciousness as: 'This is mine. I am this. This is my permanent Self.' And that person regards whatever is seen, heard, sensed, cognized, reached, looked for, pondered by the mind as: 'This is mine. I am this. This is my permanent Self.' Also, whatever standpoint for speculative views one takes, namely: 'This world [is identical to] this permanent Self. After death I will become this, which is permanent, everlasting, eternal, not liable to change, and I will remain so for eternity.' This, too, that 136
person regards as: 'This is mine. I am this. This is my permanent Self.'

"But, an instructed noble disciple, taking account of the noble ones, skilled in the *dhamma* of the noble ones, well-trained in the *dhamma* of the noble ones, taking account of the virtuous person, skilled in the *dhamma* of the virtuous person, well-trained in the *dhamma* of the virtuous person, regards the body as: 'This is not mine. I am not this. This is not my permanent Self.' Such a person regards feeling as: 'This is not mine. I am not this. This is not my permanent Self.' Such a person regards perception as: 'This is not mine. I am not this. This is not my permanent Self.' Such a person regards the dispositions to action as: 'These are not mine. I am not these. These are not my permanent Self.' Such a person regards consciousness as: 'This is not mine. I am not this. This is not my permanent Self.' And that person regards whatever is seen, heard, sensed, cognized, reached, looked for, pondered by the mind as: 'This is not mine. I am not this. This is not my permanent Self.' Also, whatever standpoint for speculative views one takes, namely: 'This world [is identical to] this permanent Self. After death I will become this, which is permanent, everlasting, eternal, not liable to change, and I will remain so for eternity.' This, too, that person regards as: 'This is not mine. I am not this. This is not my permanent Self.' That person, considering things in this way, will not be worried about what is non-existent."

9. When this had been said, a certain *bhikkhu* spoke in this way to the Exalted One: "But, sir, could there be anxiety about something that is non-existent externally?"[10]

"There could be, *bhikkhu*," the Exalted One said. "In this case, someone thinks: 'What was certainly mine before, that is definitely not mine now;

Buddha has changed the wording into the first person: *etaṃ mama, eso'ham asmi, eso me attā* ("This is mine. I am this. This is my permanent Self."). This is a major piece of evidence that much of early Buddhism developed in the context of a dialogue or debate with Brahmanist ideas, especially the *Upaniṣads*. See Gombrich, *How Buddhism Began*, pp. 38–39.

[10] *Bahiddhā*. This word could be translated also as "outwardly" or "objectively." The reference is to things considered outside the mind or self.

what certainly could have been mine, there is definitely no chance of my getting that.' That person then grieves, mourns, laments, beats one's chest, and cries out in disillusion. In that case, there is anxiety about something that is non-existent externally."

"But, sir, could there be no anxiety about something that is non-existent externally?"

"There could be, *bhikkhu*," the Exalted One said. "In this case, someone does not think: 'What was certainly mine before, that is definitely not mine now; what certainly could have been mine, there is definitely no chance of my getting that.' That person then does not grieve, mourn, lament, beat one's chest, and does not cry out in disillusion. In that case, there is no anxiety about something that is non-existent externally."

"But, sir, could there be anxiety about something that is non-existent internally?"[11]

"There could be, *bhikkhu*," the Exalted One said. "In this case, someone thinks: 'This world [is identical to] this permanent Self. After death I will become this, which is permanent, everlasting, eternal, not liable to change, and I will remain so for eternity.' Such a person hears the *dhamma* as it is taught by the *Tathāgata* or by a disciple of the *Tathāgata* for the elimination of all standpoints on speculative views that involve obstinacy, bias, prejudice, and obsessiveness; for the calming of all dispositions to action; for the forsaking of all attachments; for the destruction of craving; for dispassion; for
137 cessation; and for *nibbāna*. Such a person thinks: 'I will surely be annihilated! I will surely perish! I will surely not exist!' That person then grieves, mourns, laments, beats one's chest, and cries out in disillusion. Thus, there is anxiety about something that is non-existent internally."

"But, sir, could there be no anxiety about something that is non-existent internally?"

"There could be, *bhikkhu*," the Exalted One said. "In this case, someone does not think: 'This world [is identical to] this permanent Self. After death I will become this, which is permanent, everlasting, eternal, not liable to change, and I will remain so for eternity.' Such a person hears the *dhamma* as it is taught by the *Tathāgata* or by a disciple of the *Tathāgata* for the elimination of all standpoints on speculative views that involve obstinacy, bias, prejudice, and obsessiveness; for the calming of all dispositions to action; for the forsaking of all attachments; for the destruction of craving; for dispassion; for cessation; and for *nibbāna*. But such a person does not think: 'I will surely be annihilated! I will surely perish! I will surely not exist!' That person does not grieve, mourn, lament, beat one's chest, and does not cry out

[11] *Ajjhattaṃ*. This word could also be translated as "inwardly" or "subjectively." The reference is to things considered inside the mind or self.

in disillusion. Thus, there is no anxiety about something that is non-existent internally."

10. "*Bhikkhus,* could you take hold of some possession, such that that possession would be permanent, everlasting, eternal, and not liable to change, and would remain so for eternity? And do you see any such possession that you might take hold of that would be permanent, everlasting, eternal, and not liable to change, so that it would remain so for eternity?"

"No, sir."

"Good, *bhikkhus,* I, too, do not see any such possession that you might take hold of that would be permanent, everlasting, eternal, and not liable to change, so that it would remain so for eternity. Could there be someone grasping onto the doctrine of attachment to a Self, and, from that grasping onto the doctrine of attachment to a Self, there would not arise grief, sorrow, suffering, lamentation, and despair? Do you see a way that a person could grasp onto the doctrine of attachment to a permanent Self that would not give rise to sorrow, lamentation, pain, despair, and distress?

"No, sir."

"Good, *bhikkhus,* I, too, do not see a way that one could grasp onto the doctrine of attachment to a permanent Self that would not give rise to sorrow, lamentation, pain, despair, and distress.

"*Bhikkhus,* could you depend on a commitment to speculative views, so that for the person depending on that view there would not arise sorrow, lamentation, suffering, depression, and despair? Do you see a way that a dependence on a commitment to speculative views would not give rise to sorrow, lamentation, pain, despair, and distress?

"No, sir."

"Good, *bhikkhus,* I, too, do not see a way that a dependence on a commitment to speculative views would not give rise to sorrow, lamentation, 138
pain, despair, and distress.

11. "*Bhikkhus,* if there were a permanent Self, could it be said that: 'Something belongs to my Self?'"

"Yes, sir."

"Or, if there were what belongs to a Self, could it be said that: 'My Self exists'?"

"Yes, sir."

"*Bhikkhus,* if neither a Self nor what belongs to a Self is found,[12] in truth or in reality, then would it not also be true that this standpoint of speculative view, namely: 'This world [is identical to] this permanent Self. After death I will become this, which is permanent, everlasting, eternal, not liable

[12] That is, both the Self and what is connected to a Self are non-existent.

to change, and I will remain so for eternity' is a wholly and completely foolish doctrine?"

"Sir, how could it not be a wholly and completely foolish doctrine?"

"What do you think, *bhikkhus?* Is the body permanent or impermanent?"

"Impermanent, sir."

"And that which is impermanent, is it painful or pleasant?"

"Painful, sir."

"And in regard to that which is impermanent, painful, and subject to change, is it proper that it be viewed as: 'This is mine. I am this. This is my permanent Self.'?"

"No, indeed, sir."

"What do you think, *bhikkhus?* Is feeling permanent or impermanent?"

"Impermanent, sir."

"And that which is impermanent, is it painful or pleasant?"

"Painful, sir."

"And in regard to that which is impermanent, painful, and subject to change, is it proper that it be viewed as: 'This is mine. I am this. This is my permanent Self.'?"

"No, indeed, sir."

"What do you think, *bhikkhus?* Is perception permanent or impermanent?"

"Impermanent, sir."

"And that which is impermanent, is it painful or pleasant?"

"Painful, sir."

"And in regard to that which is impermanent, painful, and subject to change, is it proper that it be viewed as: 'This is mine. I am this. This is my permanent Self.'?"

"No, indeed, sir."

"What do you think, *bhikkhus?* Are dispositions to action permanent or impermanent?"

"Impermanent, sir."

"And that which is impermanent, is it painful or pleasant?"

"Painful, sir."

"And in regard to that which is impermanent, painful, and subject to change, is it proper that it be viewed as: 'These are mine. I am these. These are my permanent Self.'?"

"No, indeed, sir."

"What do you think, *bhikkhus?* Is consciousness permanent or impermanent?"

"Impermanent, sir."

"And that which is impermanent, is it painful or pleasant?"

"Painful, sir."

"And in regard to that which is impermanent, painful, and subject to change, is it proper that it be viewed as: 'This is mine. I am this. This is my permanent Self.'?"

"No, indeed, sir.

"Therefore, *bhikkhus,* whatever body there is—whether in the past, present, or future, internal or external, gross or subtle, inferior or superior, far or near—all body should be looked on by one who has right wisdom as: 'This is not mine. I am not this. This is not my permanent Self.'

"Therefore, whatever feeling there is—whether in the past, present, or future, internal or external, gross or subtle, inferior or superior, far or near— 139
all feeling should be looked on by one who has right wisdom as: 'This is not mine. I am not this. This is not my permanent Self.'

"Therefore, whatever perception there is—whether in the past, present, or future, internal or external, gross or subtle, inferior or superior, far or near—all perception should be looked on by one who has right wisdom as: 'This is not mine. I am not this. This is not my permanent Self.'

"Therefore, whatever dispositions to action there are—whether in the past, present, or future, internal or external, gross or subtle, inferior or superior, far or near—all dispositions to action should be looked on by one who has right wisdom as: 'These are not mine. I am not these. These are not my permanent Self.'

"Therefore, whatever consciousness there is—whether in the past, present, or future, internal or external, gross or subtle, inferior or superior, far or near—all consciousness should be looked on by one who has right wisdom as: 'This is not mine. I am not this. This is not my permanent Self.'

12. "Seeing things in this way, the learned noble disciple is disillusioned with the body, with feeling, with perception, with dispositions to action, and with consciousness. Being disillusioned, one becomes detached. Being detached, one is liberated. When (his mind) is liberated, there is the knowledge that 'it is liberated.' One understands that destroyed is birth, the holy life has been lived, done is what was to be done, there is nothing further to continue like this."[13]

"This *bhikkhu* is called one who has lifted the barrier, one who has filled in the moat, one who has pulled up the pillar, one who has withdrawn the bolt, a noble one who has put down the banner, who has laid down the burden and is unfettered.

"How is it that a *bhikkhu* is one who has lifted the barrier? In such a case, a *bhikkhu* has eliminated ignorance, cut it down to its roots, made it like a palm-tree stump, brought about its utter cessation, so that it is not liable

[13] *Itthattāyā.* That is, for an enlightened person, there is no continuance of the *saṃsāric* round of death and rebirth.

to rise again in the future. In this way, a *bhikkhu* is one who has lifted the barrier.

"How is it that a *bhikkhu* is one who has filled in the moat? In such a case, a *bhikkhu* has eliminated the round of birth that brings renewed rebirth, cut it down to its roots, made it like a palm-tree stump, brought about its utter cessation, so that it is not liable to rise again in the future. In this way, a *bhikkhu* is one who has filled in the moat.

"How is it that a *bhikkhu* is one who has pulled up the pillar? In such a case, a *bhikkhu* has eliminated craving, cut it down to its roots, made it like a palm-tree stump, brought about its utter cessation, so that it is not liable to rise again in the future. In this way, a *bhikkhu* is one who has pulled up the pillar.

"How is it that a *bhikkhu* is one who has withdrawn the bolt? In such a case, a *bhikkhu* has eliminated the five fetters belonging to the lower world,[14] cut them down to their roots, made them like palm-tree stumps, brought about their utter cessation, so that they are not liable to rise again in the future. In this way, a *bhikkhu* is one who has withdrawn the bolt.

"How is it that a *bhikkhu* is a noble one who has put down the banner, who has laid down the burden and is unfettered? In such a case, a *bhikkhu* has eliminated the conceit 'I am,' cut it down to its roots, made it like a palm-tree stump, brought about its utter cessation, so that it is not liable to rise
140 again in the future. In this way, a *bhikkhu* is one who has put down the banner, who has laid down the burden and is unfettered.

13. "So, being freed in mind, when the *devas* associated with Indra, Brahmā, or Prajāpati go searching for that *bhikkhu,* they do not find him [if they search thinking]: 'He depends on the consciousness of a *Tathāgata.*' What is the reason for this? Because, having realized the *dhamma,* I say 'a *Tathāgata* is unfathomable.'

"Because I speak and preach in this way, some recluses and Brahmins, without any basis, have vainly, falsely, and wrongly accused me, saying: 'The recluse Gotama is a nihilist.[15] He declares the annihilation, the destruction, and the non-existence of beings that actually do exist.' But I am not like that; I do not speak in that way. Truly, those venerable recluses and Brahmins are without any basis, and have vainly, falsely, and wrongly accused me, saying: 'The recluse Gotama is a nihilist. He declares the annihilation, the destruc-

[14] The five fetters belonging to the lower world keep a person tethered to *saṃsāric* existence. The five are belief in a permanent Self, perplexity, infatuation with ceremonial rituals, excitement of sensual pleasure, and ill will.

[15] *Venayiko.* Literally, "one who leads astray." That what the Buddha is accused of is actually a kind of "nihilism" derives from the explanation in the following sentence.

tion, and the non-existence of beings that actually do exist.' Both before and now, I declare only suffering and the cessation of suffering. If others, in regard to this, try to irritate the *Tathāgata,* abusing and scolding him, still the *Tathāgata* feels no anger over this, no resentment, and has no discontent in his mind.

"If others, in regard to this, were to honor the *Tathāgata,* treating him with respect and reverence, still the *Tathāgata* feels no joy over this, no delight, and has no elation in his mind. If others, in regard to this, were to honor the *Tathāgata,* treating him with respect and reverence, the *Tathāgata* would think: 'Because of what was previously known, here such praises are lavished on us.' Therefore, if others, in regard to this, try to irritate you, abusing you and scolding you, you should feel no anger over this, no resentment, and have no discontent in your minds. Therefore, if others, in regard to this, were to honor you, treating you with respect and reverence, still you should feel no joy over this, no delight, and have no elation in your minds. Therefore, if others, in regard to this, were to honor you, treating you with respect and reverence, you should think: 'Because of what was previously known, here such praises are lavished on us.'

14. "Therefore, *bhikkhus,* you should abandon that which is not yours. Abandoning that will be for your welfare and happiness for a long time. And what is not yours? The body is not yours. Abandon it. Abandoning it will be for your welfare and happiness for a long time. Feeling is not yours. Aban- 141
don it. Abandoning it will be for your welfare and happiness for a long time. Perception is not yours. Abandon it. Abandoning it will be for your welfare and happiness for a long time. Dispositions to action are not yours. Abandon them. Abandoning them will be for your welfare and happiness for a long time. Consciousness is not yours. Abandon it. Abandoning it will be for your welfare and happiness for a long time.

"What do you think about this, *bhikkhus?* Were some person in this Jeta Grove to gather grass, sticks, branches, and leaves, or were to burn them, or were to do with them as that person pleased, would you think: 'This person gathers and burns *us* as they please'?"

"No, sir. And what is the reason for this? Because, sir, that is not the Self, nor what belongs to a Self."

"In this same way, *bhikkhus,* you should abandon that which is not yours. Abandoning it will be for your welfare and happiness for a long time. And what is not yours? The body is not yours. Abandon it. Abandoning it will be for your welfare and happiness for a long time. Feeling is not yours. Abandon it. Abandoning it will be for your welfare and happiness for a long time. Perception is not yours. Abandon it. Abandoning it will be for your welfare and happiness for a long time. Dispositions to action are not yours.

Abandon them. Abandoning them will be for your welfare and happiness for a long time. Consciousness is not yours. Abandon it. Abandoning it will be for your welfare and happiness for a long time.

15. "In this way, the *dhamma* is well-taught by me, is made manifest, unveiled, made known, and has all loose ends cut off. Because the *dhamma* is well-taught by me, is made manifest, unveiled, made know, and has all loose ends cut off, those *bhikkhus* who are *arahants*, who have cut off the defilements, who dwell fulfilled, who have done what had to be done, who have laid down the burden, who have attained their true goal, and who have destroyed the fetter of rebirth are those who are freed by right knowledge. For those *bhikkhus*, the round of rebirth can no longer be discerned. . . . Because the *dhamma* is well-taught by me . . . those *bhikkhus* who have eliminated the five fetters of the lower world will all spontaneously arise [in a higher world], and will reach their final *nibbāna* there, and are not liable to return to this world. . . . Because the *dhamma* is well-taught by me . . . those *bhikkhus* who have eliminated the three fetters, and in whom lust, hatred, and delusion are reduced, will all be once-returners who, having come back to this world once, will make an end of suffering. . . . Because the *dhamma* is well-taught by me . . . those *bhikkhus* who have eliminated the three fet-
142 ters will all be stream-winners who are not liable to end up in a place of suffering and are sure to go through to enlightenment. . . . Because the *dhamma* is well-taught by me, all of those *bhikkhus* who live in conformity with the *dhamma* and live in conformity to faith are destined for enlightenment.

"In this way, the *dhamma* is well-taught by me, is made manifest, unveiled, made known, and stripped of its wrappings. Because the *dhamma* is well-taught by me, is made manifest, unveiled, made known, and has all loose ends cut off, those *bhikkhus* who have a full measure of faith in me and love for me are all destined to a place of happiness (heaven)."

16. This was said by the Exalted One. Delighted, those *bhikkhus* rejoiced in the words of the Exalted One.

10

Discourse to Vacchagotta on Fire

(*Aggivacchagotta Sutta*)[1]

Dogmatic answers to metaphysical questions comprise the core of most religious and philosophical systems. The answers to metaphysical questions, such as "does the world have a beginning?" "will the world end?" or "do human beings possess an immortal soul?" form the essential teachings of most of the world's religions and philosophies. In some religious traditions, knowledge of the deepest truths about Reality is the impetus for religious and philosophical inquiry. But this is not the case in early Buddhism. Early Buddhism is perhaps the only religious tradition that deliberately tries to avoid taking a stance on speculative metaphysical questions (*diṭṭhi*). The reasons for this avoidance are several. First, the Buddha states that such matters are irrelevant to living the religious life. Second, as an empiricist, the Buddha recognized that the scope of human knowledge is very limited and that such questions fall outside that scope. Thus, attempts at answering such metaphysical questions involve a kind of hubris on the part of the one who dogmatically clings to particular speculative views. Lastly, the motives for raising metaphysical questions often involve selfish grasping.

In the following discourse, the Buddha refers to the same ten "undeclared" views that appeared in the Shorter Discourse to Māluṅkyaputta" (Chapter 8). These ten views are presented as five pairs: (1) "the world is eternal" or "the world is not eternal"; (2) "the world is finite" or "the world is infinite"; (3) "the life principle and the body are identical" or "the life principle and the body are not identical"; (4) "the *Tathāgata* exists after death" or "the *Tathāgata* does not exist after death"; (and 5) "the *Tathāgata* both exists and does not exist after death" or "the *Tathāgata* neither exists nor does not exist." The Buddha has left these speculative views undeclared for just the reasons mentioned before. For the Buddha, knowledge claims must be justified by experience, but these ten views are beyond any possible justification in experience.

This discourse contains the Buddha's famous cross-examination of Vaccha regarding fire. When Vaccha asks where a *bhikkhu* is reborn, the Buddha explains that such a question cannot be answered because the language of the question makes certain improper metaphysical assumptions. The

[1] *Majjhima Nikāya* 1.483–488.

Buddha makes his point by drawing an analogy with fire. Using a dialectical method of questioning not so different from the "Socratic method" made famous in Plato's early dialogues, the Buddha drives Vaccha to admit that meaningful references to fire are those that can be verified in sense experience. But questions that ask about the fire after it has been extinguished—such as "which direction has the fire gone after it is extinguished?"—have no answer because the question itself is empirically empty. Such a question does not have a proper subject of reference. Any answer to questions about the fire after it has been extinguished would require treating the fire as a self-subsisting entity that remains in some mode of existence even after its extinction. Likewise, questions about where the *bhikkhu* is reborn or whether or not a *Tathāgata* exists after death—questions that might at first seem reasonable—conceal unwarranted metaphysical assumptions. The proper response to questions about the extinguished fire, and thus to the state of a *bhikkhu* after death, is that these questions "do not apply."

Discourse

483

1. Thus have I heard. At one time, the Exalted One was dwelling at Sāvatthi in the Jeta Grove in Anāthapiṇḍika's park. Vacchagotta, a religious
484 wanderer, approached the Exalted One. When he had approached the Exalted One, he exchanged pleasant greetings with him. After exchanging greetings, he sat down to one side. When he had sat down to one side, Vacchagotta said this to the Exalted One:

2. "Is it the case that venerable Gotama holds the speculative view that 'The world is eternal; this alone is true, and any other view is false'?"

"Vaccha, I do not hold the speculative view that 'The world is eternal; this alone is true, and any other view is false.'"

"Is it the case that venerable Gotama holds the speculative view that 'The world is not eternal; this alone is true, and any other view is false'?"

"Vaccha, I do not hold the speculative view that 'The world is not eternal; this alone is true, and any other view is false.'"

"Is it the case that venerable Gotama holds the speculative view that 'The world is finite; this alone is true, and any other view is false'?"

"Vaccha, I do not hold the speculative view that 'The world is finite; this alone is true, and any other view is false.'"

"Is it the case that venerable Gotama holds the speculative view that 'The world is infinite; this alone is true, and any other view is false'?"

"Vaccha, I do not hold the speculative view that 'The world is infinite; this alone is true, and any other view is false.'"

"Is it the case that venerable Gotama holds the speculative view that 'The life principle and the body are identical; this alone is true, and any other view is false'?"

"Vaccha, I do not hold the speculative view that 'The life principle and the body are identical; this alone is true, and any other view is false.'"

"Is it the case that venerable Gotama holds the speculative view that 'The life principle and the body are different; this alone is true, and any other view is false'?"

"Vaccha, I do not hold the speculative view that 'The life principle and the body are different; this alone is true, and any other view is false.'"

"Is it the case that venerable Gotama holds the speculative view that 'The *Tathāgata* exists after death; this alone is true, and any other view is false'?"

"Vaccha, I do not hold the speculative view that 'The *Tathāgata* exists after death; this alone is true, and any other view is false.'"

"Is it the case that venerable Gotama holds the speculative view that 'The *Tathāgata* does not exist after death; this alone is true, and any other view is false'?"

"Vaccha, I do not hold the speculative view that 'The *Tathāgata* does not exist after death; this alone is true, and any other view is false.'"

"Is it the case that venerable Gotama holds the speculative view that 'The *Tathāgata* both exists and does not exist after death; this alone is true, and any other view is false'?" 485

"Vaccha, I do not hold the speculative view that 'The *Tathāgata* both exists and does not exist after death; this alone is true, and any other view is false.'"

"Is it the case that venerable Gotama holds the speculative view that 'The *Tathāgata* neither exists nor does not exist after death; this alone is true, and any other view is false'?"

"Vaccha, I do not hold the speculative view that 'The *Tathāgata* neither exists nor does not exist after death; this alone is true, and any other view is false.'"

3. "Why is it that when venerable Gotama is asked the question whether he holds any of these ten speculative views,[2] he replies 'Vaccha, I do not hold that speculative view; nor that such alone is true, and any other view is false'? What danger does the venerable Gotama see so that he does not take up any of these speculative views?"

4. "Vaccha, the speculative view that 'the world is eternal' is a jungle of views, a wilderness of views, a wriggling of views, a writhing of views, the fetter of views, bringing suffering, vexation, despair, and agony. It does not

[2] In the original text, Vaccha repeats verbatim each of the ten speculative views.

lead to aversion, dispassion, cessation, calmness, higher knowledge, and *nibbāna.* The speculative view that 'the world is not eternal' is a jungle of views. . . . 'the world is finite' is a jungle of views. . . . 'the world is infinite' is a jungle of views. . . . 'the life principle and the body are identical' is a jungle of views. . . . 'the life principle and the body are different' is a jungle of
486 views. . . . 'the *Tathāgata* exists after death' is a jungle of views. . . . 'the *Tathāgata* does not exist after death' is a jungle of views. . . . 'the *Tathāgata* both exists and does not exist after death' is a jungle of views. . . . The speculative view that 'the *Tathāgata* neither exists nor does not exist after death' is a jungle of views, a wilderness of views, a wriggling of views, a writhing of views, the fetter of views, bringing suffering, vexation, despair, and agony. It does not lead to aversion, dispassion, cessation, calmness, higher knowledge, and *nibbāna.* Seeing this danger, Vaccha, I do not take up any of these speculative views."

"Is there any speculative view at all that venerable Gotama resorts to?"

"Vaccha, speculative views have been put away by the *Tathāgata.* For the *Tathāgata* has seen this: 'Such is the body, such is the origin of the body, such is the extinction of the body; such is feeling, such is the origin of feeling, such is the extinction of feeling; such is perception, such is the origin of perception, such is the extinction of perception; such are the dispositions to action, such is the origin of dispositions to action, such is the extinction of dispositions to action; such is consciousness, such is the origin of consciousness, such is the extinction of consciousness.' Therefore, I say that because of the destruction, fading away, cessation, abandoning, and relinquishing of all conceptions, all cogitations, all predispositions of I-making, mine-making, and conceit, the *Tathāgata* is without attachment."

5. "When a *bhikkhu* is liberated in mind, venerable Gotama, where is he reborn?"

"'Reborn,' Vaccha, does not apply."

"Then is he not reborn, venerable Gotama?"

"'Not reborn,' Vaccha, does not apply."

"Then is he both reborn and not reborn, venerable Gotama?"

"'Both reborn and not reborn,' Vaccha, does not apply."

"Then is he neither reborn nor not reborn, venerable Gotama?"

"'Neither reborn nor not reborn,' Vaccha, does not apply."

6. "When the venerable Gotama is asked these questions[3] about the
487 rebirth of a liberated *bhikkhu,* he says that they 'do not apply.' In this connection, I am experiencing some ignorance and confusion. The confidence in venerable Gotama that I had acquired through our earlier conversation has now disappeared."

[3] The text repeats verbatim Vaccha's four questions and the Buddha's answers.

7. "Vaccha, you might well be ignorant; you might well be confused, for this *dhamma* is profound, difficult to see, difficult to understand. It is peaceful, excellent, beyond the sphere of mere reasoning, subtle, and understood by the wise. Because you hold a different view, have a different inclination, practice a different discipline, and follow a different teacher, this is hard for you to understand. For this reason, Vaccha, I will question you in return on this matter. Answer as you see fit:

"What do you think, Vaccha, if there were a fire burning in front of you, would you know: 'there is this fire burning in front of me'?"

"Venerable Gotama, if there were a fire burning in front of me, I would know: 'There is this fire burning in front of me.'"

"What if you were asked about it in this way: 'Regarding this fire that burns in front of you, depending on what does this fire burn?' Having been asked this, what would you answer?"

"Venerable Gotama, if I were asked about it in this way: 'Regarding this fire that burns in front of you, depending on what does this fire burn?' I would answer thus: 'Regarding this fire that burns in front of me, it burns depending on grass and sticks.'"

"Vaccha, if this fire in front of you were extinguished, would you know: 'This fire in front of me has been extinguished'?"

"Venerable Gotama, if this fire in front of me was extinguished, I would know: 'This fire in front of me has been extinguished.'"

"Vaccha, if you were asked thus: 'This fire in front of you that has been extinguished, which direction has it gone, east, west, north, or south?' Having been asked this, what would you answer?"

"Venerable Gotama, it does not apply. This fire burned dependent on grass and sticks. When these had become exhausted, without receiving any more, being without fuel, it is reckoned as extinguished."

8. "So, too, Vaccha, the body, by which one describing the *Tathāgata* would describe him, has been abandoned, cut off at the root, uprooted, and utterly destroyed so that there will be no future arising for it.[4] The *Tathāgata* is liberated from being reckoned by the body. He is profound, immeasurable, and difficult to fathom like the ocean, and so 'reborn' does not apply, 'not reborn' does not apply, 'both reborn and not reborn' does not apply, 'neither reborn nor not reborn' does not apply.

"Whatever feeling . . . Whatever perception . . . Whatever dispositions 488
to action . . . Whatever consciousness, by which one describing the *Tathāgata* would describe him, has been abandoned, cut off at the root, uprooted, and utterly destroyed so that there will be no future arising for it. The *Tathāgata* is liberated from being reckoned by consciousness. He is

[4] This appears to mean that there will be no further rebirth.

profound, immeasurable, and difficult to fathom like the ocean, and so 'reborn' does not apply, 'not reborn' does not apply, 'both reborn and not reborn' does not apply, 'neither reborn nor not reborn' does not apply."

9. This having been said, Vacchagotta, the religious wanderer, said this to the Exalted One: "It is just as if there were a great sal-tree not far from either a village or a town. Its branches and leaves might fall down from impermanence. Its bark might crumble, and its sapwood might dissolve. And at another time, having removed its branches, leaves, bark, and sapwood, it would be pure, consisting entirely of the heartwood. So, too, this discourse of venerable Gotama has removed the branches, leaves, bark, and sapwood; it is pure, consisting entirely of the heartwood.

"Wonderful, venerable Gotama! Wonderful, venerable Gotama! It is just as if the venerable Gotama were to make upright what was turned upside down, or were to uncover what was covered over, or were to point out the way to those who were lost, or were to hold up an oil lamp in the darkness
489 saying 'those endowed with eyes will see the visible objects.' Thus venerable Gotama makes known the *dhamma* by diverse methods. I go to the Exalted One for refuge and also to the *dhamma* and the *Saṅgha* of the *bhikkhus.* Let the good Gotama accept me as a lay-follower who has gone for refuge from this day forth, so long as life lasts."

11

Discourse to Prince Abhaya

(*Abhayarājakumāra Sutta*)[1]

This discourse raises the age-old philosophical issues surrounding truth and its relationship to utility. In the opening scene, Prince Abhaya is encouraged to refute and discredit the Buddha by one of the Buddha's contemporaries, the Jain leader Nigaṇṭha Nātaputta (also known as Mahāvīra). Nigaṇṭha Nātaputta suggests to Prince Abhaya a question to ask the Buddha that is a logical trap.[2] The question is whether the Buddha would utter a statement that is unpleasant or disagreeable. No matter which way he answers, it appears that the Buddha would be trapped. If the Buddha would utter such a statement, then he would be no different from the ordinary, unenlightened person. If the Buddha would not utter such a statement, then he contradicts himself because, apparently, he has made some statements about Devadatta's[3] ending up in a state of misery that were disagreeable to him. Since the Buddha must either utter such statements or not (a logical tautology), then either he is no different from an ordinary person or he contradicts himself. Since neither alternative of this disjunction is something the Buddha would accept, he would be stuck in an untenable position and discredited.

The Buddha sees the logical trap and avoids it by saying that there is no "one-sided answer" to the question.[4] The Buddha's response to Prince Abhaya's question leads into a profound philosophical discussion about truth and the way that truth relates to what the Buddha teaches. To explain how Prince Abhaya's question is one-sided, the Buddha shows that the relationship between truth and his utterances (teachings) is more complex than assumed by the question posed by Prince Abhaya. The Buddha considers statements according to three categories: true or false, beneficial or unbeneficial, and agreeable or disagreeable. The Buddha's response to Prince Abhaya's question, then, is that the criteria used to determine whether or not to utter a statement are not simply a matter of agreeability or disagreeability. The full set of criteria includes this factor plus two other factors, comprising eight

[1] *Majjhima Nikāya* 1.392–394.

[2] The structure of the logical trap takes the form of a constructive dilemma.

[3] Devadatta was the Buddha's relative who, as a *bhikkhu,* tried to create a schism in the *Saṅgha* and establish himself as the leader of the *Saṅgha.* The Buddha predicted that he would likely end up in hell for a long period of time.

[4] *Majjhima Nikāya* 1.393.

possible combinations of these three factors. Prince Abhaya's question collapses these eight to just two. This is the reason his question is unanswerable as it stands.[5]

There is some debate among scholars regarding the Buddha's analysis of truth and utility in relationship to his teaching.[6] Since the discourse suggests that the Buddha teaches only what is true and beneficial, and leaves out any mention of the possibility of a statement that is false and beneficial, some scholars have argued that the Buddha held a utilitarian theory of truth. Other scholars, however, argue that since the Buddha allows that some statements are true but unbeneficial implies that the Buddha did not identify utility (being beneficial) as the criterion of truth. For these scholars, the truth of a statement, according to early Buddhism, is something established quite independent of utility.

What is clear from the discourse, however, is that what the Buddha *teaches* depends only on whether the statement is both true and beneficial, and *not* on whether it is agreeable or disagreeable. As this discourse emphasizes, the Buddha's primary motivation for teaching was compassion—even if it meant uttering things that other people did not want to hear. Hence, utilitarian considerations were key factors in determining what the Buddha would *teach,* if not necessarily in his conception of truth per se.

Discourse

392

1. Thus have I heard. At one time, the Exalted One was dwelling in Rājagaha in the Bamboo Grove in the Squirrel's Sanctuary. Then Prince Abhaya approached Nigaṇṭha Nātaputta.[7] When he had approached Nigaṇṭha Nātaputta, he saluted him and sat down to one side. When he was seated to one side, Nigaṇṭha Nātaputta said this to Prince Abhaya: "Come, prince! You should refute the doctrine of the religious wanderer Gotama. In this way, this good report will be spread about you: 'The doctrine of the religious wanderer Gotama, who has great magical power and possesses great majesty, was refuted by Prince Abhaya.'"

"But how, sir, will I refute the doctrine of the religious wanderer Gotama, who has great magical power and possesses great majesty?"

[5] A good discussion of the various permutations of truth-analysis in this discourse can be found in David Kalupahana's *A History of Buddhist Philosophy: Continuities and Discontinuities* (Honolulu: University of Hawaii Press, 1992), p. 51.

[6] See John Holder, "The Early Buddhist Theory of Truth: A Contextualist Pragmatic Interpretation," *International Philosophical Quarterly,* vol. 26, no. 4, December 1996.

[7] A leader of the Jains. Also known as Mahāvīra.

"Go, prince, and approach the religious wanderer Gotama. And having approached Gotama, speak thus: 'Sir, would the *Tathāgata* utter a statement that is unwelcome, disagreeable, and unpleasant?' If Gotama answers your question in this way: 'Prince, the *Tathāgata* would utter a statement that is unwelcome, disagreeable, and unpleasant,' then you should say to him: 'In that case, sir, what difference is there between you and the ordinary (unenlightened) person? For the ordinary person, too, would utter a statement that is unwelcome, disagreeable, and unpleasant.' If Gotama answers your question in this way: 'Prince, the *Tathāgata* would not utter a statement that is unwelcome, disagreeable, and unpleasant,' then you should say to him: 'In 393
that case, sir, why, in regard to Devadatta, have you declared: "Devadatta is in a state of misery." "Devadatta is destined for hell."[8] "Devadatta will endure hell for an eon."[9] "Devadatta is incurable." Certainly, these words offended Devadatta and displeased him.' When asked this two-horned question, the religious wanderer Gotama will neither be able to spew it out nor swallow it down. Just as if an iron barb were to get stuck in a person's throat, one would neither be able to spew it out nor swallow it down—so, too, prince, Gotama, when asked this two-horned question will neither be able to spew it out nor swallow it down."

2. "Yes, sir," Prince Abhaya replied to Nigaṇṭha Nātaputta. Having assented, he rose from his seat and saluted Nigaṇṭha Nātaputta, keeping his right side turned toward him. Then he approached the Exalted One. When he had approached the Exalted One, he greeted him courteously, and he sat down to one side. When he was seated to one side, he checked the position of the sun. Then Prince Abhaya had this thought: "The proper time for refuting the Exalted One's doctrine today has passed. I will refute the Exalted One's doctrine tomorrow at my own house." So he said this to the Exalted One: "Sir, let the Exalted One consent to taking a meal tomorrow at my house in a party of four."[10] The Exalted One consented by becoming silent. Then Prince Abhaya, having understood the Exalted One's consent, rose from his seat, saluted him, and went away keeping his right side turned toward him.

Then the Exalted One, after the passing of the night, having dressed himself in the morning and taking his robe and bowl, approached the home of Prince Abhaya. When he had approached, he sat down in the seat that was prepared. Then Prince Abhaya, with his own hands, served and satisfied the Exalted One with delicious hard and soft foods. When the Exalted One had washed his hand in the bowl to indicate that he was finished eating, Prince Abhaya took another lower seat and sat down to one side.

8 *Niraya.* Hell is a temporary place of suffering in Buddhist cosmology.

9 *Kappa* (Skt: *kalpa*). This term represents a very, very long time.

10 The "party of four" is composed of the Buddha and three others.

3. When he was seated to one side, Prince Abhaya said this to the Exalted One: "Sir, would the *Tathāgata* utter a statement that is unwelcome, disagreeable, and unpleasant?"

"There is no one-sided answer (to that question), prince."

"Already, sir, the Jains[11] have lost."

394 "Prince, why do you say this: 'Already, sir, the Jains have lost?'"

[*Then Prince Abhaya repeated in full his earlier conversation with Nigaṇṭha Nātaputta.*]

4. At that time, a young and innocent infant was sitting on Prince
395 Abhaya's lap. The Exalted One said this to Prince Abhaya: "What do think about this, prince? If this young boy, because of your negligence or that of his nurse, were to take a piece of wood or a potsherd into his mouth, what would you do to him?"

"Sir, I would take it out. If I were not able to take it out at once, I would grasp his head with my left hand, and, with a bent finger on my right hand, I would take it out, even if to do so I would have to draw blood. What is the reason for this? Because, sir, I have compassion for the boy."

"In the same way, prince, a statement that the *Tathāgata* knows to be false, inaccurate, unbeneficial, and which is also unwelcome, disagreeable, and unpleasant—that statement the *Tathāgata* does not utter. Also, a statement that the *Tathāgata* knows to be true, accurate, unbeneficial, and which is also unwelcome, disagreeable, and unpleasant—that statement, also, the *Tathāgata* does not utter. Whatever statement the *Tathāgata* knows to be true, accurate, beneficial, and which is also unwelcome, disagreeable, and unpleasant—in that case, the *Tathāgata* knows the proper time to explain that statement. Whatever statement the *Tathāgata* knows to be false, inaccurate, unbeneficial, and which is welcome, agreeable, and pleasant—that statement the *Tathāgata* does not utter. Whatever statement the *Tathāgata* knows to be true, accurate, unbeneficial, and which is also welcome, agreeable, and pleasant—that statement, also, the *Tathāgata* does not utter. Whatever statement the *Tathāgata* knows to be true, accurate, beneficial, and which is also welcome, agreeable, and pleasant—in that case, the *Tathāgata* knows the proper time to explain that statement. What is the reason for this? Prince, the *Tathāgata* has compassion for beings."

5. "Sir, whenever those learned warrior-leaders, learned Brahmins, learned householders, or learned religious wanderers prepare a question and approach the *Tathāgata* to ask it, does the Exalted One already have an answer reasoned and thought out already in his mind, such as: 'Were someone to approach me, they might ask me such-and-such a question in this

[11] *Nigaṇṭhā.*

way, and so I will explain it in this way'? Or does the answer come to mind for the *Tathāgata* on the spot?"

"In regard to that, prince, I will ask you a question in return. Give your reply as you see fit. What do you think, prince? Are you an expert in the parts of the chariot?"

"Yes, sir, I am an expert in the parts of the chariot."

"Then what do you think, prince? Were someone to approach you and ask you this: 'What is the name of this part of the chariot?' Do you already have an answer reasoned and thought out in your mind, such as: 'Were 396
someone to approach me, they might ask me such-and-such a question in this way, and so I will explain it in this way'? Or does the answer come to your mind on the spot?"

"Sir, I am a renowned charioteer who is an expert in the parts of the chariot. I know very well all the parts of the chariot. So the answer would come to my mind on the spot."

"It is exactly the same for me, prince. Whenever those learned nobles or learned Brahmins or learned householders or learned religious wanderers prepare a question and approach the *Tathāgata* to ask it, the answer comes to mind for the *Tathāgata* on the spot. What is the reason for this? Prince, the essence of the *dhamma* is thoroughly understood by the *Tathāgata,* and by means of this thorough understanding of the essence of the *dhamma,* the *Tathāgata* has the answer come to mind on the spot."

6. This having been said, Prince Abhaya said this to the Exalted One: "Wonderful, sir! Wonderful, sir! It is just as if someone were to make upright what was turned upside down, or were to uncover what was covered over, or were to explain the way to those who are lost, or were to hold up an oil lamp in the darkness, or were to hold up an oil lamp in the darkness saying 'those endowed with eyes will see the visible objects.' Just so, the Exalted One makes known the *dhamma* by diverse methods. Sir, I go to the Exalted One for refuge, to the *dhamma,* and also to the *Saṅgha* of *bhikkhus.* Let master Gotama accept me as a lay-follower who has gone for refuge from this day forth, so long as life lasts."

12

Discourse to Poṭṭhapāda

(*Poṭṭhapāda Sutta*)[1]

The Discourse to Poṭṭhapāda is among the most well-known discourses in the Pāli Canon. The discourse contains key elements of Buddhist ethics and epistemology, but it is more often studied because of its theory of human nature. In the discourse, the Buddha criticizes the prevailing views of human nature that postulate a permanent Self based on perception. In light of his refutation of arguments supporting a permanent Self, he offers his own view that human beings possess only an "acquired self."

The experience of suffering is the religious problematic not only for Buddhism but also for many of the other religious traditions of ancient India. The control of experience that leads to the elimination of suffering and brings about sublime states of joy and happiness is the ultimate goal of these religious traditions. As the opening sections of the discourse suggest, the key to controlling experience seems to have boiled down to the question of where and how does perception (of the normal sort that involves suffering) cease altogether.[2] Here the Buddha develops his own understanding of perception as a dependently arisen phenomenon, in contrast to four other theories of perception that were prevalent in his time. The four contrasting theories are that (1) perception arises and ceases without causes or conditions; (2) perceptions are the permanent Self; (3) Brahmins with magical powers can push perceptions into a person and drag them out; and (4) *devas* with magical powers can push perceptions into a person and drag them out. The Buddha rejects all four of these theories about perception, but the discourse focuses on the refutation of the first two theories.

In the discourse, the Buddha quickly dispenses with the notion that perceptions arise and cease without causes or conditions. This is completely wrong, he says, because all things that exist are part of a causal nexus of processes. Thus perceptions, like everything else, arise and cease through causes. This fact is a good thing, because if there were no causal processes involved, it would be impossible to manipulate and control perceptions in

[1] *Dīgha Nikāya* 1.178–203.

[2] The key Pāli term is *abhi-saññā-nirodha.* The PED defines *abhi-saññā-nirodha* as "trance." The translation used here is more literal: "the complete cessation of perception." But both translations may be seen as consistent, since a trancelike state may be one wherein perception ceases completely.

the way that is required to achieve religious liberation from suffering. In other words, the very possibility of effective religious training depends on the fact that perceptions arise and cease in a conditional or causal way.

This discourse raises another important point regarding Buddhist epistemology. In the middle of this discourse, the Buddha discusses the relationship of perception and knowledge. Poṭṭhapāda asks whether perception or knowledge comes first. The Buddha replies that perception comes first, then knowledge, as knowledge arises from perception. Such an account of the relationship of perception to knowledge reconfirms the Buddha's view that sense experience is the basis of all knowledge. This is further evidence that the Buddha held a form of empiricism.

The "cessation of perception," conceived as the goal of religious liberation in the Buddha's terms, is explained here as the threefold training (*tisikkhā*): moral conduct (*sīla*), mental culture (*samādhi*), and wisdom or insight (*paññā*). This training proceeds in a cumulative, developmental way. One must work gradually through the stages of training in the proper sequence, mastering earlier stages before moving on to later stages.

Training in moral conduct has a number of definite phases as it is presented in this discourse. First, a person in domestic life (a "householder") develops faith or confidence in the Buddha and his teaching. For this reason, a person might leave domestic life and take up the monastic life as a member of the *Saṅgha.* Such a person has abandoned opulent living, lives simply, and is satisfied with little. Becoming adept in moral conduct reinforces good moral habits, because such a person learns to control and guard the senses. This becomes the initial step in developing the second stage of training called "mental culture" or "concentration" (*samādhi*). By guarding the doors to the sense faculties, a person gradually takes control of one's mental life. With mental control or "mental culture," a person abandons the five psychological obstacles that lead to unwholesome actions: covetousness, ill will and anger, sloth and laziness, agitation and worry, and perplexity. Such a person achieves a sublime happiness and develops, step-by-step, the higher meditative states: the four *jhānas,* the plane of infinite space, the plane of infinite consciousness, the plane of no-thing, and, finally, the cessation of perception. Mental culture culminates with the extremely high level of mindful awareness that is necessary for the achievement of wisdom or insight into things as they truly are, that is, a full realization and understanding of the Four Noble Truths and the doctrine of dependent arising.

On the basis of the Buddha's rejection of the various theories of perception and his description of the threefold training of the Buddhist disciple, one might yet ask, does the Buddhist training eliminate perceptions altogether? Although there are some interpreters of early Buddhism who equate the goal of Buddhism with the complete cessation or elimination of perceptions, a careful study of this text suggests otherwise. In fact, the training suggested by the Buddha does not lead to the total abandonment of all perceptions, but to the arising of more wholesome perceptions when the unwholesome ones have been abandoned. In this discourse, the Buddha says explicitly that "through training, one sort of perception arises and, through training, another sort ceases."[3] So the situation of the person who is enlightened, or on the path to enlightenment, is not one in which perceptions no longer arise, but one in which the perceptions that derive from a corrupt mind and that ultimately lead to suffering are abandoned and *replaced* by perceptions of a wholesome sort.

The counterarguments to the identification of perceptions as the permanent Self in this discourse are among the Buddha's most philosophically developed attacks on the Brahmanical (Hindu) conception of *ātman.* These are also some of the most famous sections of the Pāli Canon because they purport to refute one of the most common and cherished theories of human nature, namely, that human beings have a permanent, immortal, essence (or soul).

Almost all religions, as well as many philosophies, postulate the existence of an immaterial, immortal, pure Self or soul that accounts for the true identity of a human being. Aside from the claims made by religious scriptures—claims that are grounded mainly on the authority of divinities and other higher powers—the most obvious evidence for the existence of an immaterial essence (i.e., a "soul" or "mind" in the Cartesian sense) at the core of each individual person is the firsthand experience each of us has of ourselves as a subject of perception or consciousness. For the same reasons, Poṭṭhapāda questions the Buddha to determine whether perception itself can be considered the much sought-after permanent Self (*ātman*).

When Poṭṭhapāda asks whether or not perception is the permanent Self, the Buddha recognizes that Poṭṭhapāda is assuming that there *is* such a permanent Self and that one need only determine its properties. In the course of this discussion, Poṭṭhapāda postulates three different types of pure Self: a coarse, material self consisting of the four great elements and nourished by material food; a mind-made self that is complete as to its components and not defective in any sense faculty; and an immaterial self made up of perceptions. The Buddha demonstrates to Poṭṭhapāda that none of these three candidates could be considered identical to perceptions, so that even *if* any of these three candidates were the real, permanent Self (the reality of which the Buddha rejects, anyway), perception would not be identical to the permanent Self, because, in each case, perception and the permanent Self possess different qualities or characteristics. So far, the Buddha's argument

[3] *Dīgha Nikāya* 1.183. See section 11 that follows.

proves nothing about the existence or non-existence of a permanent Self, only that such a Self and perception cannot be the same thing.

Having completed the analysis of the relationship between perception and a purported permanent Self, the Buddha turns to a criticism of those Brahmins and religious wanderers who hold the speculative view that the permanent Self is happy and healthy after death. The Buddha shows that such a position is untenable on empirical grounds: these Brahmins and religious wanderers have never seen a world that is entirely happy and healthy, not even for a single night, nor do they know of a way or practice that leads to such a world. So, without such personal knowledge, all talk about a happy, permanent Self in the afterlife turns out to be baseless speculation. Appealing to his stock analogies, the Buddha asserts that such speculation is similar to the case of a man who claims to be in love with a woman he knows nothing about, or the case of a person who has no knowledge of how a mansion will be situated building a staircase for that mansion.

Of course, the Buddha does not claim that there is no self at all. He offers, instead, a description of the self as *dependently arisen.* To do this, he describes three kinds of "acquired self": a material acquired self, a mind-made acquired self, and an immaterial acquired self. The term "acquired" seems to be particularly apt in this instance. The "self," as a dependently arisen phenomenon, is not a "fiction" but is the by-product of the complex processes that produce human perception and consciousness.

To avoid the danger of treating any of these "acquired selves" as a permanent Self, the Buddha teaches the *dhamma* as a method for "abandoning" each type of acquired self—a method whereby defiling mental states are abandoned and purified mental states grow. The training the Buddha described earlier in the discourse is precisely the path that will remove suffering through the purification of one's mental states and the development of wisdom. According to the Buddha, such training results in a life filled with sublime happiness.

Discourse

1. Thus have I heard. At one time, the Exalted One was dwelling at 178
Sāvatthi in the Jeta Grove in Anāthapiṇḍika's park. At that time, Poṭṭhapāda, a religious wanderer, together with a large contingent of about three hundred wanderers, was living at the debating hall near the *tinduka* tree in the single-halled park belonging to Queen Mallikāya.

2. Then the Exalted One, having dressed early in the morning, took his robe and bowl and entered Sāvatthi for alms. But then the Exalted One had this thought: "It is too early to wander about Sāvatthi for alms. Suppose I

were to go to the debating-hall near the *tinduka* tree in the single-halled park belonging to Queen Mallikāya and were to approach the wanderer Poṭṭhapāda." So the Exalted One went to the debating-hall near the *tinduka* tree in the single-halled park belonging to Queen Mallikāya.

3. At that time, Poṭṭhapāda was sitting together with a large assembly of religious wanderers who were tumultuous, loud, very noisy, and variously engaged in frivolous talk, such as talk about kings, thieves, ministers, armies, fears, battles, foods, drinks, stories, beds, garlands, perfumes, relatives, vehi-
179 cles, villages, towns, cities, countries, women, bravery, streets, water-well gossip, spirits of the deceased, chit-chat, legends about the creation of the world, the appearance of the sea, and talk about what exists and what does not exist.

4. Poṭṭhapāda saw the Exalted One coming from a distance. Having seen him, he called his assembly to order:

"Sirs, let there be quiet. Sirs, do not make a sound. This religious wanderer Gotama is coming. He prefers quiet. He speaks of the virtues of quiet. It would be well if, having seen this quiet assembly, he were to think that he should approach us."

This having been said, those religious wanderers became silent.

5. Then the Exalted One approached Poṭṭhapāda. At that point, Poṭṭhapāda said this to the Exalted One: "Let the Exalted One come! Welcome, Exalted One! It has been a long time, sir, since the Exalted One made his way to this place. Let the Exalted One sit down. There is a seat that has been prepared."

The Exalted One sat down on the prepared seat. Having taken another low seat, Poṭṭhapāda sat down to one side. When he was seated to one side, the Exalted One said this to Poṭṭhapāda:

"What, Poṭṭhapāda, was the matter that all of you seated here together were just now talking about? What discussion was going on among you that was interrupted?"

6. When this had been said, Poṭṭhapāda replied to the Exalted One: "Let be, sir, the matter of discussion about which those seated here were just now talking. It will not be difficult for the Exalted One to return to that later. In former days, sir, religious wanderers and Brahmins from various religious tra-
180 ditions have been sitting together assembled in a debating-hall when this discussion arose about the complete cessation of perception: 'How is there a complete cessation of perception?' In this regard, some have spoken thus: 'A person's perception arises without cause or condition and likewise it ceases. Whenever they arise, at that time, one is conscious. Whenever they cease, at that time, one is unconscious.' That is one way that they have explained the complete cessation of perception. Someone else spoke in this way: 'No, sir,

it cannot be like that. Perceptions are the permanent Self[4] of a person. It comes or it goes. Whenever it comes, at that time, one is conscious. Whenever it goes, at that time, one is unconscious.' That is one way that they have explained the complete cessation of perception. Someone else spoke in this way: 'No, sir, it cannot be like that. There are religious wanderers and Brahmins who have great power and influence. They push perception into this person or they drag it out. Whenever they push it in, at that time, one is conscious. Whenever they drag it out, at that time, one is unconscious.' That is one way that they have explained the complete cessation of perception. Someone else spoke in this way: 'No, sir, it cannot be like that. There are *devas* who have great power and influence. They push perception into this person or they drag it out. Whenever they push it in, at that time, one is conscious. Whenever they drag it out, at that time, one is unconscious.' Then, sir, this memory of the Exalted One arose, and I had this thought: 'Ah, would that the Exalted One were here! He is highly skilled in these matters! The Exalted One would know about the complete cessation of perception.' How then, sir, is there the complete cessation of perception?"

7. "Poṭṭhapāda, the case in which those religious wanderers and Brahmins spoke in this way—'a person's perception arises without cause or condition and likewise it ceases'—that idea is completely wrong. What is the reason for that? Because perceptions arise in a person *with* a cause, *with* a condition; and likewise they cease. Some perceptions arise through training. 181
And some perceptions cease through training."

"What is training?" the Exalted One said. [*A* Tathāgata *arises, a person hearing the dhamma taught by the* Tathāgata *goes forth from the domestic life to a monastic life and develops moral conduct.*[5]]

8. "Poṭṭhapāda, one who is thus accomplished in moral conduct sees no danger coming from any direction, because one is restrained by moral conduct. Just as a properly anointed king, who is a noble, having defeated his enemies, sees no danger coming from any direction, because he has conquered his enemies. In this way, a *bhikkhu* who is thus accomplished in moral conduct sees no danger coming from any direction, because he is restrained by moral conduct. He experiences internally the blameless joy that comes from being endowed with this noble practice of morality. In this way, a *bhikkhu* is accomplished in moral conduct.

[4] *Attā.*

[5] The sections on moral conduct from the *Sāmaññaphala Sutta* (*Dīgha Nikāya* 1.62–69, paragraphs 40–62) are repeated verbatim here in the *Poṭṭhapāda Sutta.* These paragraphs contain lists of specific activities that the *bhikkhu* should avoid. These sections have been omitted here (and abridged in the Pali Text Society edition) for the sake of brevity. For the full English translation of these abridged paragraphs, see *Dialogues of the Buddha,* translated by T. W. Rhys Davids and C.A.F. Rhys Davids (London: Pali Text Society, 1899–1921).

9. "How does a *bhikkhu* guard the doors of his sense faculties? In a certain case, having seen a visible object with the eye, a *bhikkhu* is not sensuously attracted to it. Nor is he attracted to its secondary attributes. If he were to live with this eye-faculty unrestricted, he would be attacked by covetousness, grief, evil, and unwholesome mental states. For this reason, he practices restraint.
182 He guards his eye-faculty and develops restraint of the eye-faculty.

"In a certain case, having heard a sound with the ear . . . having smelled a scent with the nose . . . having tasted a flavor with the tongue . . . having touched a tangible object with the body . . .

"In a certain case, having become conscious of a thought with the mind, a *bhikkhu* is not sensuously attracted to it. Nor is he attracted to its secondary attributes. If he were to live with this mind-faculty unrestricted, he would be attacked by covetousness, grief, evil, and unwholesome mental states. For this reason, he practices restraint. He guards his mind-faculty and develops restraint of the mind-faculty.

"He experiences internally the unimpaired joy that comes from being endowed with this noble practice of morality. In this way, a *bhikkhu* guards the doors of his sense faculties.

70* 9a. (65)[6] "How is a *bhikkhu* endowed with mindfulness and awareness? In this case, a *bhikkhu* when going back and forth is fully aware of his actions. When looking forward or looking backward, he is fully aware of his actions. When bending or stretching [his limbs], he is fully aware of his actions. In carrying his inner and outer robes and his bowl, he is fully aware of his actions. Whether he is drinking, eating, or tasting, he is fully aware of his actions. When he is defecating or urinating, he is fully aware of his actions. When he is walking, standing, sitting, falling asleep or awake, speaking or
71* remaining silent, he is fully aware of his actions. In this way, a *bhikkhu* is endowed with mindfulness and awareness.

9b. (66) How is a *bhikkhu* satisfied? In such a case, a *bhikkhu* is satisfied by having a robe to cover his body, by the collection of alms that attends the needs of his stomach, and he goes away, having accepted sufficient amounts from here and there. Just as a bird flies here and there, flying with only the burden of his feathers, so he is satisfied by having a robe to cover his body, by the collection of alms that attends the needs of his stomach, and he goes away, having accepted sufficient amounts from here and there. Thus, a *bhikkhu* is satisfied.

[6] Sections 9a–9j in the *Poṭṭhapāda Sutta* are repeated verbatim from the *Sāmaññaphala Sutta* (*Dīgha Nikāya* 1.70–73, paragraphs 65–74). Because the *Sāmaññaphala Sutta* occurs earlier in the first volume of the *Dīgha Nikāya,* the Pali Text Society editor has abridged the *Poṭṭhapāda Sutta,* referring the reader to the sections containing the same material in the *Sāmaññaphala Sutta.* Thus the page numbering (marked by an asterisk) and section numbers (given in parentheses) refer to the passage as it is appears in the *Sāmaññaphala Sutta.*

9c. (67) "In this way, by his being endowed with this noble aggregation of moral conduct,[7] with this noble restraint of the sense faculties, with this noble mindfulness and awareness, and with this noble satisfaction, he resorts to lodgings in a secluded place—in a forest, or at the root of a tree, in a mountain cave, in a gorge, in a cemetery, deep in a jungle, in the open air, or in a heap of straw. In the afternoon, having returned from his almsround, he sits down, having crossed his legs, keeping his body erect, and having caused mindfulness to be established before him.

9d. (68) "Having abandoned covetousness for the world, he lives with his mind freed from covetousness. He has purified his mind from covetousness. Abandoning ill will and anger, he lives with his mind freed of ill will. Being friendly and compassionate to all living beings, he purifies his mind of ill will and anger. Abandoning sloth and laziness, he lives without sloth or laziness. Being illuminated by awareness, mindful and attentive, he purifies his mind of sloth and laziness. Abandoning agitation and worry, he lives with an unagitated mind. Having calmed his mind internally, he purifies his mind of agitation and worry. Abandoning perplexity, he lives having crossed over from perplexity. Having no uncertainty regarding wholesome mental states, he purifies his mind of perplexity.

9e. (69) "Just as a man might undertake business incurring a debt, but [later] he might prosper in this business so that he abolishes the old root of this debt and there might even be extra money for him to maintain a wife—such a person would think: 'Formerly, I undertook a business that incurred a debt, I prospered in that business and abolished the old root of that debt, 72*
and now extra money remains to maintain a wife.' On account of this, that person would be delighted and attain happiness.

9f. (70) "Just as a person might be sick, suffering, and gravely ill, one's food giving one no pleasure, one's body possessing no strength, and, later, when freed of these illnesses, one's food giving one pleasure and one's body being strong—such a person would think: 'Formerly, I was sick, suffering, and gravely ill, my food gave me no pleasure, my body had no strength. But now I am free of these illnesses, my food gives me pleasure, and my body is strong.' On account of this, that person would be delighted and attain happiness.

9g. (71) "Just as a person might have been imprisoned in a jail and, later, is freed from bondage, living safely without any expenditure and without the loss of any of one's possessions. On account of this, such a person would be delighted and attain happiness.

9h. (72) "Just as a person might have been a slave—not independent, belonging to others, not able to go where one wants—and, later, is freed

[7] *Sīla-kkhandha.* The PED translates this as "all that belongs to moral practice."

from this enslavement, independent, does not belong to others, and is a free person who is able to go wherever one wants—such a person would think thus: "Formerly, I was a slave, not independent, belonging to others, not able to go where I want. But now I am freed from this enslavement, am independent, do not belong to others, and a freeman who is able to go wherever
73* I want.' On account of this, that person would be delighted and attain happiness.

9i. (73) "Just as a person who is wealthy, someone with property, might enter upon a road crossing through a wilderness, and, later, having crossed through the wilderness safely, without any expenditure, without the loss of any possessions—such a person would think: "Formerly, I was a person who was wealthy, someone with property, who entered upon a road crossing through a wilderness. And now I have crossed through the wilderness safely, without any expenditure, without the loss of any of my possessions.' On account of this, that person would be delighted and attain happiness.

9j. (74) "So, too, when a *bhikkhu* perceives that these five obstacles are not destroyed in himself, he sees them as a debt, as a disease, as a jail, as enslavement, as a road crossing through a wilderness. Just as one is free from debt, free from illness, released from bondage, freed from slavery, and in a peaceful country, so, too, a *bhikkhu* perceives the elimination of these five obstacles in himself.

182 10. "Gladness arises in him perceiving that these five obstacles have been eliminated in himself. From this gladness arises joy. From this joy, his body is calmed. From this calming of the body, he feels happiness. And from happiness, his mind is concentrated. Having become aloof from sensual pleasures, aloof from unwholesome mental states, he lives, having entered the first *jhāna,* which is accompanied by reasoning and cogitation, wherein there is joy and happiness born of detachment. Then for him that perception of sensual pleasure that he had previously passes away. At that time there is in him a perception of a subtle reality, joy, and happiness born of detachment. He is conscious of a perception of a subtle reality, that there is joy and happiness born of detachment in him at this time. Thus, through training, one sort of perception arises, and, through training, one sort of perception ceases.

"This is that training," said the Exalted One.

11. "Again, in a further case, by the calming of reasoning and cogitation, internally purified, a *bhikkhu* lives, having entered the second *jhāna,* which has a one-pointed mind that is devoid of reasoning and cogitation and wherein there is joy and happiness born of concentration.[8] Then for him that

[8] *Samādhi.*

perception of a subtle reality, joy, and happiness born of detachment, that he had previously passes away. At that time there is in him a perception of a subtle reality, joy, and happiness born of concentration. He is conscious of 183 a perception of a subtle reality, that joy and happiness born of concentration is in him at this time. Thus, through training, one sort of perception arises, and, through training, one sort of perception ceases.

"This is that training," said the Exalted One.

12. "Again, in a further case, dwelling in equanimity, and with the cessation of joy, mindful and fully aware, a *bhikkhu* lives, having entered the third *jhāna,* wherein he experiences happiness with the body and that which the noble ones describe as: 'He who has equanimity and mindfulness lives happily.' Then for him that perception of a subtle reality, joy, and happiness born of concentration, that he had previously passes away. Then at the time there is in him a perception of a subtle reality, equanimity, and happiness. He is conscious of a perception of a subtle reality, that there is equanimity and happiness in him at this time. Thus, through training, one sort of perception arises, and, through training, one sort of perception ceases.

"This is that training," said the Exalted One.

13. "Again, in a further case, abandoning both happiness and suffering, from the extinction of the elation and despair he felt formerly, a *bhikkhu* lives, having entered the fourth *jhāna,* wherein there is neither suffering nor happiness, but the purity of mindfulness and equanimity. And he is conscious of a perception of a subtle reality, that there is neither suffering nor happiness in him at this time. Thus, through training, one sort of perception arises, and, through training, one sort of perception ceases.

"This is that training," said the Exalted One.

14. "Again, in a further case, by passing completely beyond all perception of physicality, by extinguishing the perception of resistance, by giving no attention to the perceptions of diversity, thinking 'space is infinite,' a *bhikkhu* lives, having entered into the plane of infinite space. Then the perception of physicality that he had previously passes away. Then at that time there is in him a perception of a subtle reality, infinite space. He is conscious of a perception of a subtle reality, that there is in him at this time the plane of infinite space. Thus, through training, one sort of perception arises, and, through training, one sort of perception ceases.

"This is that training," said the Exalted One.

15. "Again, in a further case, by passing completely beyond the plane of 184 infinite space, thinking 'consciousness is infinite,' a *bhikkhu* lives, having entered into the plane of infinite consciousness. Then the perception of a subtle reality, infinite space, that he had previously passes away. At that time, there is a perception of a subtle reality, infinite consciousness. He is

conscious of a perception of a subtle reality, that there is in him at this time the plane of infinite consciousness. Thus, through training, one sort of perception arises, and, through training, one sort of perception ceases.

"This is that training," said the Exalted One.

16. "Again, in a further case, by passing completely beyond the plane of infinite consciousness, thinking 'there is not any thing,' a *bhikkhu* lives, having entered into the plane of no-thing. Then the perception of a subtle reality, infinite consciousness, he had previously passes away. At that time, there is a perception of a subtle reality, the plane of nothing. He is conscious of a perception of a subtle reality, that there is in him at this time the plane of no-thing. Thus, through training, one sort of perception arises, and, through training, one sort of perception ceases.

"This is that training," said the Exalted One.

17. "So, whenever a *bhikkhu* here is self-conscious, he then goes step-by-step until he gradually attains the summit of perception. When he has attained the summit of perception, he thinks in this way: 'Intentional thinking[9] is bad for me. It would be better for me to have no intentional thinking.' But if I were to go on producing intentional thoughts and mental constructions, these perceptions might pass away in me, but other, coarser perceptions might arise. Suppose I were not to produce intentional thoughts and mental constructions?' Thus, he neither produces intentional thoughts nor mental constructions. Then, for him, producing neither intentional thoughts nor mental constructions, these perceptions pass away, but other, coarser perceptions do not arise. He attains cessation. Thus, he attains deliberately, step-by-step, the cessation of perception.

18. "What do you think, Poṭṭhapāda? Have you heard this previously, that one attains deliberately, step-by-step, the cessation of perception?"

"No, sir. I understand it just as the Exalted One said it [*repeating verba-*
185 *tim section 17*]."

"Yes, that is right, Poṭṭhapāda."

19. "Sir, does the Exalted One declare that the summit of perception is one? Or does he declare that the summit of perception is many?"

"Poṭṭhapāda, I declare that the summit of perception is one. Also, I declare that the summit of perception is many."

"But how, sir, does the Exalted One declare that the summit of perception is one? And how does he declare that it is many?"

"According to someone's level of attainment of cessation, Poṭṭhapāda, that is how I declare the summit of perception. Thus, I declare that the summit of perception is one. Also, I declare that the summit of perception is many."

[9] *Cetayamāna.* This term refers to a faculty of choice or will.

20. "Sir, does perception arise first and afterward knowledge? Or does knowledge arise first and afterward perception? Or do both perception and knowledge arise at the same time, neither one earlier or later than the other?"

"Perception arises first, Poṭṭhapāda, then afterward knowledge. There is the arising of knowledge *from* the arising of perception. Thus, one knows 'conditioned by this, knowledge arises in me.' In this way, it should be understood that perception arises first and knowledge afterward. There is the arising of knowledge from the arising of perception."

21. "Sir, is perception the permanent Self[10] of a person? Or is perception one thing, and the permanent Self another?"

"What do you postulate[11] as the permanent Self, Poṭṭhapāda?" 186

"Sir, I postulate a coarse material self, consisting of the four great elements[12] and nourished by material food."

"But, Poṭṭhapāda, were there such a coarse material self, consisting of the four great elements and nourished by material food—that being the case—perception would be one thing, and the permanent Self would be another. From this way of thinking, one would have to infer that perception would be one thing and the permanent Self would be another. Granting a coarse material self, consisting of the four great elements and nourished by material food, yet certain perceptions arise in a person, and other perceptions pass away. From this way of thinking, then, one would have to infer that perception would be one thing and the permanent Self would be another."

22. "Sir, I postulate a mind-made self, complete with all of its components and not defective in any sense faculty."

"But, Poṭṭhapāda, were there such a mind-made self, complete with all of its components and not defective in any sense faculty—that being the case—perception would be one thing, and the permanent Self would be another. From this way of thinking, one would have to infer that perception would be one thing and the permanent Self would be another. Granting a mind-made self, complete with all of its components and not defective in any sense faculty, yet certain perceptions arise in a person, and other perceptions pass away. From this way of thinking, then, one would have to infer that perception would be one thing and the permanent Self would be another." 187

23. "Sir, I postulate an immaterial self made up of perceptions."

"But, Poṭṭhapāda, were there such an immaterial self made up of perceptions—that being the case—perception would be one thing, and the permanent Self would be another. From this way of thinking, one would have

[10] *Attā* (Skt: *ātman*).

[11] Or "take for granted."

[12] The "four great elements" are earth, water, fire, and air.

to infer that perception would be one thing and the permanent Self would be another. Granting an immaterial self made up of perceptions, yet certain perceptions arise in a person, and other perceptions pass away. From this way of thinking, then, one would have to infer that perception would be one thing and the permanent Self would be another."

24. "Is it possible, sir, for me to know this: 'perception is a person's permanent Self' or that 'perception is one thing; the permanent Self is another'?"

"It is difficult, Poṭṭhapāda, for someone like you to understand this—namely, whether 'perception is a person's permanent Self' or that 'perception is one thing; the permanent Self is another'—because you have a different view, a different faith, different inclinations, a different discipline, a different code of conduct."

25. "Sir, if this is difficult for me to understand, namely, whether 'perception is a person's permanent Self' or that 'perception is one thing; the permanent Self is another,' because I have a different view, a different faith, different inclinations, a different discipline, a different code of conduct, then tell me, sir, is the world eternal? Is this alone true, and any other view false?"

"I have not declared, Poṭṭhapāda, 'the world is eternal; this alone is true, and any other view is false.'"

"Sir, is the world not eternal? Is this alone true, and any other view false?"

"I have not declared, Poṭṭhapāda, 'the world is not eternal; this alone is true, and any other view is false.'"

"Sir, is the world finite? Is this alone true, and any other view false?"

"I have not declared, Poṭṭhapāda, 'the world is finite; this alone is true, and any other view is false.'"

188 "Sir, is the world infinite? Is this alone true, and any other view false?"

"I have not declared, Poṭṭhapāda, 'the world is infinite; this alone is true, and any other view is false.'"

26. "Sir, is the life principle[13] the same as the body? Is this alone true, and any other view false?"

"I have not declared, Poṭṭhapāda, 'the life principle is the same as the body; this alone is true, and any other view is false.'"

"Sir, is the life principle one thing, and the body another? Is this alone true, and any other view false?"

"I have not declared, Poṭṭhapāda, 'the life principle is one thing and the body another; this alone is true, and any other view is false.'"

27. "Sir, does the *Tathāgata* exist after death? Is this alone true, and any other view false?"

[13] *Jīva.* This term is sometimes translated as "soul."

"I have not declared, Poṭṭhapāda, 'the *Tathāgata* exists after death; this alone is true, and any other view is false.'"

"Sir, does the *Tathāgata* not exist after death? Is this alone true, and any other view false?"

"I have not declared, Poṭṭhapāda, 'the *Tathāgata* does not exist after death; this alone is true, and any other view is false.'"

"Sir, does the *Tathāgata* both exist and not exist after death? Is this alone true, and any other view false?"

"I have not declared, Poṭṭhapāda, 'the *Tathāgata* both exists and does not exist after death; this alone is true, and any other view is false.'"

"Sir, does the *Tathāgata* neither exist nor not exist after death? Is this alone true, and any other view false?"

"I have not declared, Poṭṭhapāda, 'the *Tathāgata* neither exists nor does not exist after death; this alone is true, and any other view is false.'"

28. "But, sir, why are these things not declared by the Exalted One?"

"Because, Poṭṭhapāda, these are not conducive to the goal, not conducive to the *dhamma,* and they do not lead to the taking up of the holy life, to 189
aversion, to dispassion, to calmness, to higher knowledge, to enlightenment, to *nibbāna.* For that reason, these things are not declared by me."

29. "But, sir, what is declared by the Exalted One?"

"'This is suffering,'[14] Poṭṭhapāda, has been declared by me. 'This is the origin of suffering' has been declared by me. 'This is the cessation of suffering' has been declared by me. 'This is the path going to the cessation of suffering' has been declared by me."

30. "But, sir, why are these things declared by the Exalted One?"

"Because, Poṭṭhapāda, these are conducive to the goal, conducive to the *dhamma,* and they do lead to the taking up of the holy life, to aversion, to dispassion, to calmness, to higher knowledge, to enlightenment, to *nibbāna.* For that reason, these things are declared by me."

"So it is, Exalted One. So it is, Well-Farer. Now it is time, sir, for the Exalted One to do what he thinks fit."

Then the Exalted One arose from his seat and went away.

31. Then right after the Exalted One had gone away, those religious wanderers abused Poṭṭhapāda from all sides, jeering at him with their words, saying: "Whatever this religious wanderer Gotama says, Poṭṭhapāda just agrees with him, saying, 'Yes, that is so, Exalted One. Yes, that is so, Well-Farer.' *We* do not know for certain what doctrine Gotama is teaching, whether: 'the world is eternal' or 'the world is not eternal'; 'the world is finite' or 'the world is infinite'; 'the life principle is the same as the body' or 'the life principle is

[14] *Dukkha.*

one thing and the body another'; 'the *Tathāgata* exists after death' or 'the
190 *Tathāgata* does not exist after death'; 'the *Tathāgata* both exists and does not exist after death' or 'the *Tathāgata* neither exists after death nor does not exist after death.'"

This having been said, Poṭṭhapāda said this to those religious wanderers: "I, too, do not know for certain what doctrine the religious wanderer Gotama is teaching [*in regard to these ten speculative views*].[15] But Gotama declares a path that is true, justified, real, accords with the *dhamma,* and lays out the *dhamma* in an orderly way. Given that Gotama declares a path that is true, justified, real, accords with the *dhamma,* and lays out the *dhamma* in an orderly way, how is it that a person like me would not agree that what was well said by the wise Gotama was indeed well said?"

32. Then, two or three days later, Citta, the son of an elephant trainer, and Poṭṭhapāda approached the Exalted One. When Citta had approached, he saluted the Exalted One and sat down to one side. Poṭṭhapāda engaged in courteous conversation with the Exalted One and, having exchanged greetings of friendship and courtesy, sat down to one side. When he was seated to one side, Poṭṭhapāda said this to the Exalted One:

"A few days ago, sir, right after the Exalted One had gone away, those religious wanderers abused me from all sides, jeering at me with their words, saying: 'Whatever this religious wanderer Gotama says, Poṭṭhapāda just agrees with him, saying, "Yes, that is so, Exalted One. Yes, that is so, Well-Farer." *We* do not know for certain what doctrine Gotama is teaching, whether: "the world is eternal" or "the world is not eternal"; "the world is finite" or "the world is infinite"; "the life principle is the same as the body" or "the life principle is one thing, and the body another"; "the *Tathāgata* exists after death" or "the *Tathāgata* does not exist after death"; "the *Tathāgata*
191 both exists and does not exist after death" or "the *Tathāgata* neither exists after death nor does not exist after death."'"

"This having been said, sir, I said this to those religious wanderers: 'I, too, do not know for certain what doctrine the religious wanderer Gotama is teaching [*in regard to the ten speculative views*].[16] But Gotama declares a path that is true, justified, real, accords with the *dhamma,* and lays out the *dhamma* in an orderly way. Given that Gotama declares a path that is true, justified, real, accords with the *dhamma,* and lays out the *dhamma* in an orderly way, how is it that a person like me would not agree that what was well said by the wise Gotama was indeed well said?'"

33. "Poṭṭhapāda, all of these religious wanderers are blind and lacking sight. You among them are the only one who has sight. There are some things

[15] In the original text, all ten views are repeated verbatim.

[16] In the original text, all ten views are repeated verbatim.

that I have declared in my teaching of the *dhamma* as certain. There are other things that I have declared in my teaching of the *dhamma* as uncertain. What are those uncertain things that I have declared as such in my teaching of the *dhamma?* [*Just these ten speculative views*].[17]

"And why, Poṭṭhapāda, are these declared as uncertain by me in my teaching of the *dhamma?* Because these are not conducive to the goal, not conducive to the *dhamma;* and they do not lead to the taking up of the holy life, to aversion, to dispassion, to calmness, to higher knowledge, to enlightenment, to *nibbāna.* For that reason, these things are not declared by me."

"But what has been declared as certain by me in my teaching of the *dhamma?* 'This is suffering' has been declared as certain by me in my teach- 192
ing of the *dhamma.* 'This is the origin of suffering.' . . . 'This is the cessation of suffering.' . . . 'This is the path going to the cessation of suffering' has been declared as certain by me in my teaching of the *dhamma.*"

"Why are these things declared as certain by me in my teaching of the *dhamma?* Because these are conducive to the goal, conducive to the *dhamma;* and they do lead to the taking up of the holy life, to aversion, to dispassion, to calmness, to higher knowledge, to enlightenment, to *nibbāna.* For that reason, these things are declared as certain by me in my teaching of the *dhamma.*

34. "There are some religious wanderers and Brahmins who speak in this way and hold the following speculative view: 'after death, the permanent Self is perfectly happy and healthy.' When I had approached them, I spoke in this way: 'Is it true, venerable sirs, that you speak in this way and hold the following speculative view: "after death, the permanent Self is perfectly happy and healthy"?' Thus questioned, they assented by saying 'yes.' Then I spoke to them in this way: 'Do you, venerable sirs, live knowing and seeing a world that is perfectly happy?' Having been asked this, they replied, 'No.' Then I spoke to them in this way: 'Have you, venerable sirs, experienced a single night or a single day, even a half of a night or half of a day in which you yourselves were perfectly happy?' Having been asked this, they replied, 'No.' Then I spoke to them in this way: 'Do you know, venerable sirs, "This is the way, this is the practice, for realizing a perfectly happy world"?' Having been asked this, they replied, 'No.' Then I spoke to them in this way: 'Have you, venerable sirs, ever heard the sounds of the voices of *devas* who have been reborn in a perfectly happy world saying: "Gentlemen, by a good and direct effort toward the goal, one may realize a perfectly happy world. Gentlemen, we have made such an effort and have been reborn in a perfectly happy world."' Having been asked this, they replied, 'No.' 193

[17] All ten views are repeated verbatim in the original text.

"What do you think, Poṭṭhapāda? That being the case, does not the talk of these religious wanderers and Brahmins turn out to be foolish?

35. "Just as a person might say: 'I desire the most beautiful girl in this whole country; I am in love with her.' Then some people might say to him: 'Good man, this most beautiful girl in the whole country that you desire and love, do you know whether this most beautiful girl is a member of the warrior-leader class[18] or a member of the Brahmin class or a member of the merchant-farmer class[19] or a member of the laborer class?'[20] But having been asked this question, he would say, 'No.' Then some people might say to him: 'Good man, this most beautiful girl in the whole country that you desire and love, do you know the name of this most beautiful girl or her clan? Whether she is tall or short? Whether she is black, dark, or has a fair complexion? Or where she lives, in which village, town, or city?' But having been asked these questions, he would say, 'No.' Then some people might say to him: 'Good man, then you neither know nor see this woman whom you desire and love?' But having been asked these questions, he would say, 'Certainly.' What do you think, Poṭṭhapāda? That being the case, does not the talk of this man turn out to be foolish?"

"Certainly, sir. That being the case, the talk of that man turns out to be foolish."

36. "In exactly the same way, Poṭṭhapāda, there are some religious wanderers and Brahmins who speak in this way and hold the speculative view that 'after death, the permanent Self is perfectly happy and healthy.' [*So I questioned them about this view in the way I just mentioned, showing them that*
194 *they do not have any knowledge that would justify such a claim.*][21]

"What do you think, Poṭṭhapāda? That being the case, does not the talk of these religious wanderers and Brahmins turn out to be foolish?"

"Certainly, sir. That being the case, the talk of these religious wanderers and Brahmins turns out to be foolish."

37. "Just as a person might build a staircase for climbing into a mansion at an intersection of four roads—some people might say to him: 'Good man, in regard to this mansion that you are building, do you know whether it will face an eastern direction, a southern direction, a western direction, or a northern direction? Or whether it will be tall, short, or of middling height?' But having been asked this question, he would say, 'No.' Then some people might ask him: 'Good man, then you neither know nor see this mansion for

[18] *Khattiya* (Skt: *kṣatriya*).

[19] *Vessa* (Skt: *vaiśya*).

[20] *Sudda* (Skt: *śūdra*).

[21] In the original text, the Buddha repeats the whole discussion he had with those religious wanderers and Brahmins exactly as in section 34.

which you are building a staircase that climbs into it?' But having been asked this question, he would say, 'Certainly.' What do you think, Poṭṭhapāda? That being the case, does not the talk of that man turn out to be foolish?"

"Certainly, sir. That being the case, the talk of that man turns out to be foolish."

38. "In exactly the same way, Poṭṭhapāda, there are some religious wanderers and Brahmins who speak in this way and hold the speculative view that 'after death, the permanent Self is perfectly happy and healthy.' [*So I questioned them about this view in the way I just mentioned, showing them that they do not have any knowledge that would justify such a claim.*][22] 195

"What do you think, Poṭṭhapāda? That being the case, does not the talk of these religious wanderers and Brahmins turn out to be foolish?"

"Certainly, sir. That being the case, the talk of these religious wanderers and Brahmins turns out to be foolish."

39. "Poṭṭhapāda, there are these three kinds of acquired self: the material acquired self, the mind-made acquired self, and the immaterial acquired self. And what is the material acquired self? It is material, composed of the four great elements and nourished by material food—this is the material acquired self. And what is the mind-made acquired self? It is mind-made, having all of its components and not lacking in any sense faculty—this is the mind-made acquired self. And what is the immaterial acquired self? It is immaterial, made up of perceptions—this is the immaterial acquired self.

40. "Poṭṭhapāda, I teach the *dhamma* for abandoning the material acquired self. Behaving in this way, your defiling mental states will pass away, 196
and your purifying mental states will increase. And then you will live here and now, having entered into the fulfillment and completion of wisdom when you have understood and realized this for yourself. It is possible that you might think in this way: 'Defiling mental states will pass away, and purifying mental states will increase. And then one will live here and now, having entered into the fulfillment and completion of wisdom that one has understood and realized for oneself—but living might still be suffering.' But that is not how it should be regarded, Poṭṭhapāda. If defiling mental states pass away and purifying mental states grow, so that one will live here and now, having entered into the fulfillment and completion of wisdom that one has understood and realized for oneself, then there will be delight, joy, calm, mindfulness, and awareness—living would be happiness.

41. "I also teach the *dhamma* for abandoning the mind-made acquired self. . . .[23]

[22] Again, the Buddha repeats the whole discussion he had with those religious wanderers and Brahmins exactly as in section 34.

[23] The remainder of the section is exactly as section 40.

42. "I also teach the *dhamma* for abandoning the immaterial acquired
197 self. . . .[24]

43. "If someone else were to ask: 'What, friend, is this material acquired self about which you teach the *dhamma* for its abandoning—a way of behaving whereby defiling mental states pass away and purifying mental states grow, so that one will live here and now, having entered into the fulfillment and completion of wisdom that one has understood and realized for oneself?' Having been asked this, we should explain the matter in this way: 'Friend, it is just *this* material acquired self about which we teach the *dhamma* for its abandoning—a way of behaving whereby defiling mental states pass away and purifying mental states grow, so that one will live here and now, having entered into the fulfillment and completion of wisdom that one has understood and realized for oneself.'

44. "If someone else were to ask: 'What is this mind-made acquired self about which you teach the *dhamma* for its abandoning?' . . . 'it is just *this* mind-made acquired self about which we teach the *dhamma* for its aban-
198 doning. . . .'

45. "If someone else were to ask: 'What is this immaterial acquired self about which you teach the *dhamma* for its abandoning?' . . . 'it is just *this* immaterial acquired self about which we teach the *dhamma* for its abandoning. . . .'

"What do you think, Poṭṭhapāda? That being the case, does not this statement turn out to be well-founded?"

"Certainly, sir. That being the case, this statement turns out to be well-founded."

46. "Poṭṭhapāda, just as a person might build a staircase for climbing into a mansion at an intersection of four roads—some people might say to him: 'Good man, in regard to this mansion that you are building, do you know whether it will face an eastern direction, a southern direction, a western direction, or a northern direction? Or whether it will be tall, short, or of middling height?' And he would reply in this way: 'Friend, the mansion, for which I am building the ascending staircase, has the staircase properly beneath it.'

"What do you think, Poṭṭhapāda? That being the case, does not this statement turn out to be well-founded?"

"Certainly, sir. That being the case, this statement turns out to be well-
199 founded."

47. "In exactly the same way, Poṭṭhapāda, if someone else were to ask us

[24] The remainder of the section is exactly as section 40.

about the material acquired self, the mind-made acquired self or the immaterial acquired self, we should reply [*in the way we just discussed.*][25]

"What do you think, Poṭṭhapada? These things being the case, do not these statements turn out to be well-founded?"

"Certainly, sir. These things being the case, these statements turn out to be well-founded."

48. This having been said, Citta, the son of an elephant trainer, said this to the Exalted One: "Sir, whenever the material acquired self exists, would it be false that the mind-made acquired self or the immaterial self exists? At that time, would there be only a material acquired self? And whenever the mind-made acquired self exists, would it be false that the material acquired self or the immaterial self exists? At that time, would there be only a mind-made acquired self? And whenever the immaterial acquired self exists, would it be false that the material acquired self or the mind-made self exists? At that time, would there be only an immaterial acquired self?"

49. "Citta, whenever the material acquired self exists, at that time, one does not refer to it as 'mind-made acquired self,' nor as 'immaterial acquired 200
self.' At that time, one refers to it only as 'material acquired self.' And whenever the mind-made acquired self exists, at that time, one does not refer to it as 'material acquired self,' nor as 'immaterial acquired self.' At that time, one refers to it only as 'mind-made acquired self.' And whenever the immaterial acquired self exists, at that time, one does not refer to it as 'material acquired self,' nor as 'mind-made acquired self.' At that time, one refers to it only as 'immaterial acquired self.'

"Citta, if someone were to ask you: 'Did you exist for a period of time in the past, or did you not exist? Will you exist for a period of time in the future, or will you not? Do you exist now, or do you not?' Being questioned in this way, Citta, how will you explain the matter?"

"Sir, if someone were to ask me: 'Did you exist for a period of time in the past, or did you not exist? Will you exist for a period of time in the future, or will you not? Do you exist now, or do you not?' Being questioned in this way, I would explain the matter in this way: 'I did exist for a period of time in the past; and it is not the case that I did not exist. I will exist for a period of time in the future; and it will not be the case that I will not exist. I do exist now; and it is not the case that I do not exist.' Having been questioned in this way, sir, that is how I would explain the matter."

50. "Citta, if someone were to ask you: 'Was your past acquired self your only true acquired self, and the future and present ones false? Or, will your future acquired self be your only true acquired self, and the past and present

[25] Exactly as sections 43–45.

ones false? Or, is your present acquired self your only true acquired self, and the past and future ones false?' Having been questioned in this way, Citta, how would you explain the matter?"

201 "Sir, if someone were to ask me: 'Was your past acquired self your only true acquired self, and the future and present ones false? Or, will your future acquired self be your only true acquired self, and the past and present ones false? Or, is your present acquired self your only true acquired self, and the past and future ones false?' Having been questioned in this way, sir, I would explain the matter in this way: 'My past acquired self *was,* at that time, my only true acquired self, and the future and present ones false. My future acquired self *will be,* at that time, my only true acquired self, and the past and present ones false. My present acquired self *is,* at this time, my only true acquired self, and the past and future ones false.' Having been questioned in this way, sir, this is how I would explain the matter."

51. "In exactly the same way, Citta, whenever the material acquired self exists, at that time, one does not refer to it as 'mind-made acquired self,' nor as 'immaterial acquired self.' At that time, one refers to it only as 'material acquired self.' And whenever the mind-made acquired self exists, at that time, one does not refer to it as 'material acquired self,' nor as 'immaterial acquired self.' At that time, one refers to it only as 'mind-made acquired self.' And whenever the immaterial acquired self exists, at that time, one does not refer to it as 'material acquired self,' nor as 'mind-made acquired self.' At that time, one refers to it only as 'immaterial acquired self.'

52. "Just as in the case of cow's milk—from the milk come curds, from the curds comes butter, from the butter comes ghee, and from the ghee comes the cream of ghee. Whenever there is milk, at that time, one does not refer to it as 'curds,' nor as 'butter,' nor as 'ghee,' nor as the 'cream of ghee.' At that time, one refers to it only as 'milk.' And whenever there are curds, at that time, one does not refer to them as 'milk,' nor as 'butter,' nor as 'ghee,' nor as the 'cream of ghee.' At that time, one refers to them only as 'curds.' Whenever there is butter, at that time, one does not refer to it as 'milk,' nor as 'curds,' nor as 'ghee,' nor as the 'cream of ghee.' At that time, one refers to it only as 'butter.' Whenever there is ghee, at that time, one does not refer to it as 'milk,' nor as 'curds,' nor as 'butter,' nor as the 'cream of ghee.' At that time, one refers to it only as 'ghee.' Whenever there is the 'cream of ghee,' at that time, one does not refer to it as 'milk,' nor as 'curds,' nor as 'butter,' nor
202 as 'ghee.' At that time, one refers to it only as the 'cream of ghee.'

53. "In exactly the same way, whenever the material acquired self exists, at that time, one does not refer to it as 'mind-made acquired self,' nor as 'immaterial acquired self.' At that time, one refers to it only as 'material acquired self.' And whenever the mind-made acquired self exists, at that

time, one does not refer to it as 'material acquired self,' nor as 'immaterial acquired self.' At that time, one refers to it only as 'mind-made acquired self.' And whenever the immaterial acquired self exists, at that time, one does not refer to it as 'material acquired self,' nor as 'mind-made acquired self.' At that time, one refers to it only as 'immaterial acquired self.'

"But such as these are only popular expressions, ordinary language, common ways of speaking, common designations, which the *Tathāgata* uses without being led astray."

54. This having been said, Poṭṭhapāda said this to the Exalted One: "Wonderful, sir! Wonderful, sir! It is just as if someone were to make upright what was turned upside down, or were to uncover what was covered over, or were to explain the way to those who are lost, or were to hold up an oil lamp in the darkness, saying, 'those endowed with eyes will see the visible objects.' Just so, the Exalted One makes known the *dhamma* by diverse methods. I, sir, go to the Exalted One for refuge and also to the *dhamma* and the *Saṅgha* of the *bhikkhus*. Let the Exalted One accept me as a lay-follower who has gone for refuge from this day forth, so long as life lasts."

55. Citta, the son of an elephant trainer, said this to the Exalted One: "Wonderful, sir! Wonderful, sir! It is just as if someone were to make upright what was turned upside down, or were to uncover what was covered over, or were to explain the way to those who are lost, or were to hold up an oil lamp in the darkness, saying, 'those endowed with eyes will see the visible objects.' Just so, the Exalted One makes known the *dhamma* by diverse methods. I, sir, go to the Exalted One for refuge and also to the *dhamma* and the *Saṅgha* of the *bhikkhus*. Sir, may I receive lower ordination[26] from the Exalted One, may I receive the higher ordination!"[27]

56. Citta received both the lower ordination and the higher ordination from the Exalted One. The venerable Citta, recently ordained, living alone, secluded, vigilant, ardent, and resolute, after only a short time achieved the goal for which young men of good families rightly go forth from home to 203
homelessness—and he lived, having entered that unsurpassed holy life, perfected in the here and now, having understood and realized it for himself. He knew "birth is destroyed, the holy life has been lived, done is what was to be done, there is nothing further to continue like this."[28] Indeed, the venerable Citta, the son of an elephant trainer, became another of the *arahants*.

26 *Pabbajjā*. Literally, "going forth."

27 *Upasampadā*. Literally, "obtained" or "attained."

28 *Itthattāyā*. That is, for such a person, there is no continuance of the *saṃsāric* round of death and rebirth.

13

Discourse on the Threefold Knowledge

(*Tevijja Sutta*)[1]

The sages of the early Upaniṣads claimed that the ultimate religious goal is to realize that one's permanent Self (*ātman*) is identical with *Brahman* (the one, underlying source of existence, Ultimate Reality). As the Upaniṣads assert, a person who knows *Brahman,* becomes *Brahman* (the "All").[2] In ritual practice and in later Vedic theology, *Brahman* came to be conceived as the god Brahmā, creator of the universe and among the highest *devas* in the Hindu pantheon. A theological form of salvation thus became available, conceived as "union with Brahmā" (*brahma-sahavyatā*), a kind of beatific relationship with this highest deity. According to the Vedic tradition, the study and mastery of the "threefold knowledge," which referred to knowledge of the three Vedas,[3] was considered a crucial step toward achieving "union with Brahmā." As the priestly class that possessed the sacred knowledge of the Vedic sacrifice, Brahmins were thought by many (and certainly by themselves) to have the inside track to this form of spiritual salvation. In this discourse, the Buddha criticizes the Brahmins for claiming to have a higher spiritual status on the basis of this specialized religious knowledge.

The discourse commences with the improbable circumstance of two Brahmins consulting the Buddha about which Brahmanical teacher has got it right as regards the path to union with Brahmā. But to the Brahmins' surprise, the Buddha makes no attempt to declare which teacher has the right teaching. Instead, the Buddha attempts to refute the claims of Brahmins to have salvific knowledge of this sort. Using arguments that could apply to many other religious traditions, the Buddha counters the Brahmins' claims to religious knowledge by emphasizing the fact that none of these Brahmins have the personal experience necessary to justify their claims. Where many religions invoke a leap of faith, the Buddha stressed that one should use personal experience to verify claims to knowledge. So the gist of the Buddha's argument is that because neither these Brahmins nor their teachers going back seven generations have ever seen Brahmā face-to-face, they should not

[1] *Dīgha Nikāya* 1.235–253.

[2] Richard Gombrich offers a very helpful discussion of the *Brahman* doctrine of the early Upaniṣads and its relationship to the *Tevijja Sutta* in *How Buddhism Began,* pp. 58–62.

[3] The original three Vedas are the *Rig Veda,* the *Sāma Veda,* and the *Yajur Veda.*

make claims about religious matters that they have not experienced for themselves. By means of a number of similes, the Buddha leads Vāseṭṭha to the conclusion that, without empirical support, the boasts of these Brahmins are no more than foolish talk.

The Buddha does not merely reject the Brahmin claim to religious precedence; he reconstructs the meanings of the phrase "union with Brahmā" and the concept "Brahmin." For the Buddha, "union with Brahmā" loses any connection to theology. These concepts are adapted to the Buddhist path by equating "union with Brahmā" with the ethics of living the holy life (*brahmacariya*) in the Buddhist sense. The noble disciple who achieves "union with Brahmā" is one who goes forth from domestic life to monastic life and fulfills the threefold training of moral conduct, mental culture, and wisdom. Such a person develops the *brahmavihāras,* Buddhism's highest virtues, namely, compassion (*karuṇā*), loving-kindness (*mettā*), sympathetic joy (*muditā*), and equanimity (*upekhā*). Regardless of social class, the person who lives the holy life to these high standards is truly a "Brahmin," according to the Buddha.

Discourse

235

1. Thus have I heard. At one time, the Exalted One was walking on tour in Kosala together with a large contingent of five hundred *bhikkhus.* He arrived at a Kosalan Brahmin village named Manasākaṭa. The Exalted One dwelled in Manasākaṭa on the north side of the village in the mango grove on the banks of the Aciravati river.

2. At that time, a large number of well-known and prosperous Brahmins lived in Manasākaṭa, such as Cankī, Tārukkha, Pokkharasāti, Jānussoni, and Todeyya, as well as other well-known and prosperous Brahmins.

3. Then Vāseṭṭha and Bhāradvāja, who were jungle-dwellers, were pacing back and forth and strolling along the road when this talk arose about the right and the wrong path.

4. The youth Vāseṭṭha said this: "This is the only straight path, the direct path—leading to salvation for one who follows it—to union with Brahmā, the one that is taught by the Brahmin Pokkharasāti."

5. The youth Bhāradvāja said this: "*This* is the only straight path, the 236
direct path—leading to salvation for one who follows it—to union with Brahmā, the one that is taught by the Brahmin Tārukkha."

6. Vāseṭṭha was not able to convince Bhāradvāja. Nor was Bhāradvāja able to convince Vāseṭṭha.

7. Then Vāseṭṭha said this to Bhāradvāja: "Bhāradvāja, the religious

wanderer Gotama, son of the Sakyas, who has gone forth from the Sakyan clan, is dwelling in Manasākaṭa on the north side of the village in the mango grove on the banks of the Aciravati river. This good report has been spread about concerning the venerable Gotama; the Exalted One is described as: 'an *arahant,* a fully awakened one, endowed with knowledge and virtue, a Well-Farer, a knower of the world, an unsurpassed charioteer of human beings who are like horses to be tamed, a teacher of *devas* and human beings, a Buddha, an Exalted One.' Let us go, good Bhāradvāja, and approach the religious wanderer Gotama. When we have approached him, we will ask Gotama about the meaning of this. However Gotama explains it, that we will accept as the truth."

"So be it," Bhāradvāja replied to Vāseṭṭha.

8. Then Vāseṭṭha and Bhāradvāja approached the Exalted One. When they had approached, they exchanged greetings with the Exalted One, conversed courteously with him, and having so conversed, sat down to one side. When they were seated to one side, Vāseṭṭha said this to the Exalted One:

"Here, master Gotama, we are jungle-dwellers, who were pacing back and forth and strolling along the road when this talk arose about the right and the wrong path. I spoke in this way: 'This is the only straight path, the direct path—leading to salvation for one who follows it—to union with Brahmā, the one that is taught by the Brahmin Pokkharasāti.' But Bhāradvāja spoke in this way: '*This* is the only straight path, the direct path—leading to salvation for one who follows it—to union with Brahmā, the one that is taught by the Brahmin Tārukkha.' In this case, master Gotama, there is a dispute,
237 a quarrel, regarding our different views."

9. "Vāseṭṭha, you say that: 'This is the only straight path, the direct path —leading to salvation for one who follows it—to union with Brahmā, the one that is taught by the Brahmin Pokkharasāti.' But Bhāradvāja spoke in this way: '*This* is the only straight path, the direct path—leading to salvation for one who follows it—to union with Brahmā, the one that is taught by the Brahmin Tārukkha.' So what, then, Vāseṭṭha, is the dispute? What is the quarrel? How do you hold different views?"

10. "It concerns right and wrong paths, master Gotama. Various Brahmins declare different paths—for example, the Brahmins Addhariyā, Tittiriyā, Chandokā, Chandāvā, and those Brahmins who live the holy life. But do all of these paths lead out to salvation for one who follows them, to union with Brahmā? Just as many different paths near a village or town all meet in the center of the village, is it similarly the case that the different paths declared by the various Brahmins—for example, the Brahmins Addhariyā, Tittiriyā, Chandokā, Chandāvā, and those Brahmins who live the holy life—all of these paths lead out to salvation for one who follows them, to union with Brahmā?"

11. "'They lead out,'[4] you said, Vāseṭṭha?"
"'They lead out,' master Gotama, I say."
"'They lead out,' you said, Vāseṭṭha?"
"'They lead out,' master Gotama, I say."
"'They lead out,' you said, Vāseṭṭha?"
"'They lead out,' master Gotama, I say." 238

12. "How is it, Vāseṭṭha? Is there even one of these Brahmins who possesses the threefold (Vedic) knowledge[5] who has seen Brahmā face-to-face?"

"No, master Gotama."

"How is it, Vāseṭṭha? Is there even a single teacher of these Brahmins who possesses the threefold knowledge who has seen Brahmā face-to-face?"

"No, master Gotama."

"How is it, Vāseṭṭha? Is there even a single teacher's teacher of these Brahmins who possesses the threefold knowledge who has seen Brahmā face-to-face?"

"No, master Gotama."

"How is it, Vāseṭṭha? Is there even a great ancestor of the teachers of these Brahmins who possesses the threefold knowledge going back seven generations who has seen Brahmā face-to-face?"

"No, master Gotama."

13. "How is it, Vāseṭṭha? Are there earlier sages of these Brahmins who possess the threefold knowledge, creators of the mantras, pronouncers of the mantras, whose ancient mantras and songs Brahmins possessing the threefold knowledge still sing and recite today, reciting and repeating their sayings—such as Aṭṭhaka, Vāmaka, Vāmadeva, Vessāmitta, Yamataggi, Aṅgiraso, Bhāradvāja, Vaseṭṭha, Kassapa, and Bhagu—did they speak thus: 'We know and see when, how, and where Brahmā appears'?"

"No, master Gotama."

14. "So, Vāseṭṭha, not one of the Brahmins who possesses the threefold knowledge has seen Brahmā face-to-face, not a single teacher of these Brahmins who possesses the threefold knowledge has seen Brahmā face-to-face, not a single teacher's teacher of these Brahmins who possesses the threefold
knowledge has seen Brahmā face-to-face, not a great ancestor of the teach- 239
ers of these Brahmins who possesses the threefold knowledge going back seven generations has seen Brahmā face-to-face, not even earlier sages of these Brahmins who possess the threefold knowledge, creators of the mantras,

[4] *Nīyyanti* (Skt: *niryāti*). This word means "they lead out (of *saṃsāra*)." The repetition of the question seems to mean: "are you really sure?"

[5] Intensive study of the original three Vedas (*Rig Veda, Sāma Veda,* and *Yajur Veda*) was an essential part of the training of a Brahmin. The knowledge in these sacred texts was thought to have saving power.

pronouncers of the mantras, whose ancient mantras and songs Brahmins possessing the threefold knowledge still sing and recite today, reciting and repeating their sayings—such as Aṭṭhaka, Vāmaka, Vāmadeva, Vessāmitta, Yamataggi, Aṅgiraso, Bhāradvāja, Vaseṭṭha, Kassapa, and Bhagu—they did not speak thus: 'We know and see when, how, and where Brahmā appears.' And yet those Brahmins who possess the threefold knowledge speak thus: 'We teach the way to this union (with Brahmā) which we do not know and do not see: This is the only straight path, the direct path—leading to salvation for one who follows it—to union with Brahmā.'

"What do you think, Vāseṭṭha? That being the case, does not the talk of those Brahmins who possess the threefold knowledge turn out to be foolish?"

"Certainly, master Gotama. That being the case, the talk of those Brahmins who possess the threefold knowledge turns out to be foolish."

15. "Well, then, Vāseṭṭha, there is no basis for the claim of the Brahmins who possess the threefold knowledge, who teach the way to a union (with Brahmā) that they neither know nor see; and yet they say: 'This is the only straight path, the direct path—leading to salvation for one who follows it—to union with Brahmā.' Just as a string of blind people in a line clinging to one another—neither the first one sees, nor the middle one sees, nor the last one sees. Just as in the case of the string of blind people, so it is with the talk of those Brahmins who possess the threefold knowledge—neither the first
240 one sees, nor the middle one sees, nor the last one sees. The talk of those Brahmins who possess the threefold knowledge turns out to be laughable. It turns out to be words only, empty and vain.

16. "What do you think, Vāseṭṭha? Do those Brahmins who possess the threefold knowledge see the moon and the sun as the mass of other people do? Do they go to pray, holding up clasped hands in veneration toward the places where the moon and the sun rise and set?"

"Yes, master Gotama. The Brahmins who possess the threefold knowledge see the moon and the sun as the mass of other people do. They go to pray, holding up clasped hands in veneration toward the places where the moon and the sun rise and set."

17. "What do you think, Vāseṭṭha? On the basis of the fact that those Brahmins who possess the threefold knowledge see the moon and the sun as the mass of other people do, and they go to pray, holding up clasped hands in veneration toward the places where the moon and the sun rise and set, are they able to teach union with the moon and the sun, saying: 'This is the only straight path, the direct path—leading to salvation for one who follows it—to union with the moon and the sun'?"

"No, master Gotama."

18. "So it is, Vāseṭṭha, that those Brahmins who possess the threefold knowledge see the moon and the sun as the mass of other people do, and they go to pray, holding up clasped hands in veneration toward the places where the moon and the sun rise and set, yet they are not able to teach union with the moon and the sun, saying: 'This is the only straight path, the direct path—leading to salvation for one who follows it—to union with the moon and the sun'—and not one of the Brahmins who possesses the threefold knowledge has seen Brahmā face-to-face, not a single teacher of those Brahmins who possess the threefold knowledge has seen Brahmā face-to-face, not a single teacher's teacher of those Brahmins who possesses the threefold 241
knowledge has seen Brahmā face-to-face, not a great ancestor of the teachers of those Brahmins who possesses the threefold knowledge going back seven generations has seen Brahmā face-to-face, not even earlier sages of these Brahmins who possess the threefold knowledge, creators of the mantras, pronouncers of the mantras, whose ancient mantras and songs Brahmins possessing the threefold knowledge still sing and recite today, reciting and repeating their sayings—such as Aṭṭhaka, Vāmaka, Vāmadeva, Vessāmitta, Yamataggi, Aṅgiraso, Bhāradvāja, Vaseṭṭha, Kassapa, and Bhagu—they did not speak thus: 'We know and see when, how, and where Brahmā appears.' And yet those Brahmins who possess the threefold knowledge speak thus: 'We teach the way to this union (with Brahmā) which we do not know and do not see: "This is the only straight path, the direct path—leading to salvation for one who follows it—to union with Brahmā."'

"What do you think, Vāseṭṭha? That being the case, does not the talk of those Brahmins who possess the threefold knowledge turn out to be foolish?"

"Certainly, master Gotama. That being the case, the talk of those Brahmins who possess the threefold knowledge turns out to be foolish."

"Good, Vāseṭṭha. Indeed, there is no basis for the claim of the Brahmins who possess the threefold knowledge, who teach the way to a union (with Brahmā) that they neither know nor see; and yet they say: 'This is the only straight path, the direct path—leading to salvation for one who follows it—to union with Brahmā.'

19. "Just as a person might say: 'I desire the most beautiful girl in this whole country; I am in love with her.' Then some people might say to him: 'Good man, this most beautiful girl in the whole country that you desire and love, do you know whether this most beautiful girl is a member of the warrior-leader class or a member of the Brahmin class or a member of the merchant-farmer class or a member of the laborer class?' But having been asked this question, he would say 'No.' Then some people might say to him: 'Good man, this most beautiful girl in the whole country that you desire and love, do you know the name of this most beautiful girl or her clan? Whether she 242

is tall or short? Whether she is black or dark or has a fair complexion? Or where she lives, in which village, town, or city?' But having been asked these questions, he would say 'No.' Then some people might say to him: 'Good man, then you neither know nor see this woman whom you desire and love?' But having been asked these questions, he would say 'Certainly.' What do you think, Vāseṭṭha? That being the case, does the talk of this man turn out to be foolish?"

"Certainly, master Gotama. That being the case, the talk of that man turns out to be foolish."

20. "Then, Vāseṭṭha, it is surely the same in this case. Not one of the Brahmins who possesses the threefold knowledge has seen Brahmā face-to-face. . . . And yet those Brahmins who possess the threefold knowledge speak thus: 'We teach the way to this union (with Brahmā) that we neither know nor see, saying: "This is the only straight path, the direct path—leading to salvation for one who follows it—to union with Brahmā."'

"What do you think, Vāseṭṭha? That being the case, does not the talk of those Brahmins who possess the threefold knowledge turn out to be foolish?"

"Certainly, master Gotama. That being the case, the talk of those Brahmins who possess the threefold knowledge turns out to be foolish."

"Good, Vāseṭṭha. Indeed, there is no basis for the claim of the Brahmins who possess the threefold knowledge, who teach the way to a union (with
243 Brahmā) that they neither know nor see, saying: 'This is the only straight path, the direct path—leading to salvation for one who follows it—to union with Brahmā.'

21. "Just as a person might build a staircase for climbing into a mansion at an intersection of four roads—some people might say to him: 'Good man, in regard to this mansion that you are building, do you know whether it will face an eastern direction, a southern direction, a western direction, or a northern direction? Or whether it will be tall or short or of middling height?' But having been asked this question, he would say 'No.' Then some people might ask him: 'Good man, then you neither know nor see this mansion for which you are building a staircase that climbs into it?' But having been asked this question, he would say 'Certainly.' What do you think, Vāseṭṭha? That being the case, does the talk of that man turn out to be foolish?"

"Certainly, master Gotama. That being the case, the talk of that man turns out to be foolish."

22. "It is surely the same in this case, Vāseṭṭha. Not one of the Brahmins who possesses the threefold knowledge has seen Brahmā face-to-face. . . . And yet those Brahmins who possess the threefold knowledge speak thus: 'We teach the way to this union (with Brahmā) that we do not know and do

not see: "This is the only straight path, the direct path—leading to salvation 244
for one who follows it—to union with Brahmā."'

"What do you think, Vāseṭṭha? That being the case, does not the talk of those Brahmins who possess the threefold knowledge turn out to be foolish?"

"Certainly, master Gotama. That being the case, the talk of those Brahmins who possess the threefold knowledge turns out to be foolish."

23. "Good, Vāseṭṭha. Indeed, there is no basis for the claim of the Brahmins who possess the threefold knowledge, who teach the way to a union (with Brahmā) that they neither know nor see; and yet they say: 'This is the only straight path, the direct path—leading to salvation for one who follows it—to union with Brahmā.'

24. "Just as this Aciravati river might be full of water right up to the brim,[6] then a man might come to the river wishing to cross over, to go across, desiring to go to the other shore. If he were to call out to the farther shore while standing on the near shore: 'Come here, other shore! Come here, other shore!' What do you think, Vāseṭṭha? Would his calling out, his request, his wishing, or his attempt to please serve as a cause that would cause the farther shore of the Aciravati river to come to the near shore?"

"No, master Gotama."

25. "In the same way, Vāseṭṭha, those Brahmins who possess the threefold knowledge have abandoned in the present those things that make one truly a Brahmin and have instigated in the present those things that make one a non-Brahmin. They say: 'We call on Indra, we call upon Soma, we call upon Varuna, we call upon Isāna, we call upon Prajāpati, we call upon Brahmā, we call upon Mahiddhi, and we call upon Yama.' But there is no basis to be found in the claims of those Brahmins who possess the threefold
knowledge, for they have abandoned in the present those things that make 245
one truly a Brahmin and have instigated in the present those things that make one a non-Brahmin—using such causes as calling out, requesting, wishing, and attempting to please with the intention that at the breaking up of the body after death, they will achieve union with Brahmā.

26. "Just as this Aciravati river might be full of water right up to the brim, then a man might come to the river wishing to cross over, to go across, desiring to go to the other shore. And he might be standing firmly on the near shore, bound with his hands tied behind his back with tightly fastened bonds. What do you think, Vāseṭṭha? Would such a person be able to go from the near shore of the Aciravati river to the farther shore?"

[6] *Kākapeyyā.* According to the PED, this term literally means that the river was so full that "a crow might easily drink from it."

"No, master Gotama."

27. "In the same way, Vāseṭṭha, these five characteristics of sensual pleasure are called 'fetters' or 'bonds' in the noble discipline. Which five? Material forms cognizable by the eye that are pleasing, agreeable, charming, enticing, accompanied by desire, and leading to lust. Sounds cognizable by the ear . . . Smells cognizable by the nose . . . Tastes cognizable by the tongue . . . Tangible things cognizable by the body that are pleasing, agreeable, charming, enticing, accompanied by desire, and leading to lust. These are the five characteristics of sensual pleasure that the Brahmins who possess the threefold knowledge enjoy, are bound by, are infatuated with, are guilty of, do not see the danger in, and know no escape from.

28. "Indeed, there is no basis to be found for the claim of those Brahmins who possess the threefold knowledge, because they have abandoned in
246 the present those things that make one truly a Brahmin and have instigated in the present those things that make one a non-Brahmin. These are the five characteristics of sensual pleasure that the Brahmins who possess the threefold knowledge enjoy, are bound by, are infatuated with, are guilty of, do not see the danger in, and know no escape from. Being trapped by chasing after sensual pleasures, at the breaking up of the body after death, they still believe there will be a "union with Brahmā"—but that is not possible.

29. "Just as this Aciravati river might be full of water right up to the brim, then a man might come to the river wishing to cross over, to go across, desiring to go to the other shore. This man, having covered himself up to his head, might lie down on the near shore. What do you think, Vāseṭṭha? Would this man be able to go to the farther bank of the Aciravati river from this near bank?"

"No, master Gotama."

30. "In the same way, Vāseṭṭha, according to the noble discipline there are these five obstacles that are called 'hindrances' or 'obstacles' or 'entanglements' or 'coverings.' What are the five? The obstacle of sensual pleasure, the obstacle of ill will, the obstacle of sloth and torpor, the obstacle of worry and agitation, and the obstacle of perplexity. These are the five obstacles according to the noble discipline that are called 'hindrances' or 'obstacles' or 'entanglements' or 'coverings.' Those Brahmins who possess the threefold knowledge are veiled in, enveloped by, covered over with, and entangled in these five obstacles. Indeed, those Brahmins who possess the threefold knowledge have abandoned in the present those things that make one truly a Brahmin and have instigated in the present those things that make one a non-Brahmin. Being veiled in, enveloped by, covered over with, and entangled in these five obstacles, there is no basis to be found for the claim that, at the breaking up
247 of the body after death, they will achieve union with Brahmā.

31. "What do you think, Vāseṭṭha? What have you heard spoken by the venerable old Brahmins, the teacher's teacher? Is Brahmā married or not married?"

"Not married, master Gotama."

"Does he have a mind filled with hatred, or is his mind free of hatred?"

"His mind is free of hatred, master Gotama."

"Does he have a mind filled with ill will, or is ill will absent from his mind?"

"Ill will is absent from his mind, master Gotama."

"Does he have a mind filled with impurities, or is his mind without impurities?"

"His mind is without impurities, master Gotama."

"Is he powerful or powerless?"

"Powerful, master Gotama."

32. "What do you think, Vāseṭṭha? Are the Brahmins who possess the threefold knowledge married or not married?"

"Married, master Gotama."

"Do they have minds filled with hatred, or are their minds free of hatred?"

"Their minds are filled with hatred, master Gotama."

"Do they have minds filled with ill will, or is ill will absent from their minds?"

"They have minds filled with ill will, master Gotama."

"Do they have minds filled with impurities, or are their minds without impurities?"

"Their minds are filled with impurities, master Gotama."

"Are they powerful or powerless?"

"Powerless, master Gotama."

33. "So it is, Vāseṭṭha, the Brahmins who possess the threefold knowledge are married, but Brahmā is unmarried. Do you suppose that there is a uniting and coming together between the Brahmins who possess the threefold knowledge who are married and Brahmā who is unmarried?"

"No, master Gotama."

34. "Good, Vāseṭṭha. Indeed, there is no basis to be found for the claim
of those married Brahmins who possess the threefold knowledge that, at the
breaking up of the body after death, they will achieve union with the unmar- 248
ried Brahmā.

35. "It is also the case that the Brahmins who possess the threefold knowledge have minds filled with hatred . . . minds filled with ill will . . . minds filled with impurities . . . [and] are powerless, but the mind of Brahmā is without hatred . . . ill will is absent from his mind . . . his mind is without impurities . . . [and] is powerful. Do you suppose that there is a uniting and

coming together between the Brahmins who possess the threefold knowledge whose minds are filled with hatred and Brahmā whose mind is without hatred . . . between the Brahmins whose minds are filled with ill will and Brahmā in whose mind ill will is absent . . . between the Brahmins whose minds are filled with impurities and Brahmā whose mind is without impurities . . . [and] between the Brahmins who are powerless and Brahmā who is powerful?"

"No, master Gotama."

36. "Good, Vāseṭṭha. Indeed, there is no basis to be found for the claim of those Brahmins who possess the threefold knowledge who are powerless that at the breaking up of the body after death that they will achieve union with Brahmā whose mind is without hatred . . . in whose mind ill will is absent . . . whose mind is without impurities . . . [and] is powerful.

"In this connection, Vāseṭṭha, those Brahmins who possess the threefold knowledge, having sat down together (on the bank of the river), they sink down into it; and having sunk down into it, they arrive at despair trying to think of a dry way (across the river). Therefore, the threefold knowledge of those Brahmins is called a 'desert of threefold knowledge,' a 'jungle of threefold knowledge,' a 'desolation of threefold knowledge.'"

37. This having been said, Vāseṭṭha said this to the Exalted One: "I have heard this, master Gotama: 'The religious wanderer Gotama knows the way to union with Brahmā.'"

"What do you think, Vāseṭṭha? Is this place near Manasākaṭa? Is it not far from Manasākaṭa?"

"Yes, master Gotama. This place is near Manasākaṭa and not far from it."

"What do you think, Vāseṭṭha? Consider the case of a person who was
249 born in Manasākaṭa and grew up there. If some people were to ask that person (who had never left Manasākaṭa) which was the road to Manasākaṭa, will that person who was born in Manasākaṭa and grew up there be confused and perplexed by such a question?"

"No, master Gotama. And what is the reason for this? That person, master Gotama, was born and grew up in Manasākaṭa, so all the roads of Manasākaṭa would be well-known to that person."

38. "That person, Vāseṭṭha, who was born and grew up in Manasākaṭa, may be confused or perplexed about the question in regard to the road to Manasākaṭa, but the *Tathāgata* is neither confused nor perplexed in regard to the questions about the world of Brahmā or regarding the path of conduct that leads to the world of Brahmā. I know Brahmā, the world of Brahmā, and the path of conduct leading to the world of Brahmā. I know even those who have entered the path leading to the world of Brahmā and those who have already been reborn there."

39. This having been said, Vāseṭṭha said this to the Exalted One: "I have heard this, master Gotama: 'The religious wanderer Gotama knows the way to union with Brahma.' It would be good if master Gotama were to teach the way to union with Brahmā. Let master Gotama help the offspring of Brahmā."

"Then listen to this, Vāseṭṭha. Keep your mind attentive, and I will speak."

"Yes, sir," Vāseṭṭha replied to the Exalted One. Then the Exalted One said this:

40. "Here, Vāseṭṭha, a *Tathāgata* arises in this world, an *arahant,* a fully awakened one, perfected in knowledge and virtue, a Well-Farer, a knower of the world, an unsurpassed charioteer of human beings who are to be tamed, a teacher of *devas* and human beings, a Buddha, an Exalted One. He makes
known this world—with its *devas,* Māras, Brahmās, including religious wan- 250
derers and Brahmins—to the present generation of *devas* and human beings, having understood and realized this for himself. He teaches the *dhamma,* which is beautiful in the beginning, beautiful in the middle, and beautiful in the end, in spirit as well as in letter. He makes known the pure religious life that is complete in its entirety.

41. "A householder, or the son of a householder, or a man of low birth from any of the other classes, listens to this *dhamma.* Having listened to it, he develops a faith in the *Tathāgata.* Endowed with this faith he has developed, he reasons: 'The household life is a hindrance, a defiled path, whereas going forth is like fresh air.[7] It is not easy to achieve the fullness of perfection and purity while living a household, settled life. It is a fetter to living the holy life. So, having shaved off my hair and beard and having clothed myself in orange robes, let me go forth from home to homelessness.' Later, whether he abandons a small or large amount of wealth, whether he leaves a small or large circle of family, he shaves off his hair and beard, clothes himself in orange robes and goes forth from home to homelessness.

42. "Having gone forth in this way, he dwells bringing himself under control through the monastic rules.[8] Endowed with proper conduct toward objects of sense, he takes up the training to abstain from them, seeing danger in even small affairs. By observing the training, he is endowed with wholesome actions of the body and speech. By guarding well the senses and faculties and developing the foundations of mindfulness, he has a pure livelihood, and is virtuous and happy.

[7] Literally, "open space."

[8] *Pātimokkha.* This term refers to the more than two hundred rules for the *Saṅgha* that are described in the *Vinaya Piṭaka.* They are chanted fortnightly (at new and full moons) by the *bhikkhus* in assembly.

43. "How, Vāseṭṭha, is a *bhikkhu* perfected in moral conduct? . . .[9]

76. "[This *bhikkhu*] dwells having pervaded one direction with a mind
251 endowed with loving-kindness, then a second direction, then a third direction, then a fourth direction. Likewise upwards, downwards, crosswise, everywhere in all ways and to the furthest extent, he dwells having pervaded the whole world with a mind endowed with loving-kindness—filled with it, grown great by it, boundless in it, without hatred and ill will.

77. "Just as a strong blower of the conch shell might, with little effort, be heard in all four directions, thus, a mind that is freed by the development of loving-kindness will set an example by leaving nothing in this world untouched or unaffected. This is the way to union with Brahmā.

78. "And at another time, a *bhikkhu* dwells having pervaded one direction with a mind endowed with compassion . . . with sympathetic joy . . . with equanimity, then a second direction, then a third direction, then a fourth direction. Likewise upward, downward, crosswise, everywhere in all ways and to the furthest extent, he dwells having pervaded the whole world with a mind endowed with compassion . . . with sympathetic joy . . . with equanimity—filled with it, grown great by it, boundless in it, without hatred and ill will.

79. "Just as a strong blower of the conch shell might, with little effort, be heard in all four directions, thus, a mind that is freed by the development of compassion . . . with sympathetic joy . . . with equanimity will set an example by leaving nothing in this world untouched or unaffected. This is the way to union with Brahmā.

80. "What do you think, Vāseṭṭha? Is the *bhikkhu* who lives in this way married or unmarried?"

"Unmarried, master Gotama."

"Does he have a mind filled with hatred, or is his mind without hatred?"

"His mind is without hatred, master Gotama."

"Does he have a mind filled with ill will, or is ill will absent from his mind?"

"Ill will is absent from his mind, master Gotama."

"Does he have a mind filled with impurities, or is his mind without impurities?"

"His mind is without impurities, master Gotama."

"Is he powerful or powerless?"

[9] Sections 43–75 repeat the sections on morality found in several of the early discourses of the *Dīgha Nikāya.* In the Pali Text Society edition of the *Dīgha Nikāya,* the passage is given in full in the *Sāmaññaphala Sutta,* but is abridged in this discourse. A portion of this material (paragraphs 66–75) is contained in the Discourse to Poṭṭhapāda. See paragraphs 9a–9j in Chapter 12.

"Powerful, master Gotama." 252

81. "So it is, Vāseṭṭha, that a *bhikkhu* is unmarried and Brahmā is unmarried. Do you suppose there is a uniting and coming together between a *bhikkhu* who is unmarried and Brahmā who is unmarried?"

"Yes, master Gotama."

"Good, Vāseṭṭha. Indeed, there is a basis for the claim of the unmarried *bhikkhu* that at the breaking up of the body after death that he will achieve union with Brahmā."

"So it is that a *bhikkhu* has a mind without hatred . . . ill will is absent from his mind . . . a mind without impurities . . . [and] is powerful, and Brahmā has a mind without hatred . . . ill will is absent from his mind . . . a mind without impurities . . . [and] is powerful. Do you suppose there is a uniting and coming together between a *bhikkhu* whose mind is without hatred and Brahmā whose mind is without hatred . . . between a *bhikkhu* in whose mind ill will is absent and Brahmā in whose mind ill will is absent . . . between a *bhikkhu* whose mind is without impurities and Brahmā whose mind is without impurities . . . [and] between a *bhikkhu* who is powerful and Brahmā who is powerful?"

"Yes, master Gotama."

"Good, Vāseṭṭha. Indeed, there is a basis to be found for the claim of the *bhikkhu* who has a mind without hatred . . . a mind where ill will is absent . . . a mind without impurities . . . is powerful, that at the breaking up of the body after death he will achieve union with Brahmā."

This having been said, Vāseṭṭha and Bhāradvāja said this to the Exalted One: "Wonderful, Gotama! Wonderful, Gotama! It is just as if someone were to make upright what was turned upside down, or were to uncover what was covered over, or were to explain the way to those who are lost, or were to hold up an oil lamp in the darkness, saying, 'those endowed with eyes will see the visible objects.' Just so, the Exalted One makes known the *dhamma* by diverse methods. We go to master Gotama for refuge and also to the *dhamma* and the *Saṅgha* of the *bhikkhus*. Let master Gotama accept us as lay-followers who have gone for refuge from this day forth, so long as life lasts."

14

Discourse to Assalāyana

(*Assalāyana Sutta*)[1]

This discourse presents several significant pieces of the Buddha's social philosophy, including the arguments against class hierarchy and the rejection of the Brahmin claim to class superiority. Although most societies today do not have social classes making claims to class precedence in the way the Brahmins did in the Buddha's time, class hierarchy is most certainly a present-day reality in almost all societies. The Buddha's arguments against class hierarchy, therefore, are very much relevant to issues regarding social class today.

Some scholars have portrayed the Buddha as recommending a classless society. To the extent that the classless and democratically structured *Saṅgha* represents a social ideal for any community, such interpretations may have some merit. But there is no definitive reason why lay society should be modeled on monastic social structure. In fact, the Buddha himself repeatedly referred to the four social classes (*vaṇṇā*)[2] of traditional Indian society, and throughout the vastness of the Pāli Canon there is no argument that criticizes this fourfold social structure for society in general. In other words, the Buddha's criticism of the class system in lay society does not target social division as such, but only the claims to precedence espoused by certain classes, most notably the claims of the Brahmins.

From the Buddha's perspective, social classes are functional ways to divide up the activities required to serve the needs of people. This functionalist position differs dramatically from the Brahmanical understanding that social class is determined by birth, and that birth, in turn, is karmically determined by the moral or spiritual qualities of the person formed by actions in prior births.

The Buddha did, of course, accept the law of karma (Pāli: *kamma*). According to the law of karma, one's future state of being is a product of one's actions. And yet, the Buddha denied that membership in a social class is indicative of karmic merit or demerit. This fact can be demonstrated, argues the Buddha in this discourse, by realizing that the moral qualities of actions, including the effects of such actions as determined by the law of

[1] *Majjhima Nikāya* 2.147–157.

[2] See *Dīgha Nikāya* 3.82.

karma, differ not at all among any of the four classes. In this way, the Buddha's arguments do more than criticize the Brahmin claim to class superiority; they are also attempts to refute any stratification of the social classes in terms of moral superiority.

The Brahmins' claim to class precedence based on birth derives in part from the *Puruṣa Sūkta*[3] in the *Rig Veda.* This Vedic passage describes the birth of the Brahmin class from the mouth of *Puruṣa,* the Cosmic Person. As the Brahmanical tradition developed, *Puruṣa* was replaced by Brahmā, the highest of all gods, thus explaining the Brahmins' claim in the Buddha's day that they are born of the mouth of Brahmā. In this discourse, the Buddha ridicules this Brahmin claim of a special birth from the mouth of God. After all, Brahmins are born in precisely the same way as people of other classes.

The Buddha attacks the Brahmins' claims to superiority by birth on two further grounds. First, he points out the difficulties of classifying children of mixed parentage, arguing that, were we to accept the Brahmin view, the existence of such children would be nearly as impossible as breeding between two different species. Second, since membership in the Brahmin class requires class purity going back seven generations and this is virtually impossible to verify, how could anyone know that he or she is in fact a Brahmin?

Discourse

1. Thus have I heard. At one time, the Exalted One was dwelling at Sāvatthi in the Jeta Grove at Anāthapiṇḍika's park. At that time, five hundred Brahmins from various regions were living at Sāvatthi on some sort of business. Then this thought occurred to those Brahmins: "This religious wanderer Gotama declares the purity of the four classes. Now, who would be able to dispute this claim with the religious wanderer Gotama?" 147

At that time, a certain young Brahmin by the name of Assalāyana was living at Sāvatthi. He was young, about sixteen years old, had a shaven head, and was a master of the three Vedas (with their vocabularies, ritual, division of syllables, etymology, and the histories as the fifth). Skilled as a reciter of the Veda[4] and grammar, he was well-versed in secular subjects and in the marks of a Great Person.[5] Then this thought occurred to those Brahmins: "This youth Assalāyana is young, is sixteen years old, has a shaven head, is

[3] *Rig Veda* 10.90.

[4] *Padako.* According to the PED, "versed in the *padapāṭha* of the Veda."

[5] According to ancient Indian tradition, a "Great Person"—a person destined for greatness as a political or spiritual leader—could be recognized as such by thirty-two marks on the body. The Buddha was said to have these marks. See the *Lakkhaṇa Sutta* for a further discussion of

a master of the Three Vedas. He is skilled in philology and grammar, and well-versed in science and in the marks of a Great Person. He would be able to dispute this claim with the religious wanderer Gotama."

Then those Brahmins approached the youth Assalāyana. When they had approached him, they said this to Assalāyana: "Assalāyana, this religious wanderer Gotama declares the purity of the four classes. Let master Assalāyana go and dispute this claim with the religious wanderer Gotama."

After this was said, Assalāyana said this to those Brahmins: "Surely, sirs, Gotama is one who speaks the *dhamma.* Those who speak the *dhamma* are difficult to dispute with. I am not able to dispute the claim with Gotama."

A second time, those Brahmins said this to Assalāyana: "Assalāyana, this religious wanderer Gotama declares the purity of the four classes. Let master Assalāyana go and dispute this claim with the religious wanderer Gotama.
148 Master Assalāyana lives the life of a religious wanderer."

And a second time, Assalāyana said this to those Brahmins: "Surely, sirs, Gotama is one who speaks the *dhamma.* Those who speak the *dhamma* are difficult to dispute with. I am not able to dispute the claim with Gotama."

A third time, those Brahmins said this to Assalāyana: "Assalāyana, this religious wanderer Gotama declares the purity of the four classes. Let master Assalāyana go and dispute this claim with the religious wanderer Gotama. Master Assalāyana lives the life of a religious wanderer. Do not be defeated without fighting the battle."

2. After this was said, Assalāyana said this to those Brahmins: "Surely, sirs, I am not able to do this. Gotama is one who speaks the *dhamma.* Those who speak the *dhamma* are difficult to dispute with. I am not able to dispute the claim with Gotama. Yet I will go at the behest of the venerable ones."

3. Then Assalāyana, together with a large contingent of Brahmins, approached the Exalted One. When he had approached him, he exchanged courteous greetings with the Exalted One. Having exchanged courteous greetings and having made amiable conversation, he sat down to one side. When he was seated to one side, Assalāyana said this to the Exalted One: "Brahmins, master Gotama, have spoken thus: 'Brahmins are the highest class. Those who belong to other classes are inferior. Brahmins are a fair color. Those who belong to other classes are dark. Brahmins are pure, whereas non-Brahmins are not. Brahmins are the legitimate sons of Brahmā, born of the mouth of Brahmā, created by Brahmā, and heirs to Brahmā.' What does master Gotama say about this?"

---

these thirty-two marks (*Dīgha Nikāya* 3.143–145; for an English translation of this passage, see Maurice Walshe, *The Long Discourses of the Buddha: A Translation of the Dīgha Nikāya* (Kandy, Sri Lanka: Buddhist Publication Society, 1996), pp. 441–442.

4. "Assalāyana, Brahmin women are seen to menstruate, be pregnant, bring forth children, and nurse them. And yet how is it that these Brahmins who are also born from wombs just like others have spoken thus: 'Brahmins are the highest class. Those who belong to other classes are inferior. Brahmins are a fair color. Those who belong to other classes are dark. Brahmins are pure, whereas non-Brahmins are not. Brahmins are the legitimate sons of Brahmā, born of the mouth of Brahmā, created by Brahmā, and heirs to
Brahmā'?" 149

"Although master Gotama says this, still the Brahmins think in this way: 'Brahmins are the highest class. . . .'"

5. "What do you think, Assalāyana? Have you heard that in Yona and Kamboja, and in other bordering countries, there are two classes, masters and slaves, and that masters have become slaves and slaves have become masters?"

"Yes, sir, I have heard that in Yona and Kamboja, and in other bordering countries, there are two classes, masters and slaves, and that masters have become slaves and slaves have become masters."

"Then, in this connection, Assalāyana, on what strength of argument and by whose authority do the Brahmins speak thus: 'Brahmins are the highest class . . .'?"

"Although master Gotama says this, still the Brahmins think in this way: 'Brahmins are the highest class. . . .'"

6. "What do you think, Assalāyana? Suppose a member of the warrior-leader class[6] were to kill living beings, take what is not given, conduct himself wrongly in sensual pleasures, speak falsely, speak maliciously, speak harshly, talk nonsense, be covetous, have a malevolent mind, and hold a wrong view. On the dissolution of the body after death, would only this person be likely to reappear in a state of deprivation, in an unhappy state, in perdition, even in hell, and not a Brahmin? Or suppose a member of the merchant-farmer class[7] or a member of the laborer class[8] were to kill living beings, take what is not given, conduct oneself wrongly in sensual pleasures, speak falsely, speak maliciously, speak harshly, talk nonsense, be covetous, have a malevolent mind, and hold a wrong view. On the dissolution of the body after death, would only this person be likely to reappear in a state of deprivation, in an unhappy state, in perdition, even in hell, and not a Brahmin?

[6] *Khattiya.* Today, this class is typically considered as the second class (behind the Brahmins) in terms of class hierarchy. In the Buddha's time, however, there seem to have been a number of regions where the *khattiya* class, as a class of nobles and royalty, was considered the highest class.

[7] *Vessa.* A member of the commercial or farming class. Considered the third of the four classes in Hindu society.

[8] *Sudda.* A member of the working or the servile class. Considered the lowest of the four classes in Hindu society.

"No, master Gotama. A member of the warrior-leader class who kills living beings, takes what is not given, conducts oneself wrongly in sensual pleasures, speaks falsely, speaks maliciously, speaks harshly, talks nonsense, is covetous, has a malevolent mind, and holds a wrong view, on the dissolution of the body after death, is likely to reappear in a state of deprivation, in an unhappy destination, in perdition, even in hell. Likewise, a Brahmin as well as a *vessa* or a *sudda*—in fact, anyone from any of the four classes—who
150 kills living beings, takes what is not given, conducts oneself wrongly in sensual pleasures, speaks falsely, speaks maliciously, speaks harshly, talks nonsense, is covetous, has a malevolent mind, and holds a wrong view, on the dissolution of the body after death, is likely to reappear in a state of deprivation, in an unhappy destination, in perdition, even in hell.

"Then, in this connection, Assalāyana, on what strength of argument and by whose authority do the Brahmins speak thus: 'Brahmins are the highest class . . .'?"

"Although master Gotama says this, still the Brahmins think that: 'Brahmins are the highest class. . . .'"

7. "What do you think, Assalāyana? Suppose a Brahmin were to abstain from killing living beings, from taking what is not given, from conducting oneself wrongly in sensual pleasures, from speaking falsely, from speaking maliciously, from speaking harshly, from talking nonsense, were to refrain from covetousness, were to have a mind without malevolence, and were to hold a right view. On the dissolution of the body after death, would only this person be likely to reappear in a happy state, even in a heavenly world, and not a warrior-leader, or a merchant-farmer, or a laborer?"

"No, master Gotama. A warrior-leader who abstains from killing living beings, from taking what is not given, from conducting oneself wrongly in sensual pleasures, from speaking falsely, from speaking maliciously, from speaking harshly, from talking nonsense, refrains from covetousness, has a mind without malevolence, and holds a right view, on the dissolution of the body after death, is likely to reappear in a happy state, even in a heavenly world. Likewise, a Brahmin, merchant-farmer, or laborer—in fact, anyone from any of the four classes—who abstains from killing living beings, from taking what is not given, from conducting oneself wrongly in sensual pleasures, from speaking falsely, from speaking maliciously, from speaking harshly, from talking nonsense, refrains from covetousness, has a mind without malevolence, and holds a right view, on the dissolution of the body after death, is likely to reappear in a happy state, even in a heavenly world.

"Then in this connection, Assalāyana, on what strength of argument and by whose authority do the Brahmins speak thus: 'Brahmins are the highest class . . .'?"

"Although master Gotama says this, still the Brahmins think that: 'Brahmins are the highest class. . . .'" 151

8. "What do you think, Assālāyana? Is a Brahmin alone capable of taking a loofah and bath powder and going to the river and washing away mud and dirt, but not a warrior-leader, a merchant-farmer, or a laborer?"

"Certainly, not that, master Gotama. A warrior-leader also is capable of taking a loofah and bath powder and going to the river and washing away mud and dirt. Likewise, a Brahmin, merchant-farmer, or laborer—in fact, anyone from any of the four classes—is capable of taking a loofah and bath powder and going to the river and washing away mud and dirt."

"Then in this connection, Assalāyana, on what strength of argument and by whose authority do the Brahmins speak thus: 'Brahmins are the highest class . . .'?"

"Although master Gotama says this, still the Brahmins think that: 'Brahmins are the highest class. . . .'" 152

9. "What do you think, Assalāyana? Suppose a warrior-leader who is a properly anointed king were to convene a group of a hundred men of various birth and he were to say to them: 'Come, good sirs, let those here who have been born to a warrior-leader clan or a Brahmin clan or a royal clan take an upper fire-stick of *sāl* wood, *salala* wood, sandalwood, or *padumaka* wood and produce a fire that manifests heat. Come, good sirs, let those here who have been born to an untouchable clan, a hunter clan, a basket-maker clan, a chariot-maker clan, or a scavenger clan take an upper fire stick made from a dog's drinking trough, a pig's drinking trough, a launderer's basin, or castor-oil wood and produce a fire that manifests heat.' What do you think, Assalāyana? When a fire is produced that manifests heat by someone who is born to a warrior-leader clan, a Brahmin clan, or a royal clan by taking an upper fire-stick of *sāl* wood, *salala* wood, sandalwood, or *padumaka* wood, would that fire have a flame, a color, and a radiance, and would it be possible to use it for the purposes of fire? But is it the case that when a fire is produced that manifests heat by someone who is born to an untouchable clan, a hunter clan, a basket-maker clan, a chariot-maker clan, or a scavenger clan taking an upper fire-stick made from a dog's drinking bowl, a pig's drinking bowl, a launderer's basin, or castor-oil wood, that fire would have no flame, no color, and no radiance, it would not be possible to use it for the purposes of fire?"

"No, master Gotama. When a fire is lit and heat produced by someone who is born to a warrior-leader clan, a Brahmin clan, or a royal clan by taking an upper fire-stick of *sāl* wood, *salala* wood, sandalwood, or *padumaka* wood, that fire would have a flame, a color, and a radiance, and *it would be possible* to use it for the purposes of fire. And when a fire is lit and heat produced by someone who is born to an untouchable clan, a hunter clan, a

basket-maker clan, a chariot-maker clan, or a scavenger clan takes an upper fire-stick made from a dog's drinking bowl, a pig's drinking bowl, a launderer's basin, or castor-oil wood, that fire too would have a flame, a color, and a radiance, and it would be possible to use it for the purposes of fire. For
153 all fire has a flame, a color, and a radiance, and it is possible to use all fire for the purposes of fire."

"Then, in this connection, Assalāyana, on what strength of argument and by whose authority do the Brahmins speak thus: 'Brahmins are the highest class . . .'?"

"Although master Gotama says this, still the Brahmins think that: 'Brahmins are the highest class. Those who belong to other classes are inferior. Brahmins are a fair color. Those who belong to other classes are dark. Brahmins are pure, whereas non-Brahmins are not. Brahmins are the legitimate sons of Brahmā, born of the mouth of Brahmā, created by Brahmā, and heirs to Brahmā.'"

10. "What do think, Assalāyana? In this case, a young man belonging to the warrior-leader class has sexual intercourse with a Brahmin girl, and as a result a son is born. The son having been born to a young man belonging to the warrior-leader class and a Brahmin girl, is he like his mother or like his father? Should he be called a 'warrior-leader' or a 'Brahmin'?"

"Master Gotama, were a son born to a young man belonging to the warrior-leader class and a Brahmin girl, he is both like his mother and like his father. And he should be called both a 'warrior-leader' and a 'Brahmin.'"

11. "What do think, Assalāyana? In this case, a Brahmin young man has sexual intercourse with a girl belonging to the warrior-leader class, and as a result a son is born. The son having been born to a Brahmin young man and a girl belonging to the warrior-leader class, is he like his mother or like his father? Should he be called a 'warrior-leader' or a 'Brahmin'?"

"Master Gotama, were a son born to a Brahmin young man and a girl belonging to the warrior-leader class, he is both like his mother and like his father. And he should be called both a 'warrior-leader' and a 'Brahmin.'"

12. "What do you think, Assalāyana? Consider this case: a mare was mated with a (male) donkey, and as a result of the mating, a foal was born. The foal having been born to a mare and a donkey, is it like its mother or like its father? Should it be a called a 'horse' or a 'donkey'?"

154 "It belongs to neither kind, master Gotama, it is a mule. I see a difference in this case, but in those other cases I do not see any difference."[9]

[9] The Buddha's argument is that the social classes are not fixed or inviolable categories. The fact that the crossing of a horse with a donkey yields a mule, which is neither horse nor donkey (and not *both*, as Assalāyana asserted in the case of the child of mixed parentage), analogically supports the Buddha's position.

13. "What do you think, Assalāyana? Suppose there were two young boys, brothers from the same womb. The one is studious and educated in the Vedic knowledge. The other is unskilled and uneducated. To which of these young boys would the Brahmins first serve food at such formal occasions as when making offerings for deceased relatives, rice harvest festivals,[10] sacrifices, or meals for special guests?"

"Master Gotama, the studious and educated youth would be the one whom the Brahmins would serve the food to first at such formal occasions as when making offerings for deceased relatives, rice harvest festivals, sacrifices, or meals for special guests. For what great benefit would derive from a gift to an unskilled and uneducated person?"

14. "What do you think, Assalāyana? Suppose there were two young brothers from the same womb. The one is studious and educated, but also unvirtuous and possessing an immoral character. The other is unstudious and uneducated, but is virtuous and possesses a moral character. To which of these young boys would the Brahmins first serve food at such formal occasions as when making offerings for deceased relatives, rice harvest festivals, sacrifices, or meals for special guests?"

"Master Gotama, the boy who is unstudious and uneducated, but virtuous and possesses a moral character, would be the one whom the Brahmins would serve the food to first at such formal occasions as when making offerings for deceased relatives, rice harvest festivals, sacrifices, or meals for special guests. For what great benefit would derive from a gift to a person who is unvirtuous and possesses an immoral character?"

15. "Formerly, Assalāyana, you took your stand on birth, and having given up birth, you took your stand on scriptural learning, and having given up scriptural learning, you have come to take your stand that purification is for all four classes—which is just as I describe the matter."

16. This having been said, Assalāyana sat down and became silent, downcast, dejected, his face cast down; he was overcome with disappointment and at a loss for a response.

17. Then the Exalted One, having realized that Assalāyana had become silent, downcast, dejected, his face cast down, overcome with disappointment and at a loss for a response, said this to Assalāyana: "Once upon a time, seven Brahmin sages were living together as a community in a forest haunt in huts made of leaves. An evil view such as the following arose among them: 'Brahmins are the highest class. Those who belong to other classes are infe- 155
rior. Brahmins are a fair color. Those who belong to other classes are dark. Brahmins are pure, whereas non-Brahmins are not. Brahmins are the legitimate

[10] *Thālipake.* This term refers to an occasion at which there is a large meal of milk-rice.

sons of Brahmā, born of the mouth of Brahmā, created by Brahmā, and heirs to Brahmā.' Asita Devala, the seer, trimmed his hair and beard, dressed himself in crimson-colored clothes, put on sandals with linings, took hold of a gold staff, and appeared in the courtyard of the seven Brahmin sages. Then Asita Devala, while pacing up and down in the courtyard of the seven Brahmin sages, spoke in this way: 'Now, where have the venerable Brahmin sages gone? Now, where have the venerable Brahmin sages gone?'

"Then this thought occurred to those seven Brahmin sages: 'Who is it that paces up and down in the courtyard of the seven Brahmin sages like a village idiot saying, "Where have the venerable Brahmin sages gone? Where have the venerable Brahmin sages gone?" Now we should curse him.' Then the seven Brahmin sages cursed Asita Devala in this way: 'Become ashes, vile one!' But the more the seven Brahmin sages cursed the seer Asita Devala, the more lovely, handsome, and charming he became.

"Then this thought occurred to the seven Brahmin sages: 'Religious austerity is vain. The holy life is fruitless. Earlier we cursed a person: "Become ashes, vile one!" and such a person became ashes. But when we curse this person in that way, the more we curse him, the more lovely, handsome, and charming he becomes.'

18. "'Sirs, your religious austerity is not in vain. The holy life is not fruit-
156 less. Look here, sirs. Come now, sirs, give up your ill will toward me.'

"'Whatever ill will there is, we give up. But who are you, sir?'

"'Sirs, have you heard of the seer, Asita Devala?'

"'Yes, sir.'

"'Sirs, I am he.'

19. "Then the seven Brahmin sages approached Asita Devala and saluted him. At that point, Asita Devala said this to the seven Brahmin sages: 'I have heard this, good sirs: there are seven Brahmin sages living together as a community in a forest haunt in huts made of leaves. An evil view such as the following has arisen among them: "Brahmins are the highest class. Those who belong to other classes are inferior. Brahmins are a fair color. Those who belong to other classes are dark. Brahmins are pure, whereas non-Brahmins are not. Brahmins are the legitimate sons of Brahmā, born of the mouth of Brahmā, created by Brahmā and heirs to Brahmā."'

"'So it is, sir.'

"'But, sirs, do you know whether the mother who bore you went only with a Brahmin and never with a non-Brahmin?'

"'No, sir.'

"'But, sirs, do you know whether your mother's mothers back to the seventh generation went only with Brahmins and never with non-Brahmins?'

"'No, sir.'

"'But, sirs, do you know whether the father who bore you went only with a Brahmin and never with a non-Brahmin?'

"'No, sir.'

"'But, sirs, do you know if your father's fathers back to the seventh generation went only with Brahmins and never with non-Brahmins?'

"'No, sir.'

"'But, sirs, do you know how the conception of an embryo occurs?'

"'Sir, we know how the conception of an embryo occurs. In such a case, 157
there is the sexual union of the mother and the father, a mother is fertile, and the embryo is present. Thus the union of the three is how the conception of an embryo occurs.'

'But do you know, sirs, whether the embryo belongs to the warrior-leader class, Brahmin class, merchant-farmer class, or laborer class?'

'No, sir, we do not know whether the embryo belongs to the warrior-leader class, Brahmin class, merchant-farmer class, or laborer class.'

'That being so, sirs, then, what are you?'

'That being so, sir, we do not know what we are.'

20. "Assalāyana, those seven Brahmin sages, being cross-examined, cross-questioned, and pressed for reasons by Asita Devala about the claims regarding parentage, were not able to explain themselves. So how could you here—being cross-examined, cross-questioned, and pressed for reasons by me about the claims regarding parentage—expect to explain this? After all, you have the same teachers as they (the seven Brahmin sages) and are not even fit to be their servant, Puṇṇa, the ladle holder."

21. This having been spoken, the youth Assalāyana said this to the Exalted One: "Wonderful, Gotama! Wonderful, Gotama! Let master Gotama accept me as a lay-follower who has gone for refuge from this day forth, so long as life lasts."

15

The Lion's Roar on the Wheel-Turning Monarch

(*Cakkavattisīhanāda Sutta*)[1]

This well-known discourse offers key insights into the early Buddhist view of the proper function of kingship (government) and the close connection between morality and socioeconomic conditions.

The discourse opens with an exhortation to the *bhikkhus* on self-reliance and the value of mindfulness meditation.[2] The Buddha tells the *bhikkhus* that they should strive to undertake wholesome mental states (and so avoid the clutches of Māra, the Evil One). This exhortation is repeated and expanded upon toward the close of the discourse. But the focus of this discourse, sandwiched rather awkwardly between these two addresses to the *bhikkhus,* is the Buddha's farcical tale about right-ruling kings (called "wheel-turning monarchs")[3] and the degeneration and revival of civilized life as a function of moral conduct.

The tale begins with a description of a utopia of the distant past, at which time there was a king named Daḷhenemi who was a "wheel-turning monarch" (so-called because a radiant "Wheel-gem" would appear as a public symbol of his just rule).[4] Under his good government, the people lived exceedingly long lives (eighty thousand years) and had great beauty. Eventually, however, the Wheel-gem fades (even in a Buddhist utopia, nothing is permanent!), and the king dies, but not before he teaches his son the proper functions of kingship and the duties of a wheel-turning monarch. As the old king points out to his son, the "Wheel-gem" cannot be passed down as an inheritance but must be earned by the just governance of each new king.

Most readers of the discourse interpret the duties of a wheel-turning monarch as an early Buddhist blueprint for good government—particularly the responsibilities of government to support the poor, impart justice, provide protection to the people, and model morally correct living. A certain parallel seems to be suggested between the spiritual and the sociopolitical spheres: just as the Buddha effectively guides others to *nibbāna* by his

1 *Dīgha Nikāya* 3.58–79.

2 This discourse repeats part of the opening sections of The Greater Discourse on the Foundations of Mindfulness (see Chapter 4).

3 *Cakkavatti.*

4 The "Wheel-gem" of good political leadership is likely to be the symbolic analogue to the "wheel of the dhamma" that describes the Buddha's effective spiritual doctrine.

dhamma (doctrine), there is a type of *dhamma* by which a king guides his country to peace and prosperity. In any case, the main point is clear: a good government not only looks after the safety and the material welfare of the people (and animals, too!) but also promotes the development of moral conduct among the people. Even as the wheel-turning monarch extends his dominion over adjacent (and formerly hostile) territories, these conquests are accomplished through the force of righteousness, rather than violence and bloodshed.[5] In contrast, a bad government will have proportionally deleterious effects on the material and moral well-being of the people.

The discourse offers an excellent insight into the Buddhist view of karma through the interplay of moral and social conditions. Utopia comes to an end when a certain king fails to carry out all the duties of a wheel-turning monarch. In particular, the king neglects to support the poor. The story reaches a comical pitch as the king tries to patch up his mistakes by giving money to thieves. After that strategy does not work, he becomes desperate and resorts to executing offenders. But this only makes the criminals more violent and so leads to a downward spiral of society that, by stages, reduces the life span and diminishes the beauty of the people.

At the end of this long degeneration of society (which, according to the story, will occur at some point in the distant future), there will be so little morality left that there will not even be a concept for "moral." A week-long "war of all against all," in which people attack each other like beasts, will ensue. But some people will find the violence repulsive and, after the war, will come together to commit themselves to good deeds. As a result of their good deeds, the life span and beauty of these people will increase, and at some point in the distant future, utopia will be reestablished and the normal life span will again be eighty thousand years.

At that point, a king named Saṃkha will arise and become a wheel-turning monarch, in part, because of his generosity to the needy. A future Buddha, Metteyya,[6] will arise in the world, having all the same characteristics of the current Buddha (but with a substantially larger *Saṅgha*). Saṃkha will become a disciple of Metteyya—establishing the priority of a Buddha's spiritual *dhamma* over the political-economic *dhamma* of a righteous king—

[5] Numerous modern scholars have noted that this hopelessly optimistic account of nonviolent conquest is perhaps a parody of the sickening slaughter that accompanies any real-life conquest. See T. W. Rhys Davids, *Dialogues of the Buddha,* Part III (Oxford: Pali Text Society, 1921), p. 63, and Steven Collins, *Nirvana and Other Buddhist Felicities* (Cambridge: Cambridge University Press, 1998), p. 484.

[6] The future Buddha Metteyya (better known by the Sanskrit form of his name "Maitreya") is an important figure in Mahāyāna Buddhism. This is the only reference to the future Buddha in the early Pāli discourses.

and, by following Metteyya's teachings, Saṃkha will achieve the aims of the holy life.

In the last few sections of the discourse, the Buddha applies the lessons of the story to monastic life. He describes in detail the meaning of five common virtues (life span, beauty, happiness, enjoyment, and strength) as they apply to the *bhikkhus*. A *bhikkhu's* "strength," says the Buddha, is the elimination of the defilements (an accomplishment that Māra cannot match) and thus it is a virtue tantamount to the achievement of spiritual liberation in this very world.

Discourse

58

1. Thus have I heard.

At one time, the Exalted One was dwelling among the Magadhans at Mātulā. There the Exalted One addressed the *bhikkhus*: "*Bhikkhus*." "Sir," those *bhikkhus* replied to the Exalted One.

The Exalted One then said: "*Bhikkhus*, you should live with yourself as a guiding light,[7] with yourself as a refuge, without another as a refuge; live with the *dhamma* as a guiding light, with the *dhamma* as a refuge, without another as a refuge.

"And how does a *bhikkhu* live with himself as a guiding light, with himself as a refuge, without another as a refuge; how does he live with the *dhamma* as a guiding light, with the *dhamma* as a refuge, without another as a refuge?

"Here, a *bhikkhu* lives observing the body as body, energetically, self-possessed, and mindful, having eliminated both the desire for and the despair over the world. He lives observing feeling as feeling, energetically, self-possessed, and mindful, having eliminated both the desire for and the despair over the world. He lives observing the mind as mind, energetically, self-possessed, and mindful, having eliminated both the desire for and the despair over the world. He lives observing mental phenomena as mental phenomena, energetically, self-possessed, and mindful, having eliminated both the desire for and the despair over the world.[8] In this way, a *bhikkhu* lives with himself as a guiding light, with himself as a refuge, without another as a refuge; lives with the *dhamma* as a guiding light, with the *dhamma* as a refuge, without another as a refuge.

[7] *Dīpā* can also mean "island" or "lamp."

[8] These are the "four foundations of mindfulness." These are developed in full in The Greater Discourse on the Foundations of Mindfulness. See Chapter 4.

"*Bhikkhus,* stick to your own pastures,[9] to your ancestral haunts. By sticking to your own pastures, to your ancestral haunts, Māra will not obtain access to you; Māra will have no footing. *Bhikkhus,* by undertaking wholesome mental states, this merit increases. 59

2. "Once upon a time, *bhikkhus,* there was a king named Daḷhenemi[10] who was a wheel-turning monarch, a just king who ruled by the *dhamma,* a victor over the four ends [of the earth], who had obtained the security of his country and was endowed with the seven gems. These seven gems were, namely: the Wheel-gem, the elephant-gem, the horse-gem, the jewel-gem, the woman-gem, the householder-gem, and, the seventh, the adviser-gem. He had more than a thousand sons; and they were valiant men, heroic in physical form, and conquerors of hostile armies. He lived, having conquered this earth that is bounded by the sea by *dhamma,*[11] without stick or sword.

3. "Then after many years—many hundreds and thousands of years—King Daḷhenemi addressed a certain servant: 'Good servant, when you see the sacred Wheel-gem retreating, falling away from its place, then you should inform me.'

"'Yes, sire,' that servant replied to the king.

"And after many years—many hundreds and thousands of years—that servant saw the sacred Wheel-gem retreating, falling away from its place. Having seen this, he approached King Daḷhenemi and told him: 'Good king, are you aware that the sacred Wheel-gem is retreating, falling away from its place?'

"Then King Daḷhenemi called for his eldest son, the prince, and said to him: 'My son, the sacred Wheel-gem has retreated and fallen away from its place. I have heard it said that "for a king who is a wheel-turning monarch, when the sacred Wheel-gem retreats and falls away from its place, such a king does not have much longer to live." I have enjoyed the earthly pleas- 60
ures of a human life; it is time for me to seek heavenly pleasures. Come, my dear son and prince, take control over this earth that is bounded by the sea. I will shave off my hair and beard, put on yellow robes, and go forth from home to homelessness.'

"Then, having thoroughly instructed his eldest son in kingship, King Daḷhenemi shaved off his hair and beard, put on yellow robes and went forth from home to homelessness. And seven days after the royal sage had gone forth, the sacred Wheel-gem disappeared.

[9] The commentaries suggest that this refers to the "four foundations of mindfulness" given earlier.

[10] The king's name means "strong-tire"—an amusing name for a "wheel-turning monarch."

[11] *Dhamma* here refers to "righteousness," not to the Buddha's doctrine. It is probably meant to parallel the goodness of the Buddha's doctrine in the context of kingship.

4. "Then a certain servant approached the properly anointed, warrior-leader king. When he had approached, he said to him: 'Good king, are you aware that the sacred Wheel-gem has disappeared?'

"Then the king was distressed that the sacred Wheel-gem had disappeared and made his distress known to others. He approached the royal sage (his father) and said to him: 'Sire, are you aware that the sacred Wheel-gem has disappeared?'

"This having been said, the royal sage said to the king: 'My son, do not be distressed that the sacred Wheel-gem has disappeared, and do not make your distress known to others. The sacred Wheel-gem is not a paternal inheritance. Come now, you should carry out the duties of a noble wheel-turning monarch! It is possible that by carrying out the duties of a noble wheel-turning monarch—on the *Uposatha* (full moon) day, the fifteenth day of the month, when you have washed your head and gone up to the terrace of the palace—the sacred Wheel-gem will appear with its thousand spokes,
61 rim, hub, and complete in all its functions.'

5. "'But what, sire, is this duty of a noble wheel-turning monarch?'

"'Now, my son, depending only on the *dhamma,* honoring the *dhamma,* respecting the *dhamma,* revering the *dhamma,* paying homage to the *dhamma,* and venerating the *dhamma,* having the *dhamma* as your banner and flag, ruling by the *dhamma,* you should arrange appropriate guard, protection, and safety to family members, people in military service, warrior-leaders, vassals, Brahmin householders, townspeople and country-folk, religious wanderers and Brahmins, beasts and birds. Do not allow criminal conduct to prevail in your kingdom. And to those who are in poverty, give them money. And regarding those religious wanderers and Brahmins who have abstained from sensual excess and indolence, but are devoted to patience and gentleness—each one mastering himself, calming himself, and quenching himself—when such persons approach you from time to time, you should inquire of them: "Sir, what is wholesome (moral)? What is unwholesome (evil)? What is blameworthy? What is blameless? What should be practiced? What should not be practiced? Which of my actions will lead to hardship and suffering in the long run? Which of my actions will lead to benefit and happiness in the long run?" Having listened to them, you should avoid what is unwholesome and do what is wholesome. This, my son, is the duty of a noble wheel-turning monarch.'

"'Yes, sire,' said the properly consecrated warrior-leader king. Having assented to the royal sage, the king practiced the duties of a noble wheel-turning monarch. And from the fact that he carried out the duties of a wheel-turning monarch—on the *Uposatha* (full moon) day, the fifteenth day of the month, when he had washed his head and gone up to the terrace of the palace—the sacred Wheel-gem appeared with its thousand spokes, rim, hub,

and complete in all its aspects. Having seen this, the king had this thought: 'I have heard that when such a Wheel-gem becomes manifest on the same day as the *Uposatha* (full moon) day, the fifteenth day of the month, and a king washes his head and goes up on the terrace of the palace, such a king 62
becomes a wheel-turning monarch. Now I must be a king who is a wheel-turning monarch!'[12]

6. "At that point, *bhikkhus,* the king stood up from his seat and, putting his robe over one shoulder, he took a water-vessel in his left hand and sprinkled the Wheel-gem with his right hand, saying: 'Let the Wheel-gem turn! Let the Wheel-gem conquer!' Then the Wheel-gem rolled to the eastern direction, and the wheel-turning king followed it with his fourfold army.[13] In whatever region the Wheel-gem stopped, to that land the wheel-turning king went with his fourfold army. The hostile kings from the eastern region approached the wheel-turning monarch. When they had approached him, they said: 'Come, Great King! Welcome, Great King! This [territory] is yours, Great King! Rule over us, Great King!'[14]

"The wheel-turning king said this: 'Do not take life. Do not take what is not given. Do not commit sexual misconduct. Do not lie. Do not drink intoxicants. Rule as you did before.'[15]

"Then the hostile kings from the eastern region became vassals of the wheel-turning monarch.

7. "At that point, the Wheel-gem plunged into and reemerged again from the eastern sea and then rolled to the southern direction. . . . the hostile kings from the southern region became vassals of the wheel-turning monarch. Then the Wheel-gem plunged into and reemerged again from the southern sea and then rolled to the western direction. . . . the hostile kings from the 63
western region became vassals of the wheel-turning monarch. Then the Wheel-gem plunged into and reemerged again from the western sea and then rolled to the north, and the wheel-turning king followed it with his fourfold army. In whatever region the Wheel-gem stopped, the wheel-turning king went to that land with his fourfold army. The hostile kings from

[12] The translation of the exclamation at the end of this passage I borrow from Steven Collins. For a discussion of this, see *Nirvana and Other Buddhist Felicities,* p. 484.

[13] A fourfold army is divided into elephants, cavalry, chariots, and infantry.

[14] As T. W. Rhys Davids and other translators have noted, the wheel-turning monarch apparently accomplishes his conquests without violence or bloodshed. Rhys Davids calls this accomplishment a "parody" of genuine warfare. See T. W. Rhys Davids, *Dialogues of the Buddha,* Part III (Oxford: Pali Text Society, 1921), p. 63.

[15] *Yathābhuttaṃ bhuñjatha* is difficult to translate because the simple meaning of these words refers to eating or enjoying food. Steven Collins makes the best sense of it in this context, and the translation adopted here follows his suggestion. See *Nirvana and Other Buddhist Felicities,* p. 605, footnote 12.

the northern region approached the wheel-turning monarch. When they had approached him, they said: 'Come, Great King! Welcome, Great King! This [territory] is yours, Great King! Rule over us, Great King!'

"The wheel-turning king said this: 'Do not take life. Do not take what is not given. Do not commit sexual misconduct. Do not lie. Do not drink intoxicants. Rule as you did before.'

"Then the hostile kings from the northern region became vassals of the wheel-turning monarch.

"Then the Wheel-gem, having conquered the earth that is bounded by the sea, returned to the royal city, to the inner apartments of the king, where it seemed to stand fixed in front of the courthouse, shining forth its beauty onto the king's inner apartments.

8. "Then, also, a second king who was a wheel-turning monarch . . . and a third . . . and a fourth . . . and a fifth . . . and a sixth . . . and a seventh king who was a wheel-turning monarch addressed a certain servant: 'Good servant, when you see the sacred Wheel-gem retreating, falling away from its place, then you should inform me.'

"'Yes, sire,' that servant replied to the king.

"And after many years—many hundreds and thousands of years—that servant saw the sacred Wheel-gem retreating, falling away from its place.
64 Having seen this, he approached the king and told him: 'Good king, are you aware that the sacred Wheel-gem is retreating, falling away from its place?'

"Then the king called for his eldest son, the prince, and said to him: 'My son, the sacred Wheel-gem has retreated and fallen away from its place. I have heard it said that "for a king who is a wheel-turning monarch, when the sacred Wheel-gem retreats and falls away from its place, such a king does not have much longer to live." I have enjoyed the earthly pleasures of a human life; it is time for me to seek heavenly pleasures. Come, my dear son and prince, take control over this earth that is bounded by the sea. I will shave off my hair and beard, put on yellow robes, and will go forth from home to homelessness.'

"Then, having thoroughly instructed his eldest son in kingship, the king shaved off his hair and beard, put on yellow robes and went forth from home to homelessness. And soon after the royal sage had gone forth, the sacred Wheel-gem disappeared.

9. "Then a certain servant approached the properly anointed, warrior-leader king. When he had approached, he said to him: 'Good king, are you aware that the sacred Wheel-gem has disappeared?'

"Then the king was distressed that the sacred Wheel-gem had disappeared and he made his distress known to others. But he did not approach the royal sage to ask about the duties of a wheel-turning monarch. He ruled the country by his own whim, and in so doing, the people of the country did not prosper as well as they had done previously under the kings who had conducted themselves according to the duties of a noble wheel-turning monarch.

"Then the ministers, members of the assembly, treasury officials, guards,
gatekeepers, and chanters of the mantras assembled and approached the
king, saying to him: 'You, sire, are ruling the country by your own whim, 65
and because of that, the people are not prospering as well as they had done
previously under the kings who had conducted themselves according to the duties of a noble wheel-turning monarch. Sire, there are ministers, members of the assembly, treasury officials, guards, gatekeepers, and chanters of the mantras assembled here, as well as others, who possess an understanding of the duties of a noble wheel-turning monarch. Do ask us, sire, about such duties, and we will explain them to you.'

10. "Then the king summoned these men and asked them about the duties of a noble wheel-turning monarch, and they explained them to him. Having listened to these men, he established the appropriate guard, protection, and safety, but he did not give money to the poor. By his not giving money to the poor, poverty became prevalent in the country. When poverty had become prevalent, a certain person committed what is called 'theft' by taking what another had not given. This person was arrested and brought before the king. The king was told: 'Sire, this person has committed theft by taking what another had not given.' After that was said, the king spoke to that person:

"'Is it true, good sir, that you committed theft by taking what another had not given?'

"'Yes, sire, it is true.'

"'Why did you do that?'

"'I have no means of living, sire.' 66

"Then the king gave some money to that person, saying: 'With this money, good sir, you yourself should live and take care of your mother and father, children and wife, undertake a business, and give excellent gifts to religious wanderers and Brahmins in such a way that it leads to heaven, has a pleasant result, and guides you to a place of happiness.'

"'Yes, sire,' that man replied to the king.

11. Then another person committed what is called 'theft' by taking what another had not given. This person was arrested and brought before the king. The king was told: 'Sire, this person has committed theft by taking what another had not given.' After that was said, the king spoke to that person:

"'Is it true, good sir, that you committed theft by taking what another had not given?'

"'Yes, sire, it is true.'

"'Why did you do that?'

"'I have no means of living, sire.'

"Then the king gave some money to that person, saying: 'With this money, good sir, you yourself should live and take care of your mother and father, children and wife, undertake a business, and give excellent gifts to religious wanderers and Brahmins in such a way that it leads to heaven, has a pleasant result, and guides you to a place of happiness.'

"'Yes, sire,' that man replied to the king.

12. "Then people heard about the king that: 'To whomever commits theft, taking from another what is not given, the king gives that person money.' Having heard this, they had this further thought: 'Why don't we also commit theft by taking from another what is not given?'

"Then another person committed theft. This person was arrested and brought before the king. The king was told: 'Sire, this person has commit-
67 ted theft by taking what another had not given.' After that was said, the king spoke to that person:

"'Is it true, good sir, that you committed theft by taking what another had not given?'

"'Yes, sire, it is true.'

"'Why did you do that?'

"'I have no means of living, sire.'

"Then the king had this thought: 'If I give out money to whoever commits theft, then theft will increase.' Suppose I were to fully prevent this man from such action. I will completely destroy him by having his head cut off.'

"Then the king commanded his men: 'Now, bind this man's arms behind his back firmly with rope, shave his head closely with a razor, and lead him through the streets and squares to the loud beat of a drum. Then take him out through the southern gate, and there, to the south of the city, fully prevent this man from such action. Completely destroy him by cutting off his head.'

"'Yes, sire,' those men replied to the king. And they bound this man's arms behind his back firmly with rope, shaved his head closely with a razor, and led him through the streets and squares to the loud beat of a drum. Then they took him out through the southern gate, and there, to the south of the city, fully prevented this man from such behavior. They completely destroyed him by cutting off his head.'

13. "Then the people heard the following: 'The king makes an example of those people who commit theft by taking from another what is not given by imposing an effective prohibition that destroys such behavior at its root—he has their heads cut off.' Having heard this, they had this thought: 'Suppose now that we were to have sharp weapons made, and having had them
68 made, we will commit theft by taking from another what is not given, and

[in response to the king's actions], we will fully prevent [our victims' from turning us in] by destroying them completely—we will cut off our victims' heads!'

"Those people had sharp weapons made and, after they had them made, they began to attack villages, towns, and cities. And they committed highway robbery as well. They committed theft by taking from another what was not given, and [in response to the king's actions], they fully prevented [their victims' from turning them in] by destroying them completely—they cut off their victims' heads!

14. "Thus it was, *bhikkhus,* that from not granting money to the poor, poverty became prevalent; because of the prevalence of poverty, theft became prevalent; because of the prevalence of theft, weapons became prevalent; because of the prevalence of weapons, killing became prevalent; because of the prevalence of killing, the life span of people dwindled and their beauty decreased. As a result of the dwindling life span and the decreasing beauty, the children of those who had a life span of eighty thousand years lived for only forty thousand years.

"Among those people who lived for forty thousand years, a certain person committed theft by taking from another what had not been given. That person was arrested and brought before the king. The king was told: 'Sire, this person has committed theft by taking what another had not given.'

"After this was said, the king spoke to that person: 'Is it true, good sir, that you committed theft by taking what another had not given?'

"'No, sire,' the man said, speaking a deliberate lie.

15. "Thus it was that from not granting money to the poor, poverty became prevalent; because of the prevalence of poverty, theft became prevalent; because of the prevalence of theft, weapons became prevalent; because of the prevalence of weapons, killing became prevalent; because of the
prevalence of killing, lying became prevalent; because of the prevalence of 69
lying, the life span of people dwindled and their beauty decreased. As a result of the dwindling life span and the decreasing beauty, the children of those who had a life span of forty thousand years lived for only twenty thousand years.

"Among those people who lived for twenty thousand years, a certain person committed theft by taking from another what had not been given. Then another person reported to the king that 'such-and-such a person had committed theft by taking from another what had not been given,' thereby engaging in malicious speech.

16. "Thus it was that from not granting money to the poor, poverty became prevalent; because of the prevalence of poverty, theft became prevalent;

because of the prevalence of theft, weapons became prevalent; because of the prevalence of weapons, killing became prevalent; because of the prevalence of killing, lying became prevalent; because of the prevalence of lying, malicious speech became prevalent; because of the prevalence of malicious speech, the life span of people dwindled and their beauty decreased. As a result of the dwindling life span and the decreasing beauty, the children of those who had a life span of twenty thousand years lived for only ten thousand years.

"Among those people who lived for ten thousand years, some people were handsome, and some were ugly. Those men who were ugly, being jealous of those who were handsome, committed adultery with other men's wives.

17. "Thus it was that from not granting money to the poor, poverty became prevalent; because of the prevalence of poverty, theft became prevalent; because of the prevalence of theft, weapons became prevalent; because of the prevalence of weapons, killing became prevalent; because of the prevalence of killing, lying became prevalent; because of the prevalence of lying, malicious speech became prevalent; because of the prevalence of malicious speech, sexual misconduct became prevalent; because of the prevalence of sexual misconduct, the life span of people dwindled and their beauty decreased. As a result of the dwindling life span and the decreasing beauty, the children of those who had a life span of ten thousand years lived for only five thousand years.

"Among those people who lived for five thousand years, two things became prevalent: harsh speech and frivolous chatter. Because these two things became prevalent, the life span of people dwindled and their beauty decreased. As a result of the dwindling life span and the decreasing beauty, for the children of those who had a life span of five thousand years, some lived for two thousand five hundred years, and some lived for only two thousand years.

"Among those people who lived for two thousand five hundred years, covetousness and hatred became prevalent. Because covetousness and hatred became prevalent, the life span of these people dwindled and their beauty decreased. As a result of the dwindling life span and the decreasing beauty, the children of those who had a life span of two thousand five hundred years lived for only one thousand years.

"Among those people who lived for one thousand years, wrong speculative views became prevalent. Because wrong speculative views became prevalent, the life span of these people dwindled and their beauty decreased. As a result of the dwindling life span and the decreasing beauty, the children of those who had a life span of one thousand years lived for only five hundred years.

"Among those people who lived for five hundred years, three mental states became prevalent: improper desire,[16] excessive greed, and wrong conduct. Because these three things became prevalent, the life span of these people dwindled and their beauty decreased. As a result of the dwindling life span and the decreasing beauty, for the children of those who had a life span of five hundred years, some lived for two hundred and fifty years, and some lived for only two hundred years.

"Among those people who lived for two hundred and fifty years, these states of affairs became prevalent: disrespect toward mothers and fathers, disrespect toward religious wanderers and Brahmins, as well as no respect for the elders of one's clan.

18. "Thus it was that from not granting money to the poor, poverty became prevalent; because of the prevalence of poverty, theft became prevalent; because of the prevalence of theft, weapons became prevalent; because of the prevalence of weapons, killing became prevalent; because of the prevalence of killing, lying became prevalent; because of the prevalence of lying, malicious speech became prevalent; because of the prevalence of malicious speech, sexual misconduct became prevalent; because of the prevalence of sexual misconduct, two things, harsh speech and frivolous chatter, became 71
prevalent. Because of the prevalence of two things, harsh speech and frivolous chatter, covetousness and hatred became prevalent; because of the prevalence of covetousness and hatred, wrong speculative views became prevalent; because of the prevalence of wrong speculative views, three things, improper desire, excessive greed, and wrong conduct, became prevalent; because these three things had become prevalent, disrespect for mothers and fathers, disrespect for religious wanderers and Brahmins, and lack of respect for the elders of one's clan became prevalent;[17] and because of these things, the life span of people dwindled and their beauty decreased. As a result of the dwindling life span and the decreasing beauty, the children of those who lived two hundred and fifty years lived only for one hundred years.

19. "*Bhikkhus,* there will come a time when the children of those people will live for only ten years. And for the people who have a life span of ten years, girls will come to be of marriageable age at five years old. For those people, these flavors will disappear, namely: ghee, butter, sesame oil, honey molasses, and salt. For the people who live for ten years, [low quality] *kudrūsa*-grain will be their best food. Just as rice and meat curry are the best food now, *kudrūsa*-grain will be the best food for the people who live for ten

16 The commentaries say that "improper desire" refers to incest.

17 This completes the list of what are known as the "ten bad deeds" that is found in many places in early Buddhist texts.

years. For the people who live for ten years, the ten good deeds will disappear altogether and the ten bad deeds will prevail to the utmost. For such
people, there will be no concept for 'moral.' How, then, could there be any
agent of what is moral? Among the people who live for ten years, the ones
72 who show disrespect to mothers and fathers, religious wanderers and Brahmins, and the elders of one's clan will be the ones who are honored and
praised. Just as now the ones who are honored and praised are those who
show respect to mothers and fathers, religious wanderers and Brahmins, and
the elders of one's clan—it will be like that for those showing no respect.

20. "Among those who live for ten years, there will not be any consideration for 'mothers,' 'aunts,' 'maternal uncles,' 'wives of teachers,' or 'father's
sisters-in-law'—the world will be mixed up by promiscuity just like goats
and sheep, chickens and pigs, dogs and jackals. And for those who live for
ten years, there will be terrible anger present among them, one toward
another, terrible hatred, terrible ill will, terrible thoughts of killing, mother
against child, child against mother, father against child, child against father,
brother against brother, brother against sister, and sister against brother—
there will be such terrible anger, hatred, ill will, and thoughts of killing
among them, one for another. Just as a hunter, upon seeing a beast, has terrible anger, hatred, ill will, and thoughts of killing, so, too, it will be for those
73 people who live for ten years.

21. "Among those who live for ten years, there will be a seven-day
'weapon-period,'[18] during which they will consider each other as beasts.
Sharp weapons will appear in their hands, and with these sharp weapons they
will deprive one another of life, saying: 'That is a beast!' Then there will be
some persons who will think: 'Let me not do that to anyone! Let no one do
that to me! Suppose I were to enter a grass-thicket, a jungle, a dense stand
of trees, a place made inaccessible by rivers or a mountain recess and live off
the roots and fruits of the forest.' These people will enter such places for
seven days, living off the roots and fruits of the forest. After seven days, they
will emerge from those remote places unsullied; they will embrace each other
and sing together in the assembly hall, saying: 'Good fellow, it is wonderful!
You are alive!' Then this thought will occur to those people: 'By undertaking evil mental states, we brought about the prolonged destruction of our
kinsmen, so let us now do what is good. And what good things shall we do?
Let us refrain from taking life. That is a good deed to undertake and practice.' And so they will refrain from taking life; undertaking this good deed,
they will practice it. By undertaking this good deed, their life span and
74 beauty will increase. As a result of increasing their life span and beauty, the
children of those who lived for ten years will live for twenty years.

18 That is, a war.

22. "Then those people will have this thought: 'By undertaking this good deed, we have increased our life span and beauty. Let us perform even further actions that are good. Let us refrain from taking what is not given, from sexual misconduct, from lying, from slanderous speech, from harsh speech, from frivolous chatter, and from covetousness. Let us renounce wrong speculative views, improper desire, excessive greed, and wrong conduct. Instead, let us show respect to mothers and fathers, religious wanderers and Brahmins, and to the elders of our clan[19]—in each case, this is a good deed to undertake and practice.'

"And, in fact, they will show respect to mothers and fathers, religious wanderers and Brahmins, and to the elders of their clan—and so they will undertake and practice this good deed. By undertaking good deeds, they will increase their life span and beauty. As a result of increasing their life span and beauty, those who live for twenty years will have children that live to be forty years old. Those who live for forty years will have children that live to be eighty years old. Those who live for eighty years will have children that live to be one hundred and sixty years old. Those who live for one hundred and sixty years will have children that live to be three hundred and twenty years old. Those who live for three hundred and twenty years will have children that live to be six hundred and forty years old. Those who live for six hundred and forty years will have children that live to be two thousand years old. Those who live for two thousand years will have children that live to be four thousand years old. Those who live for four thousand years will have children that live to be eight thousand years old. Those who live for eight thousand years will have children that live to be twenty thousand years old. Those who live for twenty thousand years will have children that live to be forty thousand years old. Those who live for forty thousand years will have 75
children that live to be eighty thousand years old.

23. "Among those who live for eighty thousand years, girls will reach marriageable age at five hundred years old. Among these people there will be only three afflictions: desire, hunger, and old age. For those who live for eighty thousand years, this land of Jambudīpa[20] (India) will become powerful and prosperous, and its villages, towns, and royal cities will be so close together that a rooster could fly between them. For those who live for eighty thousand years, this Jambudīpa, like the Avīci hell, will be as dense with people as a thicket of reeds or rushes. For these people, this city of Vārāṇasi (Benares) will be a powerful and prosperous royal city called Ketumatī, containing a mass of people, a crowd of people, and it will be well-supplied with

[19] These further acts complete the list of "ten good deeds" that are referred to in numerous places in the early Buddhist texts.

[20] Literally, "land of the rose-apple."

food. For those who live for eighty thousand years, there will be eighty-four thousand cities in Jambudīpa, with Ketumatī as the royal capital.

24. "For those people who live for eighty thousand years, there will arise in the royal city of Ketumatī a king named Saṃkha, a wheel-turning monarch, a just king who will rule by the *dhamma,* a victor over the four ends [of the earth], who will obtain the security of his country and will be endowed with the seven gems. These seven gems will be, namely: the Wheel-gem, the elephant-gem, the horse-gem, the jewel-gem, the woman-gem, the householder-gem, and, the seventh, the adviser-gem. He will have more than a thousand sons; and they will be valiant men, heroic in physical form, and conquerors of hostile armies. He will live, having conquered this earth that is bounded by the sea by *dhamma* alone, without stick or sword.

76 25. "Among those people who live for eighty thousand years, an Exalted One named Metteyya will arise in the world. He will be an *arahant,* a fully awakened one, endowed with knowledge and virtue, a Well-Farer, a knower of the world, an unsurpassed charioteer of human beings who are like horses to be tamed, a teacher of *devas* and human beings, a Buddha, an Exalted One, just as I am now. He will make known this world—with its *devas,* Māras, Brahmās, religious wanderers, and Brahmins—to that generation of *devas* and human beings, having understood and realized this for himself, just as I do now. He will teach the *dhamma,* which is beautiful in the beginning, beautiful in the middle, and beautiful in the end, in spirit as well as in letter, and he will make known the pure religious life that is complete in its entirety, just as I do now. He will be accompanied by a *Saṇgha* composed of many thousands of *bhikkhus,* just as I am now accompanied by a *Saṇgha* composed of many hundreds of *bhikkhus.*

26. "Then, *bhikkhus,* King Saṃkha will rebuild the palace that King Mahā-Panāda had constructed. Having lived in it and let it go, he will donate it as a gift to religious wanderers, Brahmins, beggars, and to those who are homeless or destitute. Having given this gift, he will cut off his hair and beard, put on yellow robes, and go forth from home to the homeless life under Metteyya, the Exalted One, an *arahant* and fully awakened one. Thus having gone forth as a religious wanderer, alone, withdrawn, living vigilantly,
77 arduously, and resolutely, it will not be long before he will undertake and live the unsurpassed holy life in this very world, having understood and realized this for himself, for the purpose of which young men of good families rightly go forth from home to homelessness.

27. "*Bhikkhus,* you should live with yourself as a guiding light, with yourself as a refuge, without another as a refuge; live with the *dhamma* as a guiding light, with the *dhamma* as a refuge, without another as a refuge. And how does a *bhikkhu* live with himself as a guiding light, with himself as a

refuge, without another as a refuge; live with the *dhamma* as a guiding light, with the *dhamma* as a refuge, without another as a refuge? Here, a *bhikkhu* lives observing the body as body, energetically, self-possessed, and mindful, having eliminated both the desire for and the despair over the world. He lives observing feeling as feeling, energetically, self-possessed, and mindful, having eliminated both the desire for and the despair over the world. He lives observing the mind as mind, energetically, self-possessed, and mindful, having eliminated both the desire for and the despair over the world. He lives observing mental phenomena as mental phenomena, energetically, self-possessed, and mindful, having eliminated both the desire for and the despair over the world. In this way, a *bhikkhu* lives with himself as a guiding light, with himself as a refuge, without another refuge; lives with the *dhamma* as a guiding light, with the *dhamma* as a refuge, without another refuge.

28. "*Bhikkhus,* stick to your own pastures, to your ancestral haunts. By sticking to your own pastures and to your ancestral haunts, your life span and beauty will increase, as will your happiness, enjoyment, and strength.

"And what is there for a *bhikkhu* in a life span? Here, a *bhikkhu* develops the base of power that is endowed with concentration, exertion, and impulses to action in regard to will; the base of power that is endowed with concentration, exertion, and impulses to action in regard to energy; the base of power that is endowed with concentration, exertion, and impulses to action in regard to mind; the base of power that is endowed with concentration, exertion, and impulses to action in regard to investigation. By developing and cultivating these four bases of power, he may, if he wishes, live for an eon [*kappa*] of time, or the remaining part of an eon. This is what there is for a *bhikkhu* in a life span.

"And what is beauty for a *bhikkhu?* Here, a *bhikkhu* is one who is virtuous, lives with his senses restrained by observing the rules of monastic discipline [*pātimokkha*], is perfect in his conduct and habits, sees the danger in 78
the slightest faults, and trains himself in the precepts he has undertaken. This is beauty for a *bhikkhu.*

"And what is happiness for a *bhikkhu?* Here, a *bhikkhu* who is detached from sensual pleasures and unwholesome mental states lives, having entered the first *jhāna,* which is accompanied by reasoning and cogitation, wherein there is joy and happiness born of detachment. By the calming of reasoning and cogitation, internally purified, a *bhikkhu* lives, having entered the second *jhāna,* which has a one-pointed mind that is devoid of reasoning and cogitation and wherein there is joy and happiness born of concentration. Dwelling in equanimity, and with the cessation of joy, mindful and fully aware, a *bhikkhu* lives, having entered the third *jhāna,* wherein he experiences happiness with the body and that which the noble ones describe as: 'He who has equanimity and mindfulness lives happily.' Abandoning both happiness and suffering, from the extinction of the elation and despair he felt formerly, a *bhikkhu* lives, having entered the fourth *jhāna,* wherein there is neither suffering nor happiness, but the purity of mindfulness and equanimity. This is happiness for a *bhikkhu.*

"And what is enjoyment for a *bhikkhu?* Here, a *bhikkhu* dwells having pervaded one direction with a mind endowed with loving-kindness, then a second direction, then a third direction, then a fourth direction. Likewise upward, downward, crosswise, everywhere in all ways and to the furthest extent, he dwells having pervaded the whole world with a mind endowed with loving-kindness—filled with it, grown great by it, boundless in it, without hatred and ill will. Then he dwells having pervaded one direction with a mind endowed with compassion . . . with sympathetic joy . . . with equanimity, then a second direction, then a third direction, then a fourth direction. Likewise upward, downward, crosswise, everywhere in all ways and to the furthest extent, he dwells having pervaded the whole world with a mind endowed with equanimity—filled with it, grown great by it, boundless in it, without hatred and ill will. This is enjoyment for a *bhikkhu.*

"And what is strength for a *bhikkhu?* Here, a *bhikkhu,* having destroyed the defilements, abides and dwells in the undefiled freedom of mind and freedom through wisdom, having understood and realized it for himself in this very world. This is strength for a *bhikkhu.*

"*Bhikkhus,* I do not perceive another single strength that is as difficult to
79 master as the strength of Māra. *Bhikkhus,* by undertaking wholesome mental states, that merit increases."

This was said by the Exalted One. Delighted, those *bhikkhus* rejoiced in what the Exalted One had said.

16

Discourse to the Layman Sigāla

(*Sigālovāda Sutta*)[1]

This discourse is generally regarded as the Buddha's most important statement of moral principles for the Buddhist layperson. Since the time of the Buddha, the status of a Buddhist layperson has been a subject of controversy. Can a person be committed to following the Buddhist path and yet remain a layperson? After all, the path to enlightenment taught by the Buddha seems geared to the serious, full-time, religious practitioner, that is, the *bhikkhus* or *bhikkhunīs* who have joined the *Saṅgha.* The development of moral conduct may not be beyond the capacity of the layperson, but the mental culture (*samādhi*) and wisdom (*paññā*) required for enlightenment do not appear to be attainable by those still living a domestic life. Nevertheless, when questioned about whether any of his lay-followers have achieved enlightenment, the Buddha replied that, in fact, many of his lay-followers have achieved enlightenment.

Despite the Buddha's reply, a person living a domestic life is at a significant disadvantage in regard to religious attainment compared with the person who lives a monastic life. As it stands today, most Buddhists in countries where the Theravāda tradition is prevalent think that *nibbāna* is not attainable by anyone except the most adept *bhikkhus.*[2] The layperson can only hope that sufficient merit is attained in this life so that he or she may be ordained as a *bhikkhu* in some future life and thereby have a better chance to attain enlightenment.

The discourse opens with Sigāla, a householder's son, paying homage to the six directions, the four cardinal directions, as well as the zenith and the nadir, according to his deceased father's instructions. The Buddha tells him that he is not paying homage to the six directions properly. Sigāla takes the Buddha to mean that his *practice* of the ritual could be improved, but, as usual, the Buddha has something far more radical in mind. The Buddha changes the very meaning of "paying homage to the six directions" from ritualized propitiation of the gods to a set of very specific *ethical* practices that fulfill one's social responsibilities to the six types of person upon whom one depends for support in life (parents, teachers, wife/children, friends, servants,

[1] *Dīgha Nikāya* 3.180–193.

[2] There is even widespread belief in such countries (Sri Lanka and Thailand, for example) that no one, not even a *bhikkhu* or *bhikkhunī,* has achieved enlightenment for many centuries.

and religious practitioners). These relationships are social, familial, educational, and religious. But what is most interesting about the Buddha's account of these social relationships is that they are all construed as involving *reciprocity.* For example, the son or daughter provides support to the parents in old age and keeps the family traditions, but the parents are expected to respond by providing their child moral guidance, vocational training, and eventually a proper share of the inheritance.

As one might expect, the moral principles taught to the *bhikkhus* differ from those taught to laypersons. Unlike the moral teachings intended for the *bhikkhus,* immoral conduct is not taught to the layperson as *intrinsically* bad; rather, it is shown to lead to undesirable *consequences* such as loss of a good reputation and consignment to a stint in hell after death.

The discourse offers an especially interesting account of friendship. Friendship is an important value because one's circle of associates has a significant influence on the moral quality of one's behavior. Given the Buddha's idea of socially constructed reciprocity, it is critical to have morally good and supportive friends. The Buddha's focus on friendship challenges the view that early Buddhism overemphasizes individualism. The recommendation that the layperson develop strong friendships indicates that the Buddha recognized human beings as fundamentally *social* beings.

Discourse

180

1. Thus have I heard. At one time, the Exalted One was dwelling in Rājagaha in the bamboo grove in the Squirrel's Feeding Ground. At that time, Sigāla, a householder's son, rose up early in the morning and went out of Rājagaha with wet clothes and wet hair. Holding up his clasped hands in reverence, he paid homage to the four directions—to the eastern direction, the southern direction, the western direction, the northern direction—and also to the nadir and the zenith.

2. Then the Exalted One, having dressed himself early in the morning, took his robe and bowl and entered Rājagaha for alms. The Exalted One saw Sigāla, the householder's son, rise up early in the morning and go out of Rājagaha with wet clothes and wet hair, holding up his clasped hands in reverence to the four directions—to the eastern direction, the southern direction, the western direction, the northern direction—and also to the nadir and the zenith.

Having seen Sigāla, he said to him: "Householder's son, why do you rise up early in the morning and go out of Rājagaha with wet clothes and wet
181 hair, holding up your clasped hands in reverence to the four directions—to

the eastern direction, the southern direction, the western direction, the northern direction—and also to the nadir and the zenith?"

"Sir, my father, when he was dying, said this: 'Son, you should pay homage to the directions.' And so, sir, out of honor, respect, esteem, and reverence for the words of my father, I pay homage to the four directions—to the eastern direction, the southern direction, the western direction, the northern direction—and also to the nadir and the zenith."

"But, householder's son, that is not the way to pay homage to the six directions according to the noble discipline."[3]

"How, then, sir, should one pay homage to the six directions according to the noble discipline? It would be good, sir, if the Exalted One would teach the right doctrine in regard to the correct way to pay homage to the six directions."

"Then listen to this, householder's son. Keep your mind attentive and I will speak."

"Yes, sir," Sigāla replied to the Exalted One. So the Exalted One said this:

3. "From the fact that the noble disciple has abandoned the four defilements of action, such a person does not commit evil actions based on these four defilements, and does not associate with the six causes that waste a person's wealth. By removing the fourteen evils, by covering the six directions, he practices in order to conquer both worlds. Such a person has won this world as well as the next world. After the breaking up of the body at death, that person is reborn in a good place, even a heavenly world.

"What are the four defilements of action that are abandoned? Taking life is a defilement of action. Taking what is not given is a defilement of action. Living wrongly in regard to sensual pleasures is a defilement of action. Speaking falsely is a defilement of action. These are the four defilements of action that are abandoned."

This was said by the Exalted One.

4. This having been said by the Well-Farer, the Teacher then said another thing: 182

> "It is said that taking life, taking what is not given, speaking falsely,
> And adultery, too, the wise do not commend.

5. "What are the four bases for the evil action that he does not commit? One commits evil action because one is motivated by desire. One commits evil action because one is motivated by hatred. One commits evil action because one is motivated by delusion. One commits evil action because one

[3] *Ariyassa vinaye.* This refers to the rules for Buddhist practice.

is motivated by fear. From the fact that the noble disciple is not motivated by desire, not motivated by hatred, not motivated by delusion, and not motivated by fear, such a person does not commit evil actions on account of these four bases."

This was said by the Exalted One.

6. This having been said by the Well-Farer, the Teacher then said another thing:

"Whoever transgresses the *dhamma*
Through desire, hatred, fear, and delusion
That person's reputation wanes,
As the moon wanes in the second half of the month.

Whoever does not transgress the *dhamma*
Through desire, hatred, fear, and delusion
That person's reputation waxes,
As the moon waxes in the first half of the month.

7. "What are the six ways that one might waste one's wealth that [the noble disciple] is not associated with? The wrongful practice of indulging in strong drink, liquors, and other intoxicants that lead to sloth and indolence; the wrongful practice of going about the streets at inappropriate times; attending festivals; the wrongful practice of gambling and other indolent pastimes; the practice of associating with evil companions; and the practice of laziness are the six ways that one might waste one's wealth that [the noble disciple] is not associated with.

8. "There are these six dangers regarding the wrongful practice of indulging in strong drink, liquors, and other intoxicants that lead to sloth and indolence: waste of money in the present, the increase in quarrelling, being
183 liable to illness, the development of a bad reputation, indecent exposure (of one's sexual organs), and the weakening of one's intelligence is the sixth thing. These are the six dangers regarding the wrongful practice of indulging in strong drink, liquors, and other intoxicants that lead to sloth and indolence.

9. "There are these six dangers regarding the wrongful practice of going about the streets at inappropriate times: one's person is left unguarded and without protection, one's children and wife are left unguarded and without protection, one's property is left unguarded and without protection, one becomes a suspect in crimes committed in the locality, false rumors circulate about such a person, and many other painful things confront the person. These are the six dangers regarding the wrongful practice of going about the streets at inappropriate times.

10. "There are these six dangers of attending festivals. [One is always thinking:] 'Where is there dancing? Where is there singing? Where are they playing music? Where is there reciting? Where is there hand-clapping? Where are there drums?' These are the six dangers of attending festivals.

11. "There are these six dangers regarding the wrongful practice of gambling and other indolent pastimes: victory brings forth hatred, when beaten one bewails one's lost wealth, one's money is wasted in the present, one's word is not trusted in the assembly, one is reviled by friends and associates, and one is not a desirable marriage partner because people would declare that a person who lives such a corrupt life does not have enough money to maintain a wife. These are the six dangers regarding the wrongful practice of gambling and other indolent pastimes.

12. "There are these six dangers regarding association with bad companions: any scoundrel, any harlot, any drunkard, any cheat, any trickster, and any brute is one's friend and ally. These are the six dangers regarding associ- 184
ation with bad companions.

13. "There are these six dangers regarding the practice of laziness: thinking 'it's too cold,' 'it's too hot,' 'it's too early,' 'it's too late,' 'I'm too hungry,' or 'I'm too full,' one does no work. In this way, all the things one should be doing remain undone—therefore, one receives no money, and the money one has is wasted. These are the six dangers regarding the wrong practice of laziness."

This was said by the Exalted One.

14. This having been said by the Well-Farer, the Teacher then said another thing:

"There is a friend who is called a drinking buddy
There are some who are heartily friendly to one's face
But, whoever is a friend when need arises,
That person is a real friend.
Sleeping late (after the sun has risen), committing adultery,
Being inclined to enmity, doing harm,
Bad friends, and stinginess,
These six things ruin a person.
A bad friend and a bad companion
Performs a wicked deed
In this world, and in the next world
A person will be ruined.
Gambling, strong drink, dancing and singing,
Sleeping in the daytime, going around at inappropriate times,
Bad friends and stinginess,

These six things ruin a person.
Playing dice, drinking liquor
185 And going with another's beloved wife
Attending to the inferior person, but not old people
One wanes like the moon.
The one who drinks liquor
Poor, without anything
Is still thirsty even when drinking from the well.
One plunges into debt like plunging into water
And one soon deprives oneself of one's family.
One cannot live in a household
If one is accustomed to sleeping by day and getting up at night
And if one is always intoxicated and drunk.
One does no work, saying
'Too cold! Too hot! Too late!'
Wealth eludes such a person.
But the one who does not think of cold or hot as more than weeds
Who performs humane acts
Such a person is not short of happiness.

15. "There are these four types of non-friend that should be known as one who merely appears to be a friend: the non-friend who only takes, the non-friend for whom talk is highest, the non-friend who flatters, and the non-friend who is a spendthrift companion.

186 16. "There are these four reasons why a non-friend who only takes should be known as one who merely appears to be a friend: such a person only takes things, wants much for little in return, does his or her duty out of fear, and serves only his or her own interests. These are the four reasons why a non-friend who only takes should be known as one who merely appears to be a friend.

17. "There are these four reasons why a non-friend for whom talk is highest should be known as one who merely appears to be a friend: such a person dwells on the past, dwells on the future, encourages collusion in what is useless, and points out his or her misfortune [i.e., in regard to his or her inability to render service] when an occasion for service arises. These are the four reasons why a non-friend for whom talk is highest should be known as one who merely appears to be a friend.

18. "There are these four reasons why a non-friend who is a flatterer should be known as one who only appears to be a friend: such a person consents to wrongdoing, or refrains from consenting to what is good, praises one face-to-face, but speaks ill of one behind one's back. These are the four

reasons why a non-friend who is a flatterer should be known as one who only appears to be a friend.

19. "There are these four reasons why a non-friend who is a spendthrift companion should be known as one who merely appears to be a friend: such a person is a companion when you indulge in the wrongful practice of taking strong drink and other intoxicants that lead to indolence, is a companion in the practice of going about the streets at inappropriate times, is a companion who attends festivals, and is a companion who indulges in the wrongful practice of gambling and other indolent pastimes. These are the four reasons why a non-friend who is a spendthrift companion should be known as one who merely appears to be a friend."

This was said by the Exalted One.

20. This having been said by the Well-Farer, the Teacher then said another thing:

"A friend who takes only
And a friend who makes talk the highest thing
And the one who speaks flattery
And the one who is a spendthrift companion,
These four are non-friends.
Recognizing such
The wise should avoid them from far away,
Just as if they were a terrifying path. 187

21. "There are these four kinds of friends who should be known as true friends: the friend who is a helper, the friend who remains the same in good and bad times, the friend who shows what is profitable, and the friend who is compassionate.

22. "There are these four reasons why a friend who is a helper should be known as a true friend: such a person protects one from one's own negligence, protects one's property when one is negligent, is a refuge when one is frightened, and whenever a duty arises, gives one twice the means that one needs. These are the four reasons why a friend who is a helper should be known as a true friend.

23. "There are these four reasons why a friend who remains the same in good and bad times should be known as a true friend: such a person tells one his or her secrets, keeps one's secrets, does not abandon one in misfortune, and would give up his or her life and wealth for one. These are the four reasons why a friend who remains the same in good and bad times should be known as a true friend.

24. "There are these four reasons why a friend who shows what is profitable

should be known as a true friend: such a person restrains one from doing evil, encourages one to do good, declares to one what one has not heard, and points out to one the way to heaven. These are the four reasons why a friend who shows what is profitable should be known as a true friend.

25. "There are these four reasons why a friend who is compassionate should be known as a true friend: such a person does not rejoice in one's misfortunes, rejoices in one's good fortune, restrains others who speak ill of one, and praises others who speak well of one. These are the four reasons why a friend who is compassionate should be known as a true friend."

This was said by the Exalted One.

26. This having been said by the Well-Farer, the Teacher then said another
188 thing:

"The friend who is a helper
And the friend in good and bad times
And the friend who shows what is profitable
As well as the friend who is compassionate,
These four friends are discerned as such by the wise.
One should attend on them, giving them honor
As a mother attends on her own child.
The wise, endowed with moral conduct,
He shines forth like a blazing fire,
One collects wealth like a bee flies about gathering honey
The wealth one accumulates rises up like an anthill.
Having amassed such wealth
There is sufficient wealth for the clan of the layman
The wealth should be divided in four ways
So one binds oneself to one's friends.
One part of the wealth one should enjoy oneself
Two parts one should apply to work
A fourth part one should reserve for the times when there will be misfortune.

27. "And how does the noble disciple cover the six directions? One should consider these six directions as follows: one's mother and father
189 should be known as the eastern direction; teachers should be known as the southern direction; one's children and wife should be known as the western direction; one's friends and companions should be known as the northern direction; servants, workers, and helpers should be known as the nadir; and religious wanderers and Brahmins should be known as the zenith.

28. "There are these five ways that a child should minister to his or her mother and father as the eastern direction: one thinks 'I will support those

who brought me up.' One thinks 'I will perform their duties for them, keep the family tradition, and so make myself worthy of my inheritance, and at the time of their deaths I will offer gifts in their honor.' So, when the child ministers to his or her mother and father in these five ways as the eastern direction, the child's parents will respond showing the child compassion, by restraining the child from doing evil, by encouraging the child to do good, by training the child in a craft, by marrying the child to a suitable spouse, and by handing over the child's inheritance at the right time. When the child ministers to his or her mother and father in these five ways as the eastern direction, the parents will respond showing the child compassion. In this way, one covers the eastern direction, so that it is peaceful and free from fear.

29. "There are these five ways that students should minister to their teachers as the southern direction: by rising from one's seat out of respect, by waiting on them, by being obedient to them, by giving them service, and by thoroughly learning the teachers' arts. So, when students minister to their teachers in these five ways as the southern direction, the teachers will respond showing compassion to their students by instructing them so that they are well-trained, by making them grasp tightly what should be well-grasped, by making them their equal in all the arts and lore, by speaking well of them to their friends and companions, and by protecting them in all directions. When the students minister to their teachers in these five ways as the south- 190
ern direction, the teachers will respond showing compassion to the students. In this way, one covers the southern direction, so that it is peaceful and free from fear.

30. "There are these five ways that a husband should minister to his wife as the western direction: by showing her respect, by not showing her disrespect, by not being unfaithful, by relinquishing authority to her, and by providing her with sufficient adornments. So, when a husband ministers to his wife in these five ways as the western direction, his wife will respond showing compassion to her husband by performing her work well, by keeping the servants well-organized, by being faithful, by guarding their stored goods, and by being skillful and diligent in all of her duties. When a husband ministers to his wife in these five ways as the western direction, his wife will respond showing compassion to her husband. In this way, he covers the western direction, so that it is peaceful and free from fear.

31. "There are these five ways that a young man of a good family should minister to friends and companions as the northern direction: by gifts, by kindly words, by looking after their welfare, by treating them like himself, and by being true to his word. So, when a young man of a good family ministers to his friends and companions as the northern direction, his friends and companions will respond showing compassion to him by protecting him

from his own negligence, by protecting his property from his negligence, by being his refuge when he is frightened, by not abandoning him when he meets misfortune, and by honoring the other members of his family. When a young man of a good family ministers to his friends and companions in these five ways as the northern direction, his friends and companions will respond by showing him compassion. In this way, he covers the northern direction, so that it is peaceful and free from fear.

191 32. "There are these five ways that a master should minister to servants, workers, and helpers as the nadir: by arranging their work according to the servant's strength, by supplying them with food and wages, by nursing them when they are sick, by sharing special foods with them, and by generously granting them leave at certain times. So, when a master ministers to servants, workers, and helpers as the nadir, the servants, workers, and helpers will respond showing compassion to him by rising earlier than the master, by retiring later than the master, by taking only what is given to them, by doing their work properly, and by bearing a good report about the master. When a master ministers to servants, workers, and helpers in these five ways as the nadir, the servants, workers, and helpers will respond showing compassion to the master. In this way, one covers the nadir, so that it is peaceful and free from fear.

33. "There are these five ways that a young man of a good family should minister to religious wanderers and Brahmins as the zenith: by loving-kindness in bodily action, by loving-kindness in speech, by loving-kindness in thought, by keeping his house open for them, and by supplying their material needs. So, when a young man of a good family ministers to religious wanderers and Brahmins as the zenith, there are six ways that the religious wanderers and Brahmins will respond showing compassion to him, by restraining him from doing evil, by encouraging him to do good, by showing compassion with good intentions toward him, by teaching him what he has not heard, by purifying what he has heard, and by pointing out to him the way to heaven. When a young man of a good family ministers to religious wanderers and Brahmins in these five ways as the zenith, there are six ways that the religious wanderers and Brahmins will respond showing compassion to him. In this way, he covers the zenith, so that it is peaceful and free from fear."

This was said by the Exalted One.

34. This having been said by the Well-Farer, the Teacher then said another thing:

"Mother and father are the eastern direction
192 Teachers are the southern direction

Children and wife are the western direction
Friends and companions are the northern direction
Servants and workers are the nadir
Religious wanderers and Brahmins are the zenith.
All of these directions should be honored
By a family man who has sufficient means.
Wise, endowed with moral conduct,
Gentle and intelligent,
Humble and not stubborn,
Such a person achieves a [good] reputation.
Rising early, not lazy, not flinching in adversity,
Faultless in conduct and wise,
Such a person achieves a [good] reputation.
Hospitable and maker of friends
Generous, free from stinginess
A leader, trainer, and conciliator
Such a person achieves a [good] reputation.
With generosity and kindly speech
One serves the needs of the others here in this world.
Being impartial to each person
According to what is fitting
These are the four forms of kindly behavior in the world
Like the axle pin of a chariot that is moving.
And if these four forms of kindly behavior in the world did not exist
No mother would get the respect or honor that her child is obliged to give her
Nor would a father receive what his child is obliged to give him.
But since there are four forms of kindly behavior in the world
Wise people take consideration of these kindly behaviors 193
Therefore they reach greatness
And are to be praised."

35. This having been said, Sigāla said this to the Exalted One: "Wonderful, sir! Wonderful, sir! It is just as if someone were to make upright what was turned upside down, or were to uncover what was covered over, or were to explain the way to those who are lost, or were to hold up an oil lamp in the darkness, saying 'those endowed with eyes will see the visible objects.' Just so, the Exalted One makes known the *dhamma* by diverse methods. Sir, I go to the Exalted One for refuge, and also to the *dhamma* and the *Saṅgha* of the *bhikkhus*. Let the Exalted One accept me as a lay-follower, going for refuge from this day forth, as long as life lasts."

General Glossary

aggregates (*khandhas;* Skt: *skandhas*): The five aggregates comprise a human being: bodily/organic processes (*rūpa*), feeling (*vedanā*), perception (*saññā*), dispositions to action (*saṅkhāra*), and consciousness (*viññāṇa*); the aggregates are, individually and collectively, dependently arisen and so do not form a permanent Self.

Āḷāra Kālāma: A forest-dwelling teacher (most likely in the Brahmanical tradition) who taught Siddhattha (the Buddha) higher powers and higher states of experience, such as the "plane of no-thing."

Ānanda: A *bhikkhu* who served as the Buddha's personal attendant and friend; Ānanda is credited with a recitation of the entire Discourse Basket (*Sutta Piṭaka*) of the Pāli Canon at an early council of *bhikkhus* following the Buddha's decease.

anattā: The Buddhist teaching that there is no permanent Self (*attā*) or soul.

arahant: Literally, a "worthy one"; a person who has destroyed the moral defilements (*āsavas*) and thus has attained *nibbāna,* the highest stage of religious attainment in Buddhism.

attachment (*upādāna*): Selfishly grasping onto things that arise in sensory experience or grasping after the theory of a permanent Self; a psychological state characterized by selfish craving.

attā: See "permanent Self."

becoming/rebirth (*bhāva*): The continuing and changing nature of anything in existence; reproduced into existence, hence "rebirth."

bhikkhu: A fully ordained Buddhist monk; a male member of the *Saṅgha.*

bhikkhunī: A fully ordained Buddhist nun; a female member of the *Saṅgha.*

bodhisatta: Literally, a "being in awakening"; a being on the verge of attaining *nibbāna;* in the Pāli Buddhist tradition, the term is used by the Buddha to refer to himself prior to his enlightenment as a Buddha (i.e., both in his present life and in recent past lives); in later Buddhist traditions (especially in Mahāyāna Buddhism), the term takes on a further meaning—it refers to a Buddhist saint who demonstrates an infinite compassion for all beings.

Brahman: In Hindu tradition, particularly in the early Upaniṣads (and later in Advaita Vedanta), Brahman is the ground of all that exists, and thus an understanding of Brahman is the highest spiritual goal of the path of knowledge (*jñāna-yoga*); Brahman is one and transcendent, and yet it is the mysterious source of all that is real.

Brahmā: A Hindu *deva* who is Creator of the universe; in the Buddhist tradition, a *deva* that inhabits one of the higher heavenly realms; sometimes the term refers to a class of *devas* that inhabit the Brahmā-worlds (heavens).

Brahmā Sahampati: A high *deva* who inhabits a Brahmā-world; Brahmā Sahampati convinces the Buddha to teach the *dhamma,* despite the Buddha's initial reluctance to do so.

Brahmāvihāras: Literally, "dwelling in holiness"; the four cardinal virtues in Buddhism: compassion (*karuṇā*), loving-kindness (*mettā*), sympathetic joy (*muditā*), equanimity (*upekhā*).

Brahmā-world: One of the higher realms in Buddhist cosmology, inhabited mainly by *devas* or superior beings in attendance on Brahmā.

Brahmin: The social class of priests and religious teachers in Hindu society; Brahmins are typically considered as the highest of the classes on the basis of birth, religious function, bodily appearance, and purported relationship to God (Brahmā).

Buddha: Literally, "awoken"; a person who has woken up to the highest religious life and teaches to the world the path to achieve this life; an epithet for Siddhattha Gotama, who is the Buddha of the present age.

causal link (*nidāna*): The processes of the natural world, including human psychological processes, are identifiable patterns of cause and effect; for Buddhism, the most important pattern of cause and effect is the twelvefold formula of dependent arising (*paṭiccasamuppāda*) that describes the arising and ceasing of suffering.

compassion (*karuṇā*): One of the four *brahmāvihāras* or cardinal virtues of Buddhism; the Buddha taught that one should develop an unselfish identification with the well-being of all other sentient beings.

concentration (*samādhi*): A highly focused state of meditation; together with moral conduct (*sīla*), concentration forms a necessary component in the quest for wisdom (*paññā*) and liberation; the eighth factor in the Noble Eightfold Path.

consciousness (*viññāṇa*): Awareness or self-reflective mental activity; the fifth of the five aggregates that constitute a person.

contact (*phassa*): Sometimes translated as "sensory impingement," contact refers to the coming together of a sensory faculty, a sensory object, and a sensory mode of consciousness, all three of which must be present for there to occur a sensory experience; contact suggests that the various components of a sensory experience are but *functional* elements (not self-subsistent entities); contact leads to feeling (*vedana*) in the unfolding of the pattern of dependent arising.

craving (*taṇhā*): Selfish grasping after material possessions, pleasures, non-becoming; most notoriously, attachment to the notion of a permanent Self; in the formula of dependent arising, craving arises because of feelings filtered through a selfish and morally corrupt mind; for this reason, the elimination of craving is a major focus of the Buddhist path.

decision-making (*vinicchayaṃ*): Discriminative or analytical thought, investigation.

defilement (*āsava*): Literally, "outflow"; the underlying psychological factors or propensities that corrupt human experience and lead to unwholesome (immoral) activities; there are three basic defilements: greed (*lobha*), hatred (*dosa*), and delusion (*moha*).

defilements of action (*kamma-kilesā*): Psychological factors of corruption and depravity that induce an unregenerate person to morally impure actions.

delusion (*moha*): Utter lack of comprehension, confusion; one of the three basic defilements of the mind (*āsavas*) that lead to immoral or unwholesome activities.

dependent arising (*paṭiccasamupāda*): The central insight and doctrine of Buddhism; all things exist as processes (they arise as a complex concatenation of changing factors, continue to evolve and change, and eventually pass out of existence), so nothing is a permanent, self-subsisting thing; the formulae (tenfold and twelvefold versions) for dependent arising articulate the causal pattern that accounts for the arising and ceasing of suffering (*dukkha*); insight into dependent arising was the key to the Buddha's enlightenment; from this doctrine the Buddha realized the futility of selfish attachment—because nothing is permanent, even the human person has no permanent Self or soul, and therefore, one must learn to cultivate an attitude of nonattachment.

deva: A god in the Hindu (Vedic) tradition; in Buddhism, an inhabitant of the higher realms, but a natural (not a supernatural) being, because even the gods are subject to change.

Devadatta: The Buddha's first cousin and a *bhikkhu,* Devadatta tried to create a schism in the *Saṅgha* and, from his desire for fame and power, aimed to insert himself as the leader of the *Saṅgha;* the Buddha predicted that Devadatta would go to a state of misery after his death.

***deva*-eye** (*dibbacakkhu*): A faculty of vision or insight possessed by the Buddha that is beyond normal human ability.

dhamma: The Buddha's teachings or doctrine—as such, the second of the three "refuges"; the essence or nature of a thing; in the plural (*dhammā*), the term usually refers to mental objects or ideas.

discipline (*vinaya*): The rules or precepts that guide the life of a *bhikkhu* (monk) or *bhikkhuni* (nun); for the Buddhist monastic community (*Saṅgha*), the core of the discipline is the more than two hundred monastic rules known as the "*pātimokkha.*"

dispositions to action (*saṅkhāra*): The features of the human mind that motivate a person to act, or react, to events or objects within one's experience.

dukkha: See "suffering."

energy (*viriya*): An essential element in the character of those following the noble quest for enlightenment, energy refers to the mental (and physical) strength necessary to push forward along the arduous path to higher states of experience and liberation.

enlightenment: Awakening, liberation, *nibbāna.*

equanimity (*upekhā*): One of the four *brahmāvihāras* or cardinal virtues of Buddhism; the Buddha taught that a person should maintain a balanced, fair, and objective perspective at all times.

Exalted One (*bhagavant*): An epithet indicating the status of the Buddha; some translators translate the term *bhagavant* as "Blessed One" or "Lord."

factor of enlightenment (*sambojjhaṅgaṃ*): One of seven constituents of enlightenment.

faith (*saddhā*): In the nontheistic context of early Buddhism, this term means something very close to "confidence," because it refers to a kind of resolve or commitment to living a life in accord with the Buddha's teachings (*dhamma*), rather than a belief in a supernatural being or a blind acceptance of religious dogma; having faith or confidence in the Buddha, the *dhamma,* and the *Saṅgha* is what distinguishes a person as a Buddhist; faith, in the Buddhist tradition, is the expectation that, guided by the *dhamma,* one will advance in religious terms and eventually achieve liberation (*nibbāna*).

feeling (*vedanā*): The noncognitive psychological component of human experience; there are three types of feeling: pleasant, painful, and neutral.

Four Noble Truths: The core of the Buddha's teaching and its most concise statement; the Four Noble Truths are (1) suffering; (2) the origin of suffering (suffering is caused by selfish craving and ignorance); (3) the cessation of suffering (by eliminating its causes); and (4) the "middle way"—the Noble Eightfold Path that provides a way to eliminate suffering; in effect, the Four Noble Truths are a diagnosis and therapy for the human spiritual condition.

gandhabba: Originally this term referred to a musical sprite or celestial musician, but in early Buddhism it refers to a factor in the conception of a human embryo that provides the link between a newly conceived being and its previous states of existence.

Gotama: The family name of Siddhattha (the Buddha); the custom, particularly among non-Buddhists from the higher classes, was to address the Buddha by his family name.

great elements: Earth, air, wind, and fire; the four basic constituents of the material world.

Great Person (*mahāpurisa*): According to ancient Indian tradition, a great religious teacher or a great political leader would have thirty-two marks on the body that indicate a person's high status; according to the Buddhist tradition, the marks of a Great Person were found on the infant Siddhattha (the Buddha).

greed (*lobha*): Selfish grasping after, or intense desire for, material things; one of the three basic defilements (*āsavas*) that corrupt a person's mind and lead to immoral or unwholesome activities.

hatred (*dosa*): Intense dislike of another person that often foments violence; one of the three basic defilements (*āsavas*) that corrupt a person's mind and lead to immoral or unwholesome activities.

higher knowledge (*abhiññā*): Supersensory powers; extensions of the normal senses (e.g., clairaudience—the ability to hear sounds at significant distances); includes the highest knowledge claimed by the Buddha, namely, the "knowledge of the destruction of the defilements (*āsavas*)," which is a kind of insight that is identical with achieving liberation or *nibbāna.*

higher ordination (*upasampadā*): The rite whereby a person becomes a full-fledged *bhikkhu* (monk) or *bhikkhunī* (nun).

holy life (*brahmacariya*): Living a religious life; living according to a strict code of moral conduct (*sīla*).

householder (*gahapati*): A person (usually male) living a domestic life (as opposed to a monastic life).

ignorance (*avijjā*): Lack of understanding or comprehension of deeper religious truth, especially the Buddha's central teaching of dependent arising; a causal link (*nidāna*) in the formula of dependent arising.

immaterial acquired self (*arūpa atta-paṭilābha*): Acquisition of a personality based on immaterial factors; "acquired" in the sense of obtained or attained as a product of certain conditions that have dependently arisen; it is not a permanent Self.

impermanence (*anicca*): A key corollary to the Buddha's central insight that everything that exists is but a changing process, dependently arisen, hence nothing exists eternally.

infinite consciousness (plane of) (*viññānañcayatana*): A very high level of meditative attainment that succeeds mastery of the four *jhānas.*

infinite space (plane of) (*ākāsanañcayatana*): A very high level of meditative attainment that succeeds mastery of the four *jhānas.*

intentional thought (*cetayamāna*): The mind's ability to develop an inclination or a disinclination as it regards its ideas; the mental faculty of will or choice.

Jain: A member of the religious tradition known as "Jainism"; Jainism teaches that all beings have a life principle (*jīva*), and that the life principle is bound through karma to continual rebirth in the material world—only extreme asceticism can break this bondage and lead to liberation.

jhāna: An advanced state of meditation; four stages of rapture enroute to higher religious achievement and *nibbāna.*

kappa (Skt: *kalpa*): A very great length of time; an eon.

karma (Pāli: *kamma*): Literally, "action"; the moral quality of a person's actions correlates (by strong tendency or cause) with the moral quality of the results of such actions, hence morally good actions have beneficial results, and morally bad actions lead to suffering and woe.

khattiya: A social class composed of political leaders and warriors; by birth, the Buddha belonged to the *khattiya* class.

lay-follower (male: *upāsiko* / female: *upāsikā*): A nonmonastic disciple of the Buddha; someone who takes the three refuges (Buddha, *dhamma, Saṅgha*) but remains in domestic life.

life principle (*jīva*): What gives life to, or animates, the body; sometimes translated as "soul."

loving-kindness (*mettā*): One of the four *brahmāvihāras* or cardinal virtues of Buddhism; a person should develop the same kind of intense self-sacrificing love toward all beings that a mother would have for her only child.

lower ordination (*pabbajjā*): Literally, to "go forth"; a rite whereby one leaves domestic life to join the monastic life of the *Saṅgha* as a novice monk or nun.

lust (*rāga*): Uncontrolled passion for sensual pleasures.

mantra: A sacred word used in meditation to focus the mind and realize higher truths.

Māra: The Evil One, the embodiment of such evil states as lust, greed, and hatred; the tempter who aims to prevent persons from achieving enlightenment, as in the story of the Buddha's own enlightenment under the Bo tree.

material acquired self (*oḷārika atta-paṭilābha*): Acquisition of a personality based on "coarse" or material factors; "acquired" in the sense of obtained or attained as a product of certain conditions that have dependently arisen; it is not a permanent Self.

materiality (*rūpa*): Sometimes translated as "form" or "visible object"; the biological/organic aspect of the natural world that can be seen with the eye, including the human body; the material world that is composed of the four great elements (air, water, fire, and earth).

mind (*citta*): The mind is the seat of human personality, although it is not a soul or permanent Self; in fact, the mind is usually depicted as a rapidly changing confluence of mental processes (cognitive, affective, and volitional); the path to liberation proposed by the Buddha is a process of purifying the mind.

mindfulness (*sati*): Being fully aware of the arising and passing of each factor or object in one's experience is a crucial skill in the Buddhist tradition; such a skill allows one to control one's mind by paying careful attention to the direction that experiences take as they unfold (i.e., toward wholesome or unwholesome results); on the basis of the development of mindfulness, the mind can be trained to react to the world in only wholesome ways that bring an abiding happiness (rather than in ways that inevitably lead to suffering); the seventh factor in the Noble Eightfold Path.

mind-made acquired self (*manomaya atta-paṭilābha*): Acquisition of a personality based on mental factors; "acquired" in the sense of obtained or attained as a product of certain conditions that have dependently arisen; it is not a permanent Self.

monastic rules (*pātimokkha*): A code of more than two hundred rules or precepts that define the lives of the *bhikkhus* (monks) and *bhikkhunis* (nuns) in the *Saṅgha* (monastic community); these rules are recited in assembly every two weeks (at new and full moons); the monastic rules form the core of the texts known as the *Vinaya Piṭaka* (Discipline Basket).

moral conduct (*sīla*): Following the precepts and other moral codes suggested by the Buddha; the practice of moral conduct aims to eliminate sensualism, selfishness, and other unwholesome habits of action, and to replace them with virtuous or wholesome habits, such as compassion and friendliness.

neither-perception-nor-non-perception (plane of): One of the highest levels of meditative attainment that succeeds mastery of the four *jhānas;* a state of meditation so remote from normal (perceptual) experience that it cannot be described in terms of perception at all.

nibbāna (Skt: *nirvāṇa*): The highest goal of Buddhism; literally, the extinction or "cooling" of the "flame" of moral defilements that causes suffering (*dukkha*); synonymous with spiritual liberation, it represents the highest possible meaning for a human life; release from the *saṃsāric* round of death and rebirth.

Nīgaṇṭha Nātaputta: A leading figure in the Jainist tradition and a contemporary of the Buddha; also known as "Mahāvīra."

nikāya: Literally, "collection" or "grouping"; the various collections of discourses in the Discourse Basket (*Sutta Piṭaka*) of the Pāli Canon (e.g., the *Majjhima Nikāya* or "Middle-length Collection"); in monastic structure, the term refers to a "sect" among the various monastic orders.

niraya: A hellish state in the afterlife, but not a permanent state; a place of misery; the lowest place in Buddhist cosmology.

noble disciple (*ariyasāvako*): A disciple of the Buddha who understands and faithfully follows the *dhamma*.

noble discipline (*ariya vinaya*): The rules or precepts suggested by the Buddha; a key focus in the noble discipline is the development of restraint toward sensual pleasures.

Noble Eightfold Path: The Fourth Noble Truth, the "middle way"; the Buddha's recommended therapy for eliminating suffering; the Noble Eightfold Path is composed of right view, right intention, right speech, right action, right livelihood, right effort, right mindfulness, and right concentration.

non-returner: A person who is sufficiently purified in the moral or religious sense so that there will be no further rebirth; one grade short of final enlightenment.

no-thing (plane of) (*ākiñcaññayatana*): A very high level of meditative attainment that succeeds mastery of the four *jhānas*.

nutriment (*āhāra*): Literally, "food," "fuel," or "support"; nutriment refers to the necessary ingredients that are required to support bodily and mental functions; there are four kinds of nutriment: bodily (i.e., food), contact, volition, and consciousness.

obstacles (*nīvaraṇā*): Psychological hindrances to moral and religious progress; there are five obstacles: the excitement of sense pleasures (sometimes: covetousness), ill will and anger, sloth and torpor, agitation and worry, and perplexity.

once-returner: A person who is sufficiently purified in the moral or religious sense so that there will be only one more rebirth before enlightenment; the second grade on the path to enlightenment.

perception (*saññā*): Cognition or identification of an object in human experience (including memories); recent scholarship sometimes translates this term as "apperception."

permanence (*nicca*): According to the Upaniṣadic tradition, a mark of the true Reality regarding both Self (*ātman*) and transcendent reality (*Brahman*); permanence is nowhere to be found, according to early Buddhism.

permanent Self (*attā;* Skt: *ātman*): Sometimes referred to as "soul"; the belief in and realization of a true Self having the qualities of permanence, pure agency (inner controller), and bliss is the cornerstone of the Upaniṣadic tradition; the Buddha rejected belief in a permanent Self.

Prajāpati: The Creator-god (*deva*) in the Hindu (Vedic) tradition.

psycho-physicality (*nāma-rūpa*): The combination of mental and physical aspects of a person and of reality generally; for early Buddhism, the mental is not a distinct substance from the material, nor do material things have independent essences or "kinds"; rather, the "kind" of a material thing depends on mental factors, such as conceptualization (i.e., "name"); sometimes translated as "name and form" by other translators.

recollection (*anussaraṇa*): Remembrance based on memory.

religious wanderer (*paribbājika*): A religious mendicant; a term applied to wandering holy men who belonged to a number of different religious traditions at the time of the Buddha.

right view (*sammādiṭṭhi*): The first factor in the Noble Eightfold path; it refers to the understanding of suffering via the doctrine of dependent arising and the fact that there is no permanent Self.

Sakyans: The Buddha's clan.

samaṇa: A religiously focused person who has segregated oneself (morally or literally) from domestic society.

saṃsāra: The cycle of birth, death, and rebirth; mundane, unenlightened existence; escape from *saṃsara* constitutes liberation or *nibbāna.*

Saṅgha: The "assemblage" or community of Buddhist monks and nuns; the aim of the *Saṅgha* is to preserve and teach the *dhamma,* as well as to provide an ideal of community life; the "fourfold *Saṅgha*" also includes male and female lay-followers.

Sāriputta: Perhaps the most accomplished *bhikkhu* in terms of understanding and expounding on the *dhamma;* several key discourses in the Pāli Canon are attributed to Sāriputta, rather than to the Buddha.

sense bases (*āyatana*): The sense bases are a combination of sense faculty and sense object; the six sense bases are eyes and visible objects, ears and sounds, nose and smells, tongue and tastes, body and tangibles, and mind and mental objects.

sensual desire/pleasure (*kāma*): The addictive allure of pleasures derived from sensory experiences, coupled with a lustful and selfish mind, poses one of the greatest obstacles to religious progress.

social classes (*vaṇṇas;* Skt: *varṇas*): Hindu society is divided into four social classes: priests and religious teachers (Brahmins), warriors and leaders (*khattiyas*), farmers and merchants (*vessas*), and laborers (*suddas*); class membership is determined by birth, although the class system probably emerged in ancient times from economic, vocational, and racial distinctions; in Hindu society, the classes form a hierarchy with Brahmins at the top.

specific conditionality (*idapaccayata*): Literally, "from *this* cause"; an indication of a precise causal linkage; specific conditionality is closely connected to the doctrine of dependent arising; specific conditionality implies the "conditionedness" of all things, and so denies the essentialist view that there are realities that have an independent and a self-subsisting nature.

speculative view (*diṭṭhi*): A theory or doctrine that goes beyond what can be verified; an unjustifiable metaphysical position.

stream-winner: A person who is converted to Buddhism on the basis of a fourfold attainment: faith in the Buddha, faith in the *dhamma,* faith in the *Saṅgha,* and practice of the Noble Eightfold path; the first stage on the path to enlightenment; tradition suggests that such a person is certain to eventually achieve enlightenment.

sudda: The lowest and largest of the four classes of society, composed of laborers.

suffering (*dukkha*): Perhaps better rendered as "unsatisfactoriness"; it refers mainly to psychological states of profound anxiety, unfulfillment, or unhappiness; that life is filled with suffering or unsatisfactoriness is the First Noble Truth, and, as such, suffering is the basic religious problem that Buddhism aims to solve.

sympathetic joy (*muditā*): One of the four *brahmāvihāras* or cardinal virtues of Buddhism; the Buddha taught that one should take joy in the achievements of others, rather than have an attitude of jealousy or envy.

Tathāgata: A term used by the Buddha to refer to himself as an enlightened person; literally, one who is "thus gone" or one who is "like that."

threefold (Vedic) knowledge: Sacred knowledge derived from the three Vedic texts (the *Rig Veda,* the *Sāma Veda,* and the *Yajur Veda*); mastery of the three Vedas was considered the highest goal for a Hindu Brahmin, as it was the key to liberation (construed by some as "union with Brahmā" [God]).

Uddaka Rāmaputta: A forest-dwelling teacher (most likely in the Brahmanical [Hindu] tradition) who taught Siddhattha (the Buddha) higher powers and higher states of experience such as the "plane of neither-perception-nor-non-perception."

undeclared questions (*avyākatā*): A series of questions (numbering either ten or fourteen) about metaphysical issues that the Buddha refused to answer or explain; the Buddha left such questions undeclared because they do not lead to the goals of the religious life (and may, in fact, becomes obstacles to progress in the religious life).

Vedas: The ancient texts that form the core of the Hindu tradition; the Vedas contain hymns to the numerous *devas;* "*veda*" is a Sanskrit word meaning "religious knowledge"; in Hindu tradition, mastery of the Vedic texts aims at the religious knowledge necessary to achieve spiritual liberation.

vessa: The third social class in Hindu society, composed of farmers and merchants.

visible object (*rūpa*): The biological/material aspect of a the natural world that can be seen with the eye, including the human body; sometimes translated as "form."

Well-Farer (*Sugata*): A common epithet for the Buddha.

wholesome/unwholesome (*kusala/akusala*): Sometimes translated as "skilled" and "unskilled"; these terms refer to the moral or religious qualities of actions.

wisdom (*paññā*): Religious wisdom or profound insight into the way things really are; in particular, having full knowledge of the highest teachings in the Buddhist tradition, namely, dependent arising and the Four Noble Truths.

yakkhas: Nonhuman spirits, ogres, or demons, typically associated with the forest or wilderness.

Selected Bibliography

Books and Articles

Bodhi, Bhikkhu. *The Middle Length Discourses of the Buddha: A New Translation of the Majjhima Nikāya* (Kandy, Sri Lanka: Buddhist Publication Society, 1995).

Chakravarti, Uma. *The Social Dimensions of Early Buddhism* (Oxford: Oxford University Press, 1987).

Collins, Steven. *Selfless Persons* (Cambridge: Cambridge University Press, 1982).

———. *Nirvana and Other Buddhist Felicities* (Cambridge: Cambridge University Press, 1998).

Conze, Edward. *Buddhist Thought in India: Three Phases of Buddhist Philosophy* (London: George Allen and Unwin, 1962).

Frauwallner, E. *The Earliest Vinaya and the Beginnings of Buddhist Literature* (Rome: ISMEO, 1956).

Gombrich, Richard. *Theravāda Buddhism* (London: Routledge and Kegan Paul, 1988).

———. *How Buddhism Began: The Conditioned Genesis of the Early Teachings* (London: Athlone Press, 1996).

Hallisey, Charles. "Ethical Particularism in Theravāda Buddhism," *Journal of Buddhist Ethics,* vol. 3, 1996, pp. 32–43.

Hamilton, Sue. *Identity and Experience: The Constitution of the Human Being According to Early Buddhism* (London: Luzac Oriental, 1996).

———. *Early Buddhism: A New Approach* (Richmond, Surrey: Curzon Press, 2000).

Harvey, Peter. *An Introduction to Buddhism* (Cambridge: Cambridge University Press, 1990).

Herman, Arthur. *A History of Buddhist Thought* (Lanham, MD: University Press of America, 1984).

———. *The Selfless Mind: Personality, Consciousness and Nirvana in Early Buddhism* (Richmond, Surrey: Curzon Press, 1995).

Hoffman, Frank J. *Rationality and Mind in Early Buddhism* (Delhi: Motilal Banarsidass, 1987).

Hoffman, Frank J., and Mahinda Deegalle (eds.). *Pāli Buddhism* (Richmond, Surrey: Curzon Press, 1996).

Holder, John. "The Early Buddhist Theory of Truth: A Contextualist Pragmatic Interpretation," *International Philosophical Quarterly,* vol. 26, no. 4, December 1996.

Horner, I. B. *The Early Buddhist Theory of Man Perfected* (London: Williams and Norgate, 1936).

Jayatilleke, K. N. *Early Buddhist Theory of Knowledge* (London: George Allen & Unwin, 1963).

Johansson, R.E.A. *The Dynamic Psychology of Early Buddhism* (Oxford: Curzon Press, 1979).

Kalupahana, David J. *Causality: The Central Philosophy of Buddhism* (Honolulu: University of Hawaii Press, 1975).

———. *Buddhist Philosophy: A Historical Analysis* (Honolulu: University of Hawaii Press, 1976).

———. *The Principles of Buddhist Psychology* (Albany: State University of New York Press, 1987).

———. *A History of Buddhist Philosophy: Continuities and Discontinuities* (Honolulu: University of Hawaii Press, 1992).

———. *Ethics in Early Buddhism* (Honolulu: University of Hawaii Press, 1995).

Kalupahana, David J., and Indrani Kalupahana. *The Way of Siddhartha: A Life of Buddha* (Lanham, MD: University Press of America, 1987).

Keown, Damien. *The Nature of Buddhist Ethics* (London: Macmillan, 1992).

Ñaṇananda, Bhikkhu. *Concept and Reality in Early Buddhist Thought* (Kandy, Sri Lanka: Buddhist Publication Society, reprinted 1986).

Ñāṇamoli, Bhikkhu. *The Life of the Buddha* (Kandy, Sri Lanka: Buddhist Publication Society, 1972).

Nyanatiloka, Bhikkhu. *The Significance of Dependent Origination* (Wheel No. 140) (Kandy, Sri Lanka: Buddhist Publication Society, 1969).

Piyadassi, Thera. *Dependent Origination: Paṭicca Samuppāda* (Wheel No. 15a/b) (Kandy, Sri Lanka: Buddhist Publication Society, 1959).

Rahula, Walpola. *What the Buddha Taught,* second edition (London: Gordon Fraser, 1985).

Ratnapala, Nandasena. *Buddhist Sociology* (Delhi: Sri Satguru Publications, 1993).

Rhys Davids, T. W., and W. Stede (eds.). *Pali-English Dictionary* (London: Pali Text Society, reprinted 1986).

Saddhatissa, H. *Buddhist Ethics* (New York: George Braziller, 1971).

Thomas, E. J. *The History of Buddhist Thought* (London: Routledge and Kegan Paul, 1972).

Tilakaratne, Asanga. *Nirvana and Ineffability* (Colombo, Sri Lanka: The Postgraduate Institute of Pali and Buddhist Studies, 1993).

Walshe, Maurice. *The Long Discourses of the Buddha: A Translation of the Dīgha Nikāya* (Kandy, Sri Lanka: Buddhist Publication Society, 1996).

Warder, A. K. *Indian Buddhism* (Delhi: Motilal Banarsidass, reprinted 1991).

———. *Introduction to Pali,* third edition (Oxford: Pali Text Society, reprinted 1995).

Wijesekera, O. H. de A. *Buddhism and Society* (Colombo, Sri Lanka: Bauddha Sahitya Sabha, 1951).

Electronic Resources

Access to Insight (www.accesstoinsight.org).

Buddhist Publication Society (www.bps.lk).

Buddhist Scriptures Information Retrieval (www.mahidol.ac.th/budsir/budsir-main.html).

Buddhist Studies WWW Virtual Library (www.ciolek.com/WWWVL-Buddhism.html).

Dharma Net (www.dharmanet.org/infowebt.html).

Journal of Buddhist Ethics (http://jbe.gold.ac.uk).

Pali Text Society (www.palitext.com).

Vipassana Research Institute (www.tipitaka.org).